D0186067

SHADOWS OF THE WORKHOUSE

SHADOWS OF THE WORKHOUSE

JENNIFER WORTH

ISIS
LARGE PRINT
Oxford

Copyright © Jennifer Worth, 2005

First published in Great Britain 2005
by
Merton Books

Published in Large Print 2006 by ISIS Publishing Ltd.,
7 Centremead, Osney Mead, Oxford OX2 0ES
by arrangement with
Merton Books

British Library Cataloguing in Publication Data
Worth, Jennifer, 1935–
    Shadows of the workhouse. – Large print ed.
    1. Poor – England – London – Biography
    2. Poverty – England – London – History
    – 20th century
    3. Large type books
    4. London (England) – Social life and customs
    – 20th century
    I. Title
    942.1'5084'0922

ISBN 0–7531–9368–X (hb)
ISBN 978–0–7531–9369–3 (pb)

Printed and bound in Great Britain by
T. J. International Ltd., Padstow, Cornwall

Dedicated to Pat
with my gratitude

Acknowledgements

Mysel Brar, for legal advice

Douglas May, Peggy Sayer, Betty Hawney and Helen Whitehorn for advice, proof reading, typing and checking

Philip and Suzannah, for everything

All the kind people who have written to me about the workhouse system, particularly Kathleen Daley and Dennis Strange

Chris Lloyd, Bancroft Library, Mile End, London

Jonathan Evans, Royal London Hospital Archives, London

Eve Hostettler, Island History Trust, the Isle of Dogs, London E.14

Jean Todd, Allan Young and Jeff Wright for help with archive pictures

Elizabeth Scudder, London Metropolitan Archives, London EC1

Edward Rogers, Hackney Archives, London N1

Mark Aston, Camden Local Studies and Archives Centre

Contents

Part III: The Old Soldier

All names have been changed. The Midwives of St Raymund Nonnatus is a fictional name.

Introduction

The Fight

A district midwife in Poplar, East London in the 1950s could find herself in many strange and unexpected situations. It was about 7 o'clock when I reached the tenements on a cold wet night. A sound with a menacing quality greeted me. Two women were fighting. I had never seen such a thing before and crept closer to listen to the comments of bystanders.

The fight, apparently, was over a man. Well, of course, I thought, it must be over a man. What else would two women fight about?

It was dark, but light from some of the windows illuminated the scene sufficiently to show that both women had their blouses torn off and were clawing, hitting, punching, biting and kicking each other. One had long hair that was a great disadvantage to her, as it gave her adversary something to grab hold of. Literally hundreds of people were in the courtyard, men women and children, shouting, jeering, cheering, egging them on. I wondered if one of the women would grab the skirt of the other and pull it off, so that she would be virtually naked. That didn't happen, but the woman with the long hair was forced to the ground, the other on top of her, banging her head on the cobblestones.

Just as I was thinking, Dear God, someone's got to stop this, I heard the piercing sound of police whistles and two policemen rushed into the yard, blowing their whistles and wielding their truncheons to show that they meant business. Thank God they came when they did because the woman on her back otherwise would have been seriously concussed, if not killed. The police were everywhere in the East End in those days, always on the beat — on foot, of course, as there were no such things as Panda cars. Within minutes at least another ten policemen had arrived, summoned by the shrill and distinctive sound of the whistle — there were no short-wave radios or telephone links to connect members of the force. The whistle was the only means of summoning help and, if heard, police would run in every direction towards the source of the sound. At the sight of the Law, the crowd disappeared as if by magic.

Within less than two minutes I was alone in the courtyard with the police and the two women, who had been separated. The injured one was shivering and sobbing and moaning in pain. The other one was standing above her, held by the arms by a young policeman; but that didn't stop her snarling and swearing and spitting on the woman on the ground. He said, "You'll be charged for this." She screamed, "Fuck you, see if I care," and attempted to kick him but another prevented her and said: "If you attack a policeman it will be the worse for you. And if this woman dies, it is a hanging matter."

That brought her to her senses. It had not been many years before that Ruth Ellis had been hanged for murdering her lover. It shook the nation and memories were very much alive. Even in the dark and rain, with filth streaked over her face, the woman seemed to turn pale.

I knelt down on the wet cobbles to examine the other female who lay quite still. She was covered in dirt and soaking wet. Her long, sodden hair was all over her face and shoulders. I examined her as best I could in the dark, and said, "The first thing we have to do is get some blankets, because she is in a state of shock and the cold will do her as much harm as the head injury. Then we must get her to the hospital for an X-ray."

She moaned "Nah, nah I don' wan' no 'ospi'al. I'll be all righ'."

It seemed terribly quiet, after all the noise. Not a soul was in sight.

A policeman shouted out into the night air, "Anyone who can hear me — bring a couple of blankets". His voice echoed around the four walls of the tenement courtyard.

A few minutes later several doors opened and women came out carrying blankets. They gave them to us, and retreated silently back to their flats, shutting the doors. All the lights were off by this time and faces that we could feel but not see were pressed against every window, watching and waiting.

I rubbed the prostrate woman's limbs with a blanket to try to warm her, and we wrapped another one around her. She sat up.

Her assailant perked up no end at this.

"Garn, she's all righ', the cow, she deserves more'n she got, more's the pi'y. I'd like to see 'er in 'ell."

"We're taking you to the station," said the young policeman.

"She started it, the fuckin' bitch."

Then suddenly, she changed her tune. Perhaps in the heat of the moment she hadn't realised she was half-naked and surrounded by men — or maybe the idea of a police station in her state of undress seemed an attractive one. She sidled up to the young officer and rubbed her bare breast against his arm. She gave a lewd wink and threw her head back. Her shrill voice dropped about an octave and a half, and she said huskily, "Is tha' an invitation, dearie?".

I, and most of the policemen, laughed. This dirty rain-soaked woman trying to play Delilah looked so ridiculous. But the funniest part of all was the young policeman's reaction. He could not have been a day over nineteen, young enough to be her son. He looked pink and clean and high-minded. He looked down at the substantial breast rubbing his arm and jumped like a scalded cat. We roared with laughter. All the faces watching at the windows must have been laughing too. He was covered with confusion and the fresh peaches and cream complexion turned scarlet.

He spluttered, "Where are your clothes?" in a prim Scottish accent.

I don't suppose he meant to sound pompous and priggish, but he did.

6

It was a fair question. Where indeed were her clothes? They were, of course, scattered around the place, trodden underfoot in the puddles.

She advanced on him and with each hand lifted a huge pendulous breast and waved her nipples in his face.

"Your guess is as good as mine, dearie," she said.

With a cry of alarm the young policeman leapt away. None of his colleagues was going to help him out. The scene was too good to miss or to cut short in any way. He knew he was beaten. He grabbed a spare blanket that was lying on the ground and wrapped it round his tormentor.

"In heaven's name, woman, cover your nakedness!" he said with desperate appeal. A slight accent somehow suggested the son of a Scottish Presbyterian minister. The other men fell about laughing. Things were getting out of hand, the dignity of the law had to be preserved. An older officer stepped forward.

"We are not going to charge you," he said. "Go to your flat, but I want your name and flat number."

She turned sullen again. Her bright moment of exhibitionism was over. But she gave her details.

"Now off you go, but don't let's have any more of this, or you'll be in real trouble. This is a caution."

Then he turned to his men.

"Now all of you, back to your duties. You two stay here with the nurse and the injured woman. Report if you need help."

They all left, suppressing their mirth, and I heard some pseudo "Scottish" voices saying "coverr yourr nakedness, woman!". The young Scot bit his lip, and looked on the verge of tears. He wouldn't live that one down, and he knew it.

The injured woman was sitting on the wet ground throughout this scene. As the other left she screamed out, "Look at 'er, the filthy slut. She's always like that. Throwin' 'erself around. She's no be'er than a whore. Trollop! Slut! Garbage!"

She screamed the words at the retreating figure, who made to come back to attack her again. But the second policeman barred the way.

"Now get off!" he said. "If there's any more trouble you will be charged and we would be witness that you attacked first this time."

She went and we saw her no more.

We were left with the injured woman. She had obviously got her verbal energy back, but I was concerned about her head, having seen and heard several terrible blows as her head was banged on the stones. She could easily have sustained a fracture and she must have medical treatment. I said: "We've got to get her to hospital for an X-ray."

"Nah! Nah!" she cried "I won'. I won' go to no 'ospi'al. Yer can' make me. I'll be all righ'. Jes' leave me alone."

We couldn't possibly just leave her in the rain. So we agreed that we would take her back to her flat, and then leave her. She was still shaky and weak. She pulled the blanket around her, shivering. The young Scot was very kind.

"You can lean on me," he said, "just show us the way, and we'll get you home."

There were four flights of stairs to climb and she could scarcely walk, but she managed it; grim determination was forcing her on. She kept muttering "no 'orspi'al, no 'orspi'al." I think it was that negative desire that kept her going, and the fear that if she stumbled and fell, she would be forcibly carried to hospital.

The long walk around the balconies seemed interminable. I could see the faces pressed against the windows and they retreated as we got close. A little boy's face remained at one of the windows as we passed and a hand shot out and snatched him back. I heard a curse, a heavy slap, and a yelp of pain. I winced for the child; he was only being curious.

When we got to her door, she refused to let us come in with her.

"Nah, get orf," she said, "bleed orf, I'll be all righ'."

We left, and I saw her no more. They were tough in those days, really tough. Perhaps she was so used to violence that it was all part of life. Perhaps some kind neighbour took care of her for a few days. If she did have a hairline fracture of the skull, it mended in its own time with no assistance from the doctors.

A charge was not brought against either woman. For one thing the injured woman made no official complaint and, for another, personal fights in those days were common. Police just separated the adversaries and, unless some other crime was involved, charges were seldom made.

These were the tenements of Poplar, in the 1950s. It was a time, shortly after the second world war, when the scars of the devastated city were everywhere to be seen in bomb sites, blown-out shops, closed streets and roofless houses (often inhabited). It was a time when the docks were fully operational, and millions of tons of cargo poured in and out every day. Huge merchant vessels sailed up the Thames, to be piloted into the wharves through a complex system of canals, locks and basins. It was not unusual to pass along the road within a few feet of the towering hulk of a merchant ship. Even in the 1950s about sixty per cent of all cargo was unloaded by men, and the ports were teeming with labourers. Most of them lived with their families in the little houses and tenements around the docks.

Families were large, sometimes huge and living conditions cramped. In fact, by the standards of today — the early twenty-first century — living conditions would be considered Dickensian! Most dwellings had running cold water, but no hot water. About half had an indoor lavatory, and for the other half the lavatory was outside, usually shared with other families. Very few had a bathroom. A bath was taken in a tin bath placed on the floor of the kitchen or living room, though the public bath houses were more frequently used. Most houses had electric light, but gas light was still common and I have delivered many a baby by this flickering light, as well as by torchlight or hurricane lamp.

It was a time just before the social revolution of 'the pill', and families were large. A colleague of mine delivered an eighteenth baby to a woman and I

10

delivered a twenty-fourth! Admittedly these were extreme cases, but ten babies was quite common. Although the fashion for hospitalisation for a birth was fast gaining ground, "fashion" had not affected the Poplar women, who were slow to change, and a home birth was preferred. Earlier in the century, even as little as twenty or thirty years earlier, women were still delivering each other's babies as they had done in Dickens' time, but by the 1950s, with the National Health Service in being, all pregnancies and births were attended by trained midwives.

I worked with the Sisters of St Raymond Nonnatus, a religious order of nuns with a history dating back to the 1840s. This was also a Nursing Order pioneered at a time when nurses were commonly regarded as the dregs and drunks of female society. The Sisters, bound for life by the monastic vows of poverty, chastity and obedience, had been in Poplar since the 1870s. They started at a time when there was virtually no medical help for the poorest of the poor and a woman and her baby lived or died unattended. The Sisters lived and worked a life of ceaseless dedication to their religion and to the people whom they felt were in their care. At the time when I worked at Nonnatus House, Sister Julienne was Sister-in-Charge.

All is gone. If you wander around Poplar today, as I have done, you will find virtually everything has changed in the past fifty years. Nonnatus House is still standing, but the Sisters have departed. The docks are closed, and on the land smart flats and offices have been built. The vital Cockney community has been dispersed and largely destroyed. Even the language has changed. Only memories remain and, for me, are as alive today as they were nearly half a century ago. The people, with all their comedies and tragedies, are as real to me as my next-door neighbours.

Part I

Workhouse Children

Convents tend to attract within their portals ladies of middle years who are unable to cope with life in one way or another. These ladies are always single, widowed or divorced and lonely. They are nearly always gentle, timid and shy with an immense yearning for goodness which they see in the convent but cannot find in the harsh world outside. Usually they are very devout in points of religious observance and have an unrealistic or romanticised idea of monastic life and long to be part of it. However, usually they do not have a true vocation that would enable them to take the life vows of poverty, chastity and obedience. Nor, I suspect do they possess the strength of character necessary to live within these vows. So they hover on the fringe, neither fully within the world, nor withdrawn from it.

Such a lady was Jane. She was probably around forty-five, but she looked much older. She was tall, thin, aristocratic-looking, with delicate bone structure, beautifully modelled features, and refined manners. In another context she would have been an outstanding beauty, but the habit of excessive dowdiness made her look plain and nondescript. It was almost as though she did it on purpose. Her soft grey hair could have curled prettily around her face, but she cut it herself, so that it was jagged and shapeless. Her height, which should have rendered her distinguished, she reduced by bending her shoulders, so that her carriage and walk were stooped and cringing. Her large, expressive eyes were filled with nameless anxiety and surrounded by worry-wrinkles. Her speech was so soft that it sounded like a far-off twitter and her laugh a nervous giggle.

Nervousness was her chief characteristic. She seemed frightened of everything. I noticed that, even at meals, she did not dare to pick up her knife and fork until everyone else had done so and when she did, her hands frequently shook so much that she would drop something. Then she had to apologise profusely to everyone, especially to Sister Julienne, who was always at the head of the table.

She had lived at Nonnatus House for many years and fulfilled a role that was neither nurse, nor domestic servant, but a mixture of the two. I had the impression of a highly intelligent woman who could easily have trained as a nurse, and been very good at it, but something must always have prevented her from training. No doubt it was her chronic nervousness, for she could never have taken the responsibility that is a daily part of any nurse's life. So Sister Julienne sent her out to do simple jobs, like blanket baths, or enemas, or delivering various things to patients. In doing these little jobs, Jane was all of a-twitter with anxiety, going over and over her bag obsessively, muttering to herself such things as: "Soap, towels. Have I got everything? Is

16

it all there?" Consequently it took her two or three hours to do a job that any competent nurse would achieve in twenty minutes.

When she had finished, she was pathetically eager for recognition that she had done the job, her eyes almost pleading for someone to say that she had done well. Sister Julienne always praised her small achievements, but I could see that it was a strain for her to have to be constantly alert to Jane's craving for praise.

Jane also helped the nurses and midwives in the clinical room in small ways like cleaning instruments, packing bags etc. and she was pathetically, irritatingly, eager to please. Asked for a syringe, she would rush off and get three. Asked for some cotton-wool swabs for a baby, she would bring enough for twenty babies and then almost grovel as she handed over the item with a nervous giggle. The craven urge to please brought her no rest, no comfort.

It was all very disconcerting, especially as she was old enough to be my mother, and as it generally took her about three times as long as it took me to do a job, I refrained from asking. But she intrigued me, and I watched her.

Jane was generally in the house, so one of her jobs was to take telephone messages, which she did with meticulous and needless over-attention to detail. She also helped Mrs B in the kitchen. This led to many a rumpus, because Mrs B was a quick and efficient cook, and Jane's dithering nearly drove her to distraction. She shouted at Jane to "Put a move on," and then poor Jane would be paralysed with terror, faltering. "Oh, oh dear, yes, of course, yes, quickly, of course." But her limbs wouldn't move, and she just stood stock still, whimpering.

Once I heard Mrs B tell Jane to peel the potatoes and cut them in half for roasting. Later, when she wanted to put the potatoes in the oven, she found that Jane had cut every potato into about twenty pieces. She had been so desperately anxious to please by cutting them into an exact half that she couldn't stop and every half had been cut in half again, and so on until all that was left was a mound of tiny pieces. When Mrs. B exploded Jane fell back against the wall, whimpering and pleading for forgiveness, shaking all over and white with terror. Fortunately, Sister Julienne came into the kitchen at that moment, saw the situation, and rescued Jane with, "Never mind, Mrs B, we'll have mash today. They are just the right size for steaming. Jane, come with me, will you, please? The laundry has just come back and needs checking."

Poor Jane's eyes said it all — her fears, her grief, her gratitude and her love. I watched her go, and wondered what had happened to make her such a mess.

Despite the kindness always shown to her by the Sisters, she seemed to live in a world of unfathomable loneliness.

She was very devout, attending Mass every day. She also attended most of the five monastic offices of the nuns as well. I have seen her in Chapel, her fingers twitching, her eyes earnestly fixed on the altar, half-intoning the words, "Jesus loves me, Jesus loves me," over and over again, a hundred times or more. It is easy to scoff at such devotion. Women like Jane can be seen everywhere. They are always fair game for a cheap laugh.

I was with Jane on one occasion in Chrisp Street Market. It was just before Christmas and stalls were laden with cheap nick-knacks and curios — obvious Christmas presents. We approached one of these stalls. Lying in the centre, was a small wooden object, about five or six inches long. It was nearly, but not quite, round and smooth, with a slight ridge running up the under side towards a pronounced rim. The tip was rounded, smooth and polished, with a small hole in the centre.

Jane picked up the object and held it between thumb and forefinger for everyone to see.

"Ooh, what's this?" she said enquiringly.

Everyone became silent and stared at Jane and the object. No one laughed.

The stall-holder was a fast-talking, streetwise coster of about fifty, who had been selling bric-a-brac most of his life. With a theatrical gesture he pushed his cap to the back of his head, took the fag out of his mouth and stubbed it out slowly on the edge of his stall. He glanced at his audience and opened his eyes wide with surprised innocence before answering:

"Wha' is it, lady? Wha' is it? Why, lady, haven' chew seen one o' these 'ere fings afore?"

Jane shook her head.

"Why, it's a honey stirrer. Vat's what it is, lady. An 'oney-stirrer — for stirrin' 'oney."

"Really? How interesting!" murmured Jane.

"Well, yerse, werry interestin', it is. They're werry old, you know, lady. Been around a long time, they 'ave. I'm surprised you ain't come across one 'afore now."

"No, never. You learn something new every day, don't you? How do you use it?"

"How do you use it? Ah, well now, allow me to show you, lady, if you wouldn't mind."

He leaned forward and took the object from Jane's outstretched hand. The crowd, which had grown considerably in numbers, pressed silently forward, eager not to miss a word.

"Let me show you, lady. You sticks vis 'ere 'oney-stirrer in yer 'oney pot, and you stirs yer 'oney like vis . . . . . ." and he made a slight movement of the wrist, ". . . .an the 'oney, it catches on vis here li'l rim — you see vis li'l rim 'ere, lady . . . ?" (rubbing his fingers appreciatively around it) ". . . well, ve honey, it catches on the rim, an' drips off, like."

"Really?" said Jane, "how fascinating. I would never have thought of it. I suppose it must be used a lot by country people who keep bees."

"Ooh, yerse, country people, vey use it all ve time, wha' wiv all vem birds an' bees an' all."

"Well, I'm sure it must be very useful. Sister Julienne likes honey. I think I will buy this for her as a Christmas present. I am sure she would appreciate it."

"Ooh yerst, yerst. Sister Julienne will appreciate it all right, not 'arf she won't. If you asks my opinion, lady, you couldn't get Sister Julienne a Christmas present as wha' she would appreciate more, you couldn't. Now, I was askin' four shillins for vis 'ere remarkable honey-stirrer, but seein' as how it's you, lady, wot's buyin' it for Sister Julienne for Christmas, I'll let you 'ave it for two shillin' and sixpence, an' you' got a real bargain, I can tell you."

The coster beamed benignly.

"That's very good of you," exclaimed Jane as she handed over the money. "I must say I'm delighted, and I'm sure Sister will be delighted when she sees it."

"No doubt abaht' vat. No doubt at all. It's bin a pleasure doin business with you, madam, an' I must say you've made my day you 'ave, madam."

"Have I really?" said Jane with a sweet, sad smile. "I can't think how, but I'm so glad. It's always nice to give pleasure to someone, isn't it?"

Christmas day arrived — a major feast day, and a high festive occasion in a convent. We returned from morning church and prepared the dining room for Christmas lunch. A tableau of angels adorned the table centre. Our presents were exchanged at lunchtime and were placed on the dining table beside each person's plate. I found it hard to take my eyes off a small box, wrapped in silver paper, decorated with a red ribbon, resting beside Sister Julienne's plate. What was going to happen?

We were fourteen to lunch that Christmas day, including two visiting nuns from North Africa, beautiful in their white habits. Grace was said, with a special remembrance for the gifts of the Magi and we all sat down to open our presents. A chorus of "oohs" and "ahs" and little squeaks and giggles arose from the table, as kisses were exchanged between the ladies.

Sister Julienne picked up the silver box with: "Now what can this be?" and my heart stood still. She removed the paper and opened the box. Just the flicker of an eyebrow, instantaneous and then gone, was all that betrayed her. She carefully put the lid back on the box and turned to Jane with a radiant smile her eyes alight with pleasure.

"How very kind. A most charming thought, Jane. It is just what I have always wanted, and I am truly grateful. I will treasure it always."

Jane leaned forward eagerly.

"It's a honey-stirrer. They are very old."

"Oh yes, I know. I saw that at once. A delightful gift and so like you, Jane, to be so thoughtful."

Sister Jocelyn kissed her gently, with another murmur of appreciation and quietly tucked the box away beneath her scapular.

To all appearances Jane was a bit of a dimwit. It was her reading that gave me the clue that she was in fact exactly the opposite. Jane was a voracious, almost obsessive reader. Books were her only self-indulgence, and these she handled with loving care. I took to spying on her authors — Flaubert, Dostoevsky, Russell, Kierkegaard. I was astonished. Predictably, she had a daily discipline of Bible reading, but beyond the Old and New Testaments her devotional reading was formidable: St. Thomas Aquinas, Augustine, St John of the Cross. I looked at her with new eyes. Aquinas for recreation! This was no dimwit.

Yet if anyone came into the room she would jump up, all of a dither and throw down her book guiltily,

22

saying something like: "Do you want anything? Can I get you anything?" or, on one occasion: "I was just about to lay the table for breakfast. I haven't been idle, really I haven't." This was not the behaviour of an intelligent woman.

Later I discovered that Jane had spent twenty years in domestic service. She had been put into service at the age of fourteen, when life for a humble servant girl was very hard indeed. She had to be up at about 4a.m. to fetch the wood and coal, clear the grates and light the fires. Then it would be a day of constant heavy work, at the beck and call of the mistress of the house, until 10 or 11 at night, when she would be allowed to go to bed.

Jane was hopeless at the job. However hard she tried she could never master the skills of simple housework. Consequently the mistress was always cross with her. She became increasingly nervous, breaking things, bungling things. She lived in a state of sheer terror that she would do something wrong, which she always did, so she was continually getting the sack and would have to find another position — where it started all over again.

Few domestic servants can have been less suited to the job than Jane. Her incompetence was monumental. It is not uncommon for highly intellectual people to be baffled and defeated by the practicalities of everyday life.

Poor Jane! I saw her once trying to light a gas mantle. It took her forty minutes. First she spilled the matches all over the floor, and at the end she had broken the mantle, broken the glass shade, cut herself, set fire to a tea towel and scorched the wallpaper!

At Nonnatus House one day Jane spilled a drop of milk on the floor. She trembled and whimpered, "I'll clean it up. I'll clean it up. I'll do it."

She then proceeded to wash the entire kitchen floor, including moving all the tables and chairs, when all that was necessary was to wipe up the small patch of milk. No-one could stop her. She insisted on doing the whole kitchen, and I asked Sister Julienne why she behaved like that.

"Jane was utterly crushed as a child," explained Sister, "she will never get over it."

Jane very seldom went out, and never left Nonnatus House for a night. The only person she was ever known to visit was Peggy, who lived on the Isle of Dogs with her brother Frank.

No-one could describe Peggy as plump. Voluptuous would be a better description. Her softly rounded curves spoke eloquently of ease and comfort. Her large grey eyes, fringed with dark curling lashes, had a sensuous quality in their dreamy depths. Her smooth clear skin glowed with radiance and every time she smiled, which was often, dimples enhanced her beauty, making you want to look upon her more often. 'Allure' might well have been her middle name.

Yet Peggy was not an idle lady of leisure preserving her beauty with creams and lotions, and toying with men for her own amusement. Peggy was a charwoman. What with office cleaning in the early hours of the morning, her "ladies" in Bloomsbury and Knightsbridge, restaurants and banks each afternoon, she was always busy.

Peggy cleaned at Nonnatus House three mornings a week and the house always smelled sweetly of wax polish and carbolic soap when she left. Everyone liked her. Her beauty was refreshing, and her smile raised the spirits. Furthermore, she sang quietly to herself all the while as she polished and scrubbed. She had a pretty voice, and sang in tune. Her repertoire consisted of old-fashioned folksongs and hymns, the sort that children used to learn in schools and Sunday Schools; it was a delight to listen to. Her speaking voice was equally charming, and she did not sound like a Cockney, although apparently she was one.

She was kind to everyone, and never seemed to get ruffled. I recall once when I had been out half the night, (in my memory, babies always seem to have been born in the middle of the night when it was raining!) and came in wet and muddy. I had been obliged to wait in Manchester Road for forty minutes, whilst the swing bridge was open for cargo boats to pass and, consequently, was tired and ill-tempered. I crossed the hallway leading to the Clinical Room, not even conscious that I was leaving wet and muddy foot-marks all over the fine Victorian tiles that Peggy had just buffed up to glow with warm light. Something made me turn at the top of the stairs and I saw the mess I had made of her hard work.

"Oh, gosh — sorry!" I said, feebly.

Her eyes sparkled with laughter, and she was down on her knees in a trice.

"Don't give it another thought," she said, affably.

Peggy was a good deal older than she looked. Her beautiful skin, in which the only wrinkles were laughter lines around her eyes, made her look about thirty, but in fact she was around forty-five. Her supple body was as agile as a young girl and she was graceful in all her movements. Many women of forty-five would wish to look so youthful, so what was her secret, I wondered? Was it a sort of inner glow, a secret joy which she cherished all the time, which irradiated her features, making her look youthful and sensuous?

Although they were the same age, Peggy looked at least twenty years younger than Jane. Her softly rounded curves contrasted with Jane's stiff, angular bones; her clear, youthful skin with the other's dried-out wrinkles; her pretty blonde hair with Jane's ill-cut greyness. Her easy-going laughter was infectious, whilst Jane's nervous giggle was irritating. Peggy treated the tall, angular woman with great tenderness, made allowances for her nervous twitter and general silliness, and often made her laugh in a way that no-one else could. Jane seemed more relaxed when Peggy was in the house; she smiled more readily and seemed, if possible, less apprehensive.

Peggy's brother Frank was a fishmonger, known to all as "Frank the Fish". By common consent he kept the best wet-fish stall in Chrisp Street market. Whether his ability to sell his fish was due to the excellence of the fish, the ebullience of his personality or his committed hard work, was not known. Probably his success was due to a combination of all three.

He slept little, and rose about 3 o'clock each morning to go to Billingsgate fish market. He had to push his barrow along the quiet streets, as very few working men had a van in those days. At Billingsgate he personally selected all his fish, having an encyclopaedic knowledge of his customers' likes and dislikes, and he was back at Chrisp Street by 8a.m. to set up his stall.

He was an effervescent bundle of energy and he loved his work. He brought fun and laughter to hundreds of people, and many dockers were served kippers for tea, simply because their good wives couldn't resist the bantering flirtation that fell from his lips as he slipped the slippery fish into their outstretched hands, with always a wink and a squeeze.

He shut up the stall at 2p.m. every day, and started on his delivery round. He kept no books, but carried in his head a detailed knowledge of his customers' requirements on a daily basis. He never made a mistake. He called at Nonnatus House twice every week and he and Mrs B, who was not a great admirer of men, were best of friends.

Frank was a bachelor and, because he was comparatively well off and always good-natured, half the ladies of Poplar were after him — but he just wasn't interested. "E's wedded to 'is fish," they grumbled.

Frank seemed an unlikely friend for Jane, who was pathologically shy of men. If the plumber or the baker called at the house and Jane opened the door, she would go to pieces. She would chirrup and twitter around them, trying desperately to be pleasant, but merely succeeding in being ridiculous.

But with Frank she was different somehow. His ready banter and Cockney wit were tempered by gentleness and consideration, to which Jane responded with a shy, sweet smile and eyes filled with gratitude. Or was it love, my colleagues Cynthia and Trixie wondered. Did repressed, dried-up Jane harbour a secret passion for the extrovert fishmonger?

"Could be," reflected Cynthia. "How romantic! And how tragic for poor Jane! He's wedded to his fish."

"Not a chance," said Trixie, the pragmatist. "If it was a case of unrequited love, she would go to pieces with him even more than she does with other men."

Once, after Jane had been to visit Peggy and Frank, she said wistfully, "If only I had a brother. I would be happy if I had a brother." Later, Trixie said, acerbically, "It's a lover she needs, not a brother." We all had a good laugh at Jane's expense.

In the pages that follow, my narrator is largely Peggy, with some input from Frank. I have not exaggerated or embellished anything. The story is their own. The most I have allowed myself in writing it down is to invent dialogue as seemed appropriate for the flow of the narrative.

Jane, Peggy, and Frank were brought up in the workhouse. The two girls were nearly the same age, Frank was four years older. Jane and Peggy were best friends. They shared everything. They slept in adjacent beds in a dormitory of seventy girls. They sat next to each other in the refectory, where meals for three hundred girls were taken. They went to the same school. They shared the same household chores. Above all they shared each other's thoughts and feelings and sufferings, as well as small joys.

The following is the account of the formative years of their lives.

Jane

"We'll have to watch that one. Saucy little madam. Did you hear the way she spoke out of turn at breakfast?"

"Don't you worry, my dear. I'll break her before she leaves here."

The Master and Mistress were talking about Jane, who had been in the workhouse since birth. It was rumoured that her father was a high-class gentleman, distinguished in Parliament and at the Bar. When his wife found him and a servant-girl in bed together, the girl was immediately dismissed and went to the workhouse, where Jane was born.

The baby stayed with her mother to be breast-fed, but was removed when weaning commenced and taken to the infants' nursery. The mother returned to the women's section of the workhouse and saw her baby no more. Thus Jane was entirely reared by the institution and knew no other life, nor could her child's mind conceive of any other.

It was a harsh, repressive life, but no amount of smacks or punishments could subdue Jane's bubbling laughter and *joie de vivre*. In the playground she chased the other children, or hid and jumped on them

30

with a delighted 'boo'. In the dormitory she crept under the beds and poked the mattresses of sleeping children with a stick. It caused uproar and an officer would run in with smacks and orders for quietness. Jane always got smacked, being the cause of all the trouble. But she cried herself to sleep and then giggled and did it again.

As she grew bigger, her high spirits got her into endless trouble. Docility and instant obedience were expected at all times from the children, and if there was any deviation from this, naughty little Jane could generally be found at the centre of it. Who was it who tied Officer Sharp's shoelaces together as she sat darning socks, so that she fell over when she stood up and took a step? No-one knew for certain, but as Jane had been seen around her skirts, the little girl got a good smacking for it. Who was it who climbed the drainpipe in the playground? Why, Jane, of course. And who mixed up all the boots in the dormitory so that everyone had the wrong sizes? If it wasn't Jane it might well have been, so she got the punishment.

Jane's great misfortune was that she stood out. In a group of children she could not be overlooked. She was a good deal taller than average and also prettier, with her dark curls and clear blue eyes. Worse than this, (which was bad enough) she was a great deal more intelligent than most of the other children and the Master and Mistress feared an intelligent child. They told the Officers to keep an eye on her.

"Keep in line, don't straggle. Heads up, now. Don't slouch."

Officer Hawkins would show them how to do it!

The girls were marching to church one Sunday morning. It was a very long crocodile, consisting of nearly one hundred girls. Jane, halfway along on the outside, watched fat old Officer Hawkins strutting along like a penguin and with an instinctive gift for mimicry copied the walk, head thrown back, arms flapping, feet splayed. The girls behind started to giggle. A hand shot out and hit Jane on the head with such force that she fell through the column of girls into the road on the other side. She was hauled up and hit again and then pushed into line to continue marching. Her ears were ringing and lights were darting before her eyes, but she had to keep marching. She was six years old.

"Where did it come from?" demanded the Master, his eyes bulging, his face turning red. "Who is guilty of this piece of insolence?"

He was looking at a sketch of himself, on a page torn from an exercise book. It was a remarkable drawing for a child, but the Master couldn't see it that way. All he could see was himself with an exaggerated moustache, a square head, small eyes, and an exceedingly large stomach. The picture had been circulating among the girls for three days, causing endless amusement, which added to the Master's fury.

He assembled all the girls in the hall and addressed them from the pulpit. He reminded them that they were paupers, who must respect and obey their betters.

No act of disobedience, disrespect or insubordination would be tolerated. He held up the pencil drawing.

"Who did this?" he demanded, menacingly.

No one moved.

"Very well. Every single girl in this room will be beaten, starting now, with the first row."

Jane stood up.

"I did it, sir," she whispered.

She was taken to the discipline room — a small, square room with no windows and no furniture, but one stool. Several canes were hanging on the wall. Jane was beaten severely on the bare bottom. She could not sit down for several days. She was only seven years old.

This will be enough to break her spirit, thought the Master to himself with satisfaction. But it didn't. He couldn't understand it. Why, with his own eyes, the very next morning, he had seen her dancing across the playground, as though she hadn't a care in the world.

The reason why Jane's spirit was not broken was because she had a secret. It was her own special secret and she had told no one else except Peggy. It was locked in her heart and she hugged it to herself. It was this glorious secret that filled her with irrepressible joy and exhilaration. It was to be the cause of her greatest disaster, and her life-long grief and pain.

The rumour that her father was a high-born gentleman who was in Parliament must have reached Jane's ears when she was a very little girl. Perhaps she had heard the Officers talking about it. Perhaps another child had heard the adult conversation and told her. Perhaps Jane's mother had told another workhouse inmate, who had passed it on. One can never tell how rumours start.

To Jane, it was not a rumour. It was an absolute fact. Her Daddy was a high-born gentleman, who one day would come and take her away. She fantasised endlessly about her Daddy. She talked to him, and he talked to her. She brushed her hair, and cast a flirtatious eye at her father, who was looking over her shoulder admiring her curls. She ran down the playground as fast as she could, because he was standing at the other end, admiring her strength and speed. He was always with her. He was everywhere.

She had a very clear picture of him in her mind. He was not like any other man she had seen at the workhouse, not like the coal man, nor the baker, nor the boiler-man. They were ugly and short, wearing rough working-mens' clothing and cloth caps. He was not like the Master or any of the Officers. Jane's little nose wrinkled with disgust at the thought. Her Daddy was quite different. He was tall and slim with fine features and pale skin. He had long fingers; she looked at her own slender hands and knew that she had inherited her Daddy's fingers. He had lots of hair (she didn't like bald men) and it was a soft, grey colour, always clean and nicely brushed. His clothes were nothing like the awful stuff worn by the few workmen she saw, and her Daddy didn't smell of sweat like they did. He always wore beautiful suits smelling of lavender, and he wore a top hat and carried a walking-cane with a gold crest on top.

She knew just what his voice sounded like also — after all he was always talking to her — it was not rough and grating like other men's voices; it was musical and deep, with laughter in the tone. She knew this because he was always laughing with her and making fun of the Master and the Officers. His eyes had twinkled with amusement, and he had called her 'his clever girl' when she had drawn a funny picture of the Master.

So how could Jane be unhappy? The more they beat her the closer she drew to her Daddy. He comforted her when she cried at night. He dried her tears and told her to be a brave girl. She swallowed her tears quickly, because she knew that he liked to see her smiling and happy, and she made up a funny story to amuse him, because she knew that he liked her funny stories.

She had invented his house. It was a beautiful house with a long drive and fine trees in the grounds. There were steps up to the front door and, inside, the rooms smelled of beeswax and lavender. There were pictures on the walls and fine rugs on the floors. Her Daddy took her by the hand and led her through the rooms, one by one, and told her that one day he would come and take her away from the workhouse, and they would live together in the beautiful house with the long drive and fine trees.

Jane was seven years old when she went to the local council school. She was very proud of it — it was a big, proper school for big girls and Jane loved it. It brought her into contact with a life outside the workhouse, which she had not suspected existed. It introduced her to learning, which she loved. Her young mind began to expand. She realised that there were thousands of things that she could learn and she absorbed and retained her lessons quickly and thoroughly. Excellent reports of her progress were sent back to the workhouse. The Master was not impressed. A request from the school's headmistress for Jane to be allowed to take piano lessons, as she showed an unusually good ear for music, was refused, the master saying that no workhouse pauper should be singled out for special treatment. A request that Jane should be allowed to take the role of Mary in the school's nativity play was refused for the same reason.

Jane was bitterly disappointed at this, chiefly because her Daddy would have been so proud to see her playing Mary, and she cried herself to sleep about it for several nights, until he whispered to her that the silly old nativity at school was not worth crying over. She would have the chance to perform in many more, much nicer plays when she came to live with him in the beautiful house with the long drive.

The workhouse girls were kept apart, as much as possible, from the other girls at the school. This was because several local mothers had complained that they did not want their daughters mixing with 'them workhouse bastards'. This segregation was a source of great pain to many of her friends, but not to Jane. She laughed at the rule that workhouse girls should not play in the same playground as the others, and tossed her dark curls scornfully. Just let them wait. She would show them. All those dreary girls whose fathers were dustmen, and street sweepers, and costermongers. They would be sorry one day when they saw her Daddy, a high-born gentleman, drive up to the school in a carriage. She would run up to him, and all those dreary girls would see her. He would pick her up, kiss her, and take her to the waiting carriage, and all the girls would see and be jealous. The teachers would say to each other: "we always knew that Jane was different somehow".

Jane was fortunate in the class teacher she had at school. Miss Sutton was young, well educated and eager. In fact, to say that she possessed a missionary zeal in teaching the poorest of the poor children would not be overstating her dedication and enthusiasm. She saw in the vivacious Jane unusual qualities which she was determined to promote and foster. The child learned to read and write in about a quarter the length of time that it took the other children, so whilst she (Miss Sutton) was engaged with the bulk of the class, who were learning the alphabet and painstakingly spelling out words, she asked Jane to write stories for her. Jane did so with great joy and fluency, picking on any subject Miss Sutton suggested, and weaving a delightful child's story around it. Several of these stories were shown to the headmistress, who commented "there is an unusual mind at work here," and she obtained a copy of A Child's Garden of Verses which she handed to Miss Sutton for Jane's use. The child was enraptured by the rhythm of the words and quickly learned many of the poems by heart, which she recited to her Daddy when they were alone together.

Miss Sutton also introduced Jane to history and geography, using a children's encyclopaedia as her textbook. These lessons had to be surreptitious, because Miss Sutton was employed to teach reading, writing and arithmetic to the bulk of the class. Furthermore, she was canny enough to suspect that if she requested extra lessons for Jane, the request would be refused. That would be the end of history and geography for Jane.

Miss Sutton took the wise step of introducing one volume at a time to Jane, with the words, "I think you will enjoy reading about this. When you have done so, write me a story about it, and we will talk about it at lunchtime."

Jane adored Miss Sutton, and their lunchtime conversations about kings and queens and faraway places were the high point of her day.

The children's encyclopaedia was her intellectual treasure. There were ten large volumes, each beautifully bound in dark blue with gold lettering. She was given one at a time and she poured over it with a hungry mind. She loved the books, their feel and touch and smell, and wanted to keep them always, but she knew she couldn't. They were kept locked in the classroom cupboard, but she knew that Miss Sutton would let her see them any time. To Jane these books were more sacred than Holy Writ to a seer. Every word she read was — must be — gospel truth, because it was written in the " 'cyclopaedia".

One day she came across a long word she had not met before. She traced it with her finger and tried to say it to herself. 'PAR' — that was easy; 'LIA' — what did that mean? 'MENT' — that was easy, too, but what was it all together? Suddenly, like a lightening stroke, it came to her: *Parliament*. Her Daddy was in Parliament. She devoured the written pages as though her life depended on it. In the background the other children were reciting C-A-T, D-O-G. Jane heard nothing. She was pouring over the pages on Parliament and the British Constitution. She didn't understand it, but that didn't matter, it was about her Daddy. Like one possessed she read on. She turned a few pages; and then she saw him. The picture leaped towards her. It was her Daddy, as she had always known he would look; tall and slim, with slightly grey hair, a thoughtful face, but kindly. He was wearing a beautiful frock coat with tails, just as she had always known he would, with slender, drainpipe trousers and elegant shoes. He was carrying a top hat and a walking-cane with a gold crest. He had long, slender fingers just like she had. Her head fell onto the book, and she kissed the page.

The lunch bell sounded. Miss Sutton came up and roused her.

"Come on, Jane, time for lunch."

"What is Parliament?" demanded the child.

"The Houses of Parliament are where His Majesty's Government sits. Now come along to lunch."

"Where are these Houses? Can I go? Will you take me?"

Miss Sutton laughed. An eager pupil is the breath of life to a dedicated teacher.

"I will tell you as much as I know about Parliament. But you must have your lunch first. You want to grow to be a big strong girl, don't you? Go back to the classroom after lunch, and I will come."

After lunch Miss Sutton did her best to explain to the understanding of a seven-year-old that the Members of Parliament made the rules that govern the country.

"Are they very important people, and very important rules?" the child enquired.

"Very; there are none higher in the land."

"More important than the Workhouse Master?"

"Oh, much. The Members of Parliament are the highest in the land, after the King."

Jane's breath was coming fast. She seemed unable to contain her excitement. Miss Sutton was watching her closely, with astonishment. Jane was looking down at the book, tracing long words with her finger. She looked up at her teacher, her blue eyes flashing through dark lashes (extraordinary, the vivid combination of blue eyes and dark hair, thought Miss Sutton). Jane's white teeth showed, as she bit her lower lip. One of her milk teeth had come out and she drew air in through the gap with a sucking sound. She poked her tongue through the gap and wiggled it around. A secret smile spread across her face, as she whispered, confidentially:

"My Daddy is in Parliament."

Miss Sutton was, to say the least, taken aback. She was too fond of the child to say "don't be silly", but she felt it necessary to say something to dispel this illusion.

"Oh, come now, Jane, that cannot possibly be."

"But he is, he is, he's here in the book. I've seen him."

She turned a few pages on, showing the artist's impression of a Member of Parliament.

"That's my Daddy. I know it is. I've seen him lots and lots of times."

"But Jane, that's only a drawing. That is not a real man. That's just a drawing to show the clothes that a Member of Parliament might wear. That's not your Daddy, dear."

"It is, it is, I know it is!"

Jane began to cry, and jumped up.

"You don't know anything. You don't know my Daddy. I do, and I know it's him."

Jane ran from the classroom in tears. Poor Miss Sutton was troubled by this scene, and discussed it with the headmistress. They agreed that it was just the longing of a highly imaginative child for a father she had never known. The headmistress advised channelling Jane's thoughts in other directions and not mentioning Parliament again. That way she would forget about it.

Alone, by herself, Jane had decided upon a similar course. She would never again mention her father to anyone, except Peggy. No one, not even Miss Sutton, was worthy to be let into the secret. She pretended she had forgotten all about the lunchtime conversation and carried on as though it had never occurred.

Her great joy now was that she knew the book and the page where her Daddy was to be found. Whenever she could, she went to the cupboard and opened the page, to gaze upon him with rapture in her heart. If anyone came near, she turned the page quickly, pretending she was looking at something else.

Sir Ian Astor-Smaleigh

Sir Ian Astor-Smaleigh was a true philanthropist. He was an Oxford man who had devoted most of his life and a considerable part of his fortune to the improvement of living conditions and life expectancy of children in the poorest areas of London. He was a founder member of the Oxford Movement for the London Poor, having formed a charity dedicated to the provision of holidays for workhouse children. This work was also close to the heart of his wife, Lady Lavinia. They had made a systematic study of the workhouse system, and though they acknowledged that conditions had much improved since the 1850s, they had seen with their own eyes hundreds of grey, unsmiling children crowded into workhouses and orphanages. They were determined to do something about it. The idea of an annual holiday was Lady Lavinia's. Surely, she argued, two weeks by the sea for unwanted children, with healthy air and sunshine, was not too much to ask of society? The opposition was loud in its scorn. "Holidays! For pauper children! What next? Let them learn to be grateful that they were given food and shelter."

Sir Ian and his lady battled on. When it was proved that one of the causes of rickets was lack of sunlight they knew that this information could be used to further their cause. Were not half the workhouse children afflicted with rickets? And were they not advocating a holiday in sunshine?

They won the debate and, to their overwhelming relief, the committee passed, by a narrow majority, the resolution that money should be set aside for holidays for the children of one London workhouse. Additional funds were approved for a further five, if the experiment proved to be successful.

Suitable premises were found in Kent. This consisted of a series of large barns and sheds, which could be adapted as dormitories for the children, sleeping on straw mattresses on the floor. One of the sheds could be converted into a kitchen. The sheds were situated in fields which ran down to the sea. Sir Ian and members of the committee travelled to Kent to inspect the site and the accommodation. It all seemed perfect.

Sir Ian's next visit was to the workhouse selected for the experiment, in order to address the children himself and tell them of their good fortune. He wasn't going to hand over that pleasant task to anyone else, he told his wife. Was it not he who had haggled with the committee, hour after hour? So he was going to have the reward and pleasure of seeing the children's faces when they were told.

Accordingly Sir Ian had taken the train from Oxford, and was in a cab bound for his destination in the East End. He told the cabman to halt about a mile from the workhouse, because he wanted to walk the rest of the way in order to absorb the atmosphere. He attracted much attention in the London Streets. He was tall and slim and well dressed. He was also clean. "Vere's a toff, nah, do-goodin' " was one of many of the whispers as he passed. Sir Ian was unaware of any of the sideways glances. His mind was fixed on his mission and he was determined that in years ahead the holiday project would be expanded to all workhouse children, nation-wide.

The crocodile of little girls was returning from school. Jane was about halfway along the line, humming to herself as she marched along. She was looking at the pigtails of the little girl in front of her, watching them bounce up and down and wondering why they bounced more times than each step. "There must be some reason" she was thinking. She looked up, and her heart stopped beating. Pigtails, marching, the street, the buildings, the very sky itself vanished from her universe. Her Daddy was on the other side of the street walking straight towards the workhouse. She stood stock-still. The girls behind piled into her, causing commotion in the line.

"Get along there," shouted Officer Hawkins and hit her on the head. She neither heard nor felt a thing. Her father had turned into the workhouse gate and was walking straight towards the main door. She knew that it was he. Not a shadow of doubt. He was exactly as she had always known he would look, and exactly like the picture in the book, tall, slim, grey trousers, a frock coat, a top hat and a walking cane. He had come to take her away, as he had always said he would.

Joy, unspeakable joy, flooded over Jane, with a rush of love impossible for any mere adult to describe. The intensity of a child's feelings is quite beyond our understanding, though we have all been children. Jane was almost suffocating with the power of her emotions. She felt that something huge and unknown was inside her and was going to burst or break open, or do something strange and frightening.

"Get on there, I told you."

Another clout round the head, and Jane ran a few steps to catch up with the others. The door had closed behind her Daddy, and the girls marched round the back to their usual entrance and stood in line for inspection before being told that they were to go into the hall.

Jane didn't stand in line with the others. She rushed straight upstairs to the dormitory and collided with an officer on the stairway. She was flushed and breathless, but she grabbed the officer's hand, almost shouting.

"Quick, quick! I must have a clean dress and a clean apron!"

The officer was not used to being spoken to by a child in that manner. She shook her off.

"Don't be stupid. You have a clean dress on Sunday. Not before."

The child stamped.

"But I must, I must! My Daddy's downstairs, and I want a clean dress and apron before I see him."

"Your what?"

"My Daddy. He's downstairs. He's in the Master's office. I saw him go in."

There was something so intense, so urgent and compelling about the child, that the officer gave in, and Jane was supplied with a clean dress and apron, against all the rules. She rushed to the washroom and washed her face and hands, and brushed her hair until her curls shone, then flew downstairs to join the other children.

The officer plodded downstairs and told her colleagues of this extraordinary scene. They agreed that the child was mad, but one, with a snigger, said, "She may be right. Everyone says Jane's father was a high-born gentleman. Well, there's a fancy-lookin' gent gone in Master's office. We don't know what for." And she rubbed the side of her nose suggestively.

The girls filed into the hall and sat in rows, the youngest at the front, and the oldest girls at the back. Jane sat in the fifth row, about central. She sat with her eyes fixed on the door where she knew her Daddy would enter. She was burning with expectation.

The door opened and her father walked in followed by the Master. Her heart stopped beating again. Yes, it was him, the same grave yet kindly face, the same smooth grey hair, and the same deep-set eyes with a smile at the corners. She had always known he would look like that.

She sat up straight and tall. She was taller than the other girls anyway, but she increased her height by her posture. Her eyes were aflame with love. Her mouth was slightly opened, her teeth gleamed white as she smiled. An aura of light seemed to radiate from her.

Sir Ian spoke to the children from the pulpit. He could see right down the long hall and the massed young faces staring at him. Most of the faces looked glum and unresponsive, and it is always difficult to address an audience from whom the speaker feels no wave of sympathy. He had a joyful message to impart; he hoped for a joyful response. But most of the girls looked straight ahead, no emotion registering on their features. However, there was one little girl, sitting in the middle near the front, who looked really animated. Sir Ian therefore did what many public speakers do; he fixed his attention on one face in the audience and spoke to that one person alone.

He spoke of the summer coming and how hot London gets at that time of year, and said: "I am going to take you away in the summer."

The little girl stifled a gasp of joy, her eyes alight. He spoke of the countryside and the seaside, and said: "I am going to take you to a beautiful place by the sea."

The little girl could scarcely contain her emotion, as he continued: "You will be able to paddle and swim, and build sand-castles and collect shells."

The little girl in the fifth row was now breathing fast, and clenching and stretching her fingers.

Sir Ian said, "We will do all this when the summer comes."

The little girl gave a shuddering sigh of joy as he stepped down from the pulpit. He felt pleased with himself. Overall, it had been a good address and a good response.

48

The Master had also seen Jane's reaction and made a silent note to reprimand her about exhibitionism. He had not yet heard from his subordinate officers the story about the clean dress and apron.

The girls stood up to leave the hall. One by one they filed passed the Master and Sir Ian. It was at this point that Jane lost all control of herself. As she passed them she rushed out of line and flung her arms around Sir Ian's waist, crying, "Thank you, Daddy, thank you, thank you," and she burst into tears, sobbing into his waistcoat.

He was surprised by this, and not a little touched. He ruffled her pretty hair and murmured, "There, there, my child. Don't take on so. You'll go to the sea-side, and have a lovely time."

The Master tried to apologise and pull Jane away, but Sir Ian restrained him, saying that it was to the child's credit that she showed so much gratitude. He patted her hair and shoulders and took out a fine lawn handkerchief to wipe her eyes.

"There, now, dry your tears. You can't be spoiling your pretty little face with tears. Let's see you smile, now. That's better."

The girls continued to file past, and Jane still clung to him. The master was standing beside them, seething with fury. All the girls had left the refectory and Sir Ian disentangled Jane's arms from around him.

"There now, little one," he said, "off you run now. Join your playmates. And I promise you will go to the seaside in the summer time."

Jane reached upwards and touched his face, and breathed the words: "Oh Daddy, I love you Daddy, I love you so much."

She whispered it very softly, for him alone, but the master heard every word, and said out of the side of his mouth to an officer.

"Take her to the punishment room."

He then escorted his guest to the boys' section where Sir Ian gave his second address.

Jane ran to where the girls were assembled. They were agog with excitement and she was the centre of attention. She entered, proud and confident, her eyes dancing.

"That's my Daddy. He's going to take me away."

They crowded around, chattering. Most girls believed her. Some of the older ones didn't.

"Don't be silly. We're all going on holiday, not just you."

Jane replied haughtily.

"Oh well, perhaps he will take some of you others as well. He's very rich. But he's my Daddy and he's taking me specially. After that we will live together in his big house."

An officer was standing right behind her. Jane did not know it while she spoke, but she saw the girls looking over her shoulder, and she turned round. The officer grabbed her shoulder.

"You come along with me, my girl. The Master wants to see you."

Jane's heart leaped. Her bright eyes looked over to the other girls.

"There, you see. My Daddy's going to take me away, now. That's why the Master wants to see me."

The officer looked grim and most of the girls looked nervous. Only Jane was happy. She walked confidently away with the officer.

She was taken to the punishment room. The door was opened, she was pushed in and then the door was locked from the outside.

Jane was surprised, even startled, to find herself in a small room, about eight feet square, with no windows except a slit of a fan-light high up on one wall. There was no furniture, except a three-legged stool alone on the stone floor. Around the wall hung several canes of different lengths and a leather-thonged whip which had three tails, with a small lead pellet attached to the end of each tail.

She couldn't understand it. Why should they want her to wait here? Still, what did it matter, she thought to herself. She could still feel her Daddy's kind, warm hands as he caressed her hair, and the sound of his voice as he called her "my child". What did it matter? What did anything in the world matter, but that she had told him she loved him and he had called her his child and promised to take her away.

Jane sat down on the stool to wait.

Sir Ian Astor-Smaleigh returned to Oxford that evening full of philanthropic satisfaction and happiness. It had been a wonderful day. All the arrangements had been agreed with the workhouse master, the dates settled, the travelling arranged, catering organised, even the clothing supplier contracted. No wonder he was pleased. Over three hundred desperately poor children would benefit. He would be able to give a full and satisfactory report to his committee.

Lady Lavinia read his face as he entered the house. She shared her husband's happiness. The maid brought in a late meal and they sat down to discuss the day's work. He told her how he had addressed the children, twice; firstly the girls and then the boys. They were poor, grey little things, he said, with very little life or vitality in them, not like our own children, who tumble all over the place, and can't be contained. She protested that their children were not all that bad, "But do go on, dear".

"However," he said, "there was one little girl who seemed different. She was full of life. She was hanging on to my every word as I spoke. She didn't take her eyes off me and she was obviously overcome with joy at what I had been telling the girls. In fact she ran up to me afterwards to thank me."

Sir Ian had been on the point of saying that the little girl had called him 'Daddy' but then he thought better of it. After all, women were funny creatures and you never knew what they might think once they got an idea into their heads.

Lady Lavinia asked what the child was like.

"Oh, I don't know. Those damnation workhouse uniforms make all children look alike. I know she had dark hair. That's all I can say. But one thing I do know for certain — she was the only one to come up and say 'thank you' personally."

Lady Lavinia smiled fondly at her husband.

"It does her much credit," she said, "and you can be sure of another thing also — there is one little girl for whom this will be a day to remember."

A Day to Remember

Jane waited for nearly two hours in the punishment room. This was because the Master had to accompany Sir Ian to the boys' section, for his second address, after which many practical arrangements had to be sorted out. Then the Master wanted his supper, and a chance to discuss Jane's wickedness with his wife.

Two hours is a long time for a small child to wait alone in a closed room (Jane was eight years old). She got hungry and fidgety. She was not particularly worried or frightened, in fact her mind was buoyant and happy. Her Daddy had cuddled her and called her "my child".

She heard a key in the lock, and jumped up expectantly, smoothing out her apron, and running her fingers through her curls, her face eager. The Master and a male officer entered. Her face fell.

"Where's my Daddy?" she asked in a little voice.

The Master was bent on vengeance, and this added fuel to his fury. He took two steps across the room, and hit her full in the face. She fell against the wall.

"You wicked girl. I'll knock that nonsense out of you."

54

But Jane was a girl of spirit, and she had her protector now. She wasn't afraid of anyone. Her eyes gleaming, she faced the Master.

"I'll tell my Daddy of you," she shouted.

The Master hit her again, harder this time, and stood over her when she fell.

"Sir Ian Astor-Smaleigh is not your father. Do you understand? Now say it after me: 'Sir Ian Astor-Smaleigh is not my father'. Say it."

Now at this point a very curious thing happened. Curious to an adult, that is, but logical to the mind of a child. Children frequently hear something quite different to what has actually been said, particularly if it is something new and unrelated to anything else in their experience. (For example, throughout her childhood, my daughter thought our telephone number was 'fried potato'. She had heard us say '53280'.)

Jane thought the Master said: "See a nasty smelly is not my father." It didn't make sense. She stared at him in sullen amazement.

"Say it, say it," shouted the Master.

She didn't say a word, but just looked at him. The Master repeated the whole sentence, and demanded she say it, his hand raised threateningly. The child stared at him in amazement.

"A nasty smelly?" she exclaimed, her tone lifting enquiringly.

"You insolent little bastard," the man roared. "First you insult Sir Ian, and now you insult me."

To the officer, "undress her."

The officer grabbed her and started to undo the buttons of her dress. At this Jane really became alarmed and tried to pull away.

"Stop it, let me go. I'll tell my Daddy of you, I will."

"Oh, the wickedness! Has she no shame?" muttered the officer, and continued to undress Jane until she stood naked before them. She was crying and frightened now, but still she resisted as much as her puny strength would allow.

"Hold her hands tight and turn her around," ordered the Master, selecting the leather-thonged whip from the wall. Jane saw him take it down, and screamed.

"No! No! Don't! Let me go! Da . . ."

The first lash fell across her back, knocking all the breath out of her. Pain like fire shot through her body, and the second stroke fell before she had time to breathe. When the third fell, with excruciating pain, Jane realised what was happening. She gathered all her strength and pulled hard at the hands holding her screaming

"No, stop it. Daddy, Da . . ."

The fourth lash fell with added force and weight. The three lead pellets at the end of the thongs cut into her back. The pain was like nothing we can imagine.

A flogging across the back and shoulders causes indescribable pain because the bones, which are a mass of sensitive nerve endings, are only just beneath the skin surface, and there is very little soft tissue protecting them. Anyone who has banged the shinbone hard will know a little of the pain that Jane experienced every time the lash fell. The leather thongs were hard and brittle and cut the skin, exposing the bones to further pain and injury. The lead pellets struck in random places, tearing the flesh.

By the fifth lash, Jane was losing consciousness. All her weight had fallen on to the arms of the officer who held her, and she vomited down his trousers.

"Dirty little thing," he exclaimed, and jerked his knee upwards, catching her in the mouth. Her teeth clamped together over her tongue, which was lolling forward, and blood trickled out of her mouth.

Still the Master continued his self-appointed task. He had intended twenty lashes of the whip, but his wife had cautioned him, saying, "You don't want to kill her. Questions might be asked. Ten lashes will be enough to teach the girl the lesson she deserves."

Jane felt no more pain. She was only conscious of a terrible jolt to her body each time the lash fell. She could hear and see nothing beyond a red mist that swam all around her.

Eight . . . . nine . . . . ten. The Master brought down the last stroke with satisfaction. The officer let go of her hands, and she fell to the floor. She had wet herself, and she slid into the urine, mixed with vomit and blood.

"Get a couple of the women to take her to the dormitory. She is to come to my office at eight o' clock tomorrow morning, before she goes to school."

The Master issued the orders, hung the whip on the hook, and left the punishment room.

A nurse and a female officer came to collect Jane to take her up to the dormitory. The nurse was shocked with what she saw but the officer, who had seen it all before, was very blasé.

"She'll get over it. A good beating never did a child any harm. 'Spare the lash and spoil the child.' Come on. Get up on your feet you lazy girl and put your dress on."

The nurse was horrified.

"You can't put a dress on her back like that. She needs lint and gauze and ointments."

"Well you won't get them," said the officer, with finality in her voice. "The Master would never stand for favouritism."

The nurse took off her apron and wrapped the child in it. Jane could barely stand, let alone walk, so the nurse carried her upstairs to the dormitory. She laid her on the bed, face downwards, and fetched a bowl of cold water. She sat beside the bed for hours, bathing the girl's back with cold water to reduce the blood flow and restrict the terminal capillaries, so reducing the inflammation.

In spite of the pain Jane fell asleep. The nurse continued to bathe her back and all the girls crept into the dormitory, subdued and silent. They crept into bed, and only a few whispers were heard. One of their number, the brightest and liveliest, had been most terribly flogged, and a wave of shock and horror united them in silence.

A little girl with blonde hair crept up to the nurse. She was crying piteously. She said her name was Peggy and she laid her fair hair against Jane's dark curls, whispering to her, kissing her, and sobbing. She asked the nurse if she could help, and so she took a cold sponge and bathed Jane's back just as the nurse showed her. Together, the stunned and silent nurse and the weeping little girl ministered to the stricken Jane, until Peggy was so tired that she fell asleep, and the nurse lifted her up and put her to bed.

It was probably this action on the part of the nurse and her child helper that saved Jane's life.

All night she drifted in and out of consciousness, and the nurse sat up with her through the long hours, whilst the other girls slept. Sometimes Jane moaned in pain, and moved her limbs. Sometimes she let out a weak cry of "Daddy". Sometimes she took the nurse's hand, and held it fast. The blood on the back was clotting, the nurse noted with satisfaction and the child could obviously move her legs, so at least the spine had not been broken. The hours slipped past.

The Master had ordered that Jane should report to his office at 8 a.m. before school. But Jane could not be roused. The Mistress was called and she, although secretly shocked by the child's appearance, declared that she was shamming, and pulled the mattress so hard that Jane fell out of bed onto the floor on the other side where she lay, immobile. The Mistress then looked coldly at her, turned her with her foot and declared that she could have the day in bed, but must be ready for school the following morning.

Thinking to be helpful, the nurse, (who knew nothing of the background) said to the Mistress, as she was leaving. "The child has been calling for her Daddy all night long, madam. Do you think it would be helpful if we were to fetch him?"

To her surprise the Mistress exploded.

"Her Daddy! Oh, the iniquity, the sinfulness! Will there be no end to this child's wickedness?", and she stormed off to tell the Master of this latest revelation. Something else must be done to purge Jane of her lies and wicked stories.

Jane was not able to go to school the next day, nor for many days after that. Gradually the pain eased, and her mind cleared a little. She was able to stand, and to take a little food. She barely spoke, and barely raised her eyes from the ground.

The Mistress came to the dormitory to tell her that all this shamming would not be tolerated a moment longer and she must go to school, but first the Master wished to see her. Jane went deathly white and started to shake all over. She attempted to follow the Mistress out of the dormitory, but her legs gave way, and she sank to the floor. An officer hauled her to her feet and dragged her downstairs. As they approached the door of the Master's office Jane vomited the contents of her stomach. It trickled all down her dress. The Mistress was furious.

"We'll soon have that dress off you." she shouted.

The Master sat at his desk and eyed Jane up and down. The officer kept hold of her, or she would probably have fallen.

"You wicked child. You monstrous liar. It seems there is no end to your depravity. In spite of just chastisement you still persist in calling Sir Ian Astor-Smaleigh your father. If you ever do so again, I will flog you again. But, at my wife's request, I will not do so now. You see how good and kind the Mistress is to you, and how little you deserve it. For the time being, as a reminder to you of your wickedness and as an example to the others, you will be deprived of your dress and apron, and you will wear a sack. Now go. And remember, if you say again that Sir Ian Astor-Smaleigh is your father, I will flog you again. And the next time I will show no mercy."

Jane was taken away to the laundry room and her dress and apron removed. A sack with three holes, for head and arms, was put on her with string around the waist. Her hair was shorn as close as possible, so that she looked nearly bald. She was sent to school like that.

If Miss Sutton was horrified at her appearance, she was even more horrified at the change in the child's behaviour. The little girl sat shivering and cringing and saying absolutely nothing. If Miss Sutton went up to her, she reacted with terror. In fact she seemed terrified of everyone, even the other children who spoke to her. She did not read, and she barely joined in any of the lessons. If she held a pencil, her hand shook so much that she was unable to write. The most alarming feature was her total silence. For two whole weeks she said absolutely nothing, but only looked up at people with terrified eyes.

The headmistress wrote to the Master of the workhouse, asking what had happened. He replied to the effect that he had absolute authority over the workhouse children and was answerable to no one. He reminded the headmistress that he was a member of the Board of Governors of the school. If there was any interference he was in a strong position to complain to the Chairman about the conduct and competence of the headmistress. No further action was taken.

Humiliations were heaped upon Jane. She started bedwetting. The workhouse punishment for this was for the offending child to be stood on the detention platform, which was at the front of the dining hall, visible to everyone, holding her wet sheet. The child had no breakfast that day. Morning after morning, throughout the winter and spring, Jane, shorn of her hair and wearing a sack tied with string, stood miserably, conspicuously on that platform, clutching a wet sheet. Day after day she went to school with no breakfast. This morning penance continued with monotonous regularity.

The scars on Jane's back healed more quickly than the scars on her mind. In fact, her mind and personality never did really recover. She was never again seen to smile, nor heard to laugh. Her buoyant, bouncing step changed to a cringing shuffle. Her flashing blue eyes were never seen, because she would look up briefly, fearfully, and then down again quickly. Her voice changed to a whisper. Her precocious level of schoolwork changed to average or below average in the class. Miss Sutton was heartbroken, but however much she tried to encourage Jane to write stories for her, as in the old days, she had no success. Jane put her hands up to her mouth and cast fearful sideways glances at her teacher, and whispered: "Yes, Miss Sutton". But after half an hour the page was blank.

Jane's mind was largely blank as well. She had very little memory of events leading up to her flogging, and she hadn't the faintest idea why it had occurred. She went through it all in her mind, over and again, round and round, endless thought repetition that got her nowhere. Everything was confused. Nothing made sense.

She was clear in her mind that it had something to do with the day her Daddy came to the workhouse and told her that he would take her away in the summer. But why had the Master been so cross with her? Her Daddy wasn't cross, so why should the Master be cross? Why had he flogged her, and made her wear the sack? She tried and tried to think what she had done wrong, but could think of nothing. And why had the Master shouted several times: "See a nasty smelly is not your father?". This was the biggest puzzle of all. "A nasty smelly?" What did it mean? Her Daddy wasn't a 'smelly'. Her Daddy smelled of lavender as she had always known he would. She had cuddled him and smelled the lavender. She had never called the Master or Mistress nasty smellies. So why had he flogged her? Like a swarm of wasps these thoughts buzzed in her mind, all the time, day and night, until she felt she would go mad with their buzzing.

She crept around the workhouse and school, hardly speaking, barely lifting her eyes from the ground, conscious only of sick fear deep inside her lest she should again incur the Master's wrath, and the lash would again fall on her scarred back.

Not for one moment did Jane, in her thoughts, impute any blame to her father, or cease to love him. In fact her love was stronger and more real because she had seen him and touched him and he had stroked her hair and called her "my child", and said he would take her away in the summer time. The spring came, and Jane knew that the summer would come next. It would not be long now. She only had to endure and be good, and not get into any more trouble and her Daddy would come, as sure as the summer sunshine, and take her away from the workhouse forever. This fragile dream she clung to. It was her one solace in her misery and bewilderment.

May, June, July. The summer days were drawing out. There was a buzz of excitement amongst the workhouse girls — they were going on holiday. It had never happened before, and they were the first to experience this. Jane's crushed spirits rose a little, and she allowed herself to lift her eyes from the floor a bit.

August came, and preparations were made. Summer dresses and sandals were provided. The girls could talk of nothing else. They were in a fever pitch of excitement. The day for departure arrived.

The girls were standing in the dining hall after breakfast. Everything was ready. The Mistress entered.

"Right, now. Form a line and march quietly out. We will proceed to the station."

The girls stepped forward.

"Not you. Stay where you are."

The Mistress pointed to Jane. The girls marched out.

Sick disappointment took possession of Jane. She saw the last girl leave, as she stood in her place. She heard footsteps echo down the corridors and doors bang. Then silence.

Now it was that Jane's heart broke. Hitherto her suffering had been physical. Now the torture was mental, emotional, and spiritual. The utter desolation of rejection was hers to savour. Her Daddy was not going to take her away. Her Daddy did not love her, or want her. That was why she was there in the workhouse. He had put her there, because he did not want her. She would never see him again. She knew it in her heart.

Throughout the livelong summer, alone but for the porter's wife who brought her food twice a day, Jane lived with this bitter knowledge. She had nothing to do, day after day; no books, no toys, no pencils and paper. She cried herself to sleep alone in the dormitory; ate alone in the huge refectory; went out alone in the yard (euphemistically called a playground) and walked around the walls. She spoke to no one except the porter's wife, twice a day.

The other girls returned, sun-browned and happy. Jane heard stories of the seaside and paddling and catching crabs and building sandcastles. She didn't say a word. The knowledge of rejection, of being unwanted, is more terrible to live with than anything else, even bereavement, and a rejected child will usually never get over it. A physical pain entered Jane's body, somewhere in the region of the solar plexus, which ached all the time, and from which she was destined never to be free.

Unknown to Jane, Sir Ian and Lady Lavinia visited the children's holiday camp. They played with the children by the sea, organised races for them across the sands, hired a man with a donkey to give them rides and read them stories in the evening. They were very happy with their work, which was uniquely successful.

At the end of the day Sir Ian asked the Master.

"I have not seen that pretty child who came up to thank me when I first met you all. Where is she?"

The Master was nonplussed, but his resourceful wife stepped forward with a curtsey.

"The child has an aunt, sir, who always takes her on holiday each year. I assure you, sir, at this very moment the child is playing happily on a beach somewhere in Devon."

She curtsied again.

"I am glad to hear it," said Lady Lavinia, "but for my part, I am sorry not to see the child. My husband spoke most highly of her."

After they had left, the Master said.

"What a blessing we did not bring that wretched child. If she had gone running up to that man, in front of his wife, and clung to him and called him Daddy and told him she loved him, Heaven knows what trouble it would have stirred up."

And on this occasion — who can tell — the Master may have been right.

Frank

"Give me a boy for the first five years
of his life, and I will make the man."
Rousseau

Frank had but a dim recollection of his father. He remembered a tall, strong man, whom he held in awe. He remembered his big voice and huge, rough hands. He could remember once tracing the veins on the back of this vast hand with his little fingers, and looking at his own smooth white skin and wondering if he would ever have hands like that. To be like his father was his only aim and ambition and he worshipped him. In the later, sadder years of his childhood he tried desperately to remember what his father was like, but a phantom that comes and goes could not have been more elusive and only the dimmest memory remained.

He remembered his mother much more clearly; his sweet, gentle mother who was never strong because she was always coughing. He remembered the sound of her voice as she sang songs to him and played with him. Above all, he remembered her cuddles as she put him to bed and lay down beside him.

In the winter his mother hardly went out of doors because of her weak chest and his father would say, as he went off to work, "Now you look after your mother while I'm away, Frank lad. I'm relying on you to take care of her for me."

And Frank would look up at his god with big solemn eyes and accept the task as a sacred duty.

When a tiny baby was born — so tiny that everyone said she would not live — Frank was four years old. He had been an only child all his life and could not conceive of any other child entering his world. Many boys of that age become very jealous of a new-born baby, but not Frank. He was mesmerised and fascinated by this tiny creature, hardly bigger than a teacup, who could move and cry, and who needed so much care. Not for a moment did he resent the hours of attention given to the baby. In fact he liked to help. The most fascinating thing of all was to watch his mother breast-feeding the baby, and he tried never to be far away when this mysterious and beautiful ritual was going on. He kept very quiet, and crept close to his mother, and watched, spellbound, the baby sucking and the milk oozing from the nipple.

The baby was premature and sickly, and for a long while her life hung in the balance. His father had said to him, many times: "You've got a special job to do, young man. You've got to look after your little sister. That's your job now, lad."

So he watched over her all the time, and hardly went out to play with the other boys in the court, because he was so busy looking after his little sister.

The baby didn't die. She gained strength and became quite robust, although she always remained small. She was christened Margaret and was called

Peggy, because Margaret seemed too long a name for such a small baby, and his father said, after the christening, "You done a good job there, son, and I'm proud on yer."

Catastrophe struck. In those years typhoid was raging through East London. His huge, strong father, who had never known a day of illness in his life, was struck by the epidemic and died within a few days. His mother, who had never been strong, was spared and so was the baby. His mother went out to work, office cleaning. She left home in the early hours of each morning, and again each evening, leaving Frank to look after Peggy, who was now a toddler.

One day Frank ran home from school (he didn't think much of school, regarding it as a waste of time) to take over the domestic responsibilities from his mother, so that she could go out to her job. It was cold and she was coughing badly, but she went nonetheless. Money had to be earned, or they would be homeless. Frank did as he had so often done before: put some wood that he had found on his way home from school onto the fire. He made some tea for himself and Peggy, played with her and as the fire was dying, he undressed her and put her to bed creeping in beside her for warmth.

In the middle of the night he woke up, aware that something was wrong. It was pitch black, and the quietness was terrifying. He could hear Peggy breathing, but that was all. Something was missing. Sick terror seized him as he realised that his mother was not there. In panic he felt all over the bed, but the side where his mother slept was empty. He called, in a small voice so as not to wake Peggy, but there was no reply. He crept out of bed and found the matches. He struck one and the flame leapt up, lighting the whole room momentarily. His mother was not there. Blinded by tears, and choking down his sobs and his terror, he crept back into bed and held Peggy in his arms.

The cold had badly affected his mother as soon as she stepped outside. She was asthmatic and bronchitic, and had been fighting down a chest infection for several weeks. She had a mile to walk to the bus, and the freezing mist rising off the river got into her lungs. She was thankful for the brief respite of sitting in the bus, but by the time she got to the building where she was employed, she felt more dead than alive. She went to the cleaning cupboard to get out her things, but the bucket felt so heavy that she could hardly move it. She asked permission to make herself a cup of tea, saying she would feel better with something warm inside her. The tea was indeed comforting, but the building was cold and she sat shivering in the basement, pulling her shawl around her shoulders, and coughing. One by one the office workers left and she was alone.

She had about three hours of work, normally. After one hour, she had scarcely achieved one tenth of it. She felt so weak she could scarcely drag herself around, and there was still the scrubbing to do. She returned to the basement to get the bucket — the one that had felt impossibly heavy when empty — and filled it with water. She pushed it along the floor with her feet and then lifted it up the stairs one by one, resting it on each stair as she did so. She reached the second storey this way, and then her failing strength must have given out. She fell down the stairs that she had so laboriously climbed, knocking the bucket over as she fell. She was drenched with water and lay on the stone floor all night. In the morning they found her dead at the bottom of the stairs.

Frank had never spent a night away from his mother. There was only one bed so they had all slept together even when his father was alive. He had never even contemplated a time without the comforting warmth of her body beside him. Now, in the dark and cold of the room, the bed felt like a hostile and alien territory, and he wanted to run away from it and run to the next-door neighbours, screaming. But there was Peggy to think of. She was quietly sleeping, unaware that anything was wrong. So he bit his lips and rubbed his fists into his eyes and cuddled up close to her.

He was six years old.

He must have slept, because it was daylight when he was awoken by Peggy crying. There was some milk and water left from the night before but it was cold and she pushed it away. He did not know what to do. He took a wet nappy off her, as he had seen his mother do, and then didn't know what to do with it, so hid it under the bed. There was no more wood for a fire. He drank the cold milk himself and crept back into bed with her. They fell asleep again.

He awoke as a crowd of neighbouring women entered the room.

"Oh. it's a shame, oie tells ya."

"Poor li'le kids. Vey didn' ask 'a be born.'

"Both dead in six months."

"It makes yer wanna cry, don' it?"

Frank looked around him in bewilderment and held Peggy defensively, pulling the blanket up higher.

A man entered the room.

"Are these the children of the deceased?" he enquired.

A chorus of voices answered.

"Yeah, more's the pity."

"Poor li'le lambs."

"Vey don' know wha's 'appened."

"And is there no relative to look after them?"

'No' as 'ow I knows on, do you, Lil?"

"Nah, no-one."

"They will have to come with me, and the effects sold to contribute to the Guardians' expenses."

He looked around the room at the meagre furniture — one bed, one table, and two chairs, a small cupboard, a washing bowl, a chamber pot, a candle stick, some tin plates and cups — all back-breakingly acquired by the father, to provide for his family.

"Will someone get them ready while I take an inventory?"

Two women stepped forward, and Frank grabbed the back of the bed, clutching Peggy.

"Where's mummy?" he demanded.

"Yer mum's dead, luvvy, more's the pity."

"No, my dad's dead," he insisted.

"An so's yer mum, dearie, found dead vis mornin' in ve office."

"Blue, she was," chorused the women to each other.

"Frozen stiff, vey say, an' soakin' wet."

"Wet froo, an' all, and 'er wiv her weak chest."

"No' surprisin' aint it?"

Frank looked from one to another, and horror struck his heart. Was his mother dead? And he had promised his father that he would look after her! What had gone wrong? Peggy was beginning to whimper and he held her tight. Kind hands were placed upon him. He caught the bars of the bedstead with all his strength and turned his back on the women, holding Peggy, who was beginning to scream now, between his body and the bed-head.

"You will have to get him free," said the man. "They cannot stay here alone."

It took four women to loosen his fingers from the bars. A child's fingers can be incredibly strong if they are curled around something. Eventually two women were holding him and Peggy in their arms. He was biting and scratching and kicking in an hysteria of fear and rage. He shouted at the woman holding Peggy, "Give her to me. She's my sister. Don't take her away". Tears were streaming down his face.

"We will have to go. Does anyone know where the key is kept?" said the man.

The door of the room was locked, and they made their way downstairs. The woman holding Frank was badly bruised. They walked through the streets, collecting a crowd of onlookers as they went.

They were admitted to the infants' section of the workhouse, where boys and girls under seven years of age were housed. They were undressed and bathed and were not unkindly treated. In fact, Peggy's tiny stature and wispy blonde hair evoked a stream of sympathy from the women who received them. Frank had exhausted his fury, and sullenly allowed himself to be washed and his hair examined for fleas.

"We'll have to cut it off. You know the rules."

He submitted to having his head shaved, but when he saw a large woman doing the same to Peggy, he rushed at her and butted her in the stomach with his head. She collapsed onto a chair winded, then grabbed the boy and thrashed him soundly, whilst another officer shaved Peggy.

"It's a shame, cutting this pretty hair. But it will soon grow again."

Poor little Peggy looked like a tiny Martian when they had finished, and Frank sobbed in impotent rage.

They were dressed in workhouse clothes and taken to the playroom where the other children were. We would not call it a playroom today, because there was nothing to play with. It was just a large, bare room, about 40 feet long by 20 feet wide with high, uncurtained windows, and rough floorboards.

"Now you play quietly with the others until tea-time."

The door was shut, and the officer left.

They stood shyly in the doorway, looking at about forty other children, all wearing the same clothes. Frank, acutely self-conscious that he and Peggy had no hair, tried to hide her under his jacket. A boy of about his age ran up to them, shouting.

74

"You're new. You're new. Where've you come from? What's your name, baldy? An' who's this little squirt, then?"

He pulled at Peggy's arm and tickled her scalp. Frank flung himself upon the boy, fighting with cold and savage fury. All his rage, which had been building up during the day, was concentrated in the attack upon his tormentor. The other children stood back to watch the fun. The boy was no slouch when it came to fighting and they were evenly matched. There were no adults in the room to stop them.

Peggy was terrified and ran screaming to a corner, where she crouched down, hiding her head. A little girl with dark hair left the others and came over to her, and put her small arms around the sobbing child.

"Don't cry, please don't cry. They're only fighting. Boys are always fighting. Boys are awful. But don't cry. Here, sit on my knee."

The girl sat down on the floor and Peggy climbed on her knee. She played with a long, dark ringlet hanging down near to her face, and laughed when she pulled it and it bounced up again.

The girl smiled happily, and cuddled Peggy.

"You're like a little doll. I've never had a doll, but I've seen them, and you are like one. But you're better than a doll, because you're real, and dolls are only pretend. Will you be my friend? My name's Jane, and I'm three. What's yours?"

Peggy didn't say anything, but her tears stopped and she played with the ringlets. Jane sat quietly, cuddling Peggy, and laughing to herself as she watched the fight.

The boys were roughly the same age and weight, but Frank had the advantage of cold, calculated fury in defence of his sister. He glanced at the other boys who were egging them on, and knew instinctively that if he lost the fight Peggy would never be safe from their torments. After a few minutes Frank's adversary was on the floor in a corner, and called out.

"Truce. Give in. Hold 'im off."

Frank turned to face the others. He raised his fists defiantly.

"Anyone else want a go?"

No one stepped forward.

Frank swaggered his way over to the corner where Peggy sat on Jane's knee. "Thanks," he said; "she's only two, and she's scared. Her name's Peggy and she's my sister. I'm Frank."

The girl had a merry laugh, open features and piercing blue eyes. Frank liked her, he liked the way she was nursing Peggy and he saw the contentment with which the little girl responded to the older one, and he knew that he could trust her. "Let's be friends," he said.

Over the next few weeks the reality of his mother's death dawned upon Frank.

He would never see her again and pain inside reduced him to tears. Other boys laughed and jeered at him, but he only had to stick out his jaw and raise his fists aggressively, and they quickly backed off. Peggy did not seem so unhappy, because Frank was always there and had been her companion and protector from the time she was born. Also, Jane had taken to her and petted and fussed her, calling her "my little doll". Jane was indisputably the leader among the girls, so her protection meant a good deal.

Jane was good for Frank also. He liked her with instinctive childhood affection for a kindred spirit. He approved of her gentle ways with Peggy, and he trusted her. He also liked her naughtiness. She was always playing tricks and pranks, making everyone laugh. She would jump out from behind a door when the officer opened it, shouting "boo", and then run away laughing. She was always caught and smacked, but nothing seemed to quench her high spirits, and she was into the next lot of mischief before her bottom had finished smarting. The day she climbed the water pipe in the playground and sat on the gutter and wouldn't come down was one of the funniest Frank could ever remember. Fat old officer Hawkins was on duty that day and got onto a ladder, and then lumbered up it, with all the boys crowding around underneath, trying to see her knickers. When she finally got Jane down, she thrashed her soundly in the playground, and then again in the evening before bedtime, but Jane just rubbed her bottom, and shook her curls defiantly, and did not seem to care. Frank openly admired the vivacious Jane, and she, flattered by a bigger boy's attention and with a little girl's instinct for flirtation, drew him towards her.

The night times were the worst for Frank. Alone in a small hard bed, with darkness all around, he sobbed silently for his sweet mother, whom he had adored with all the passion of boyhood. He missed the warmth of her body, he missed the smell of her skin, the touch of her hand, the sound of her breathing. He would creep over to Peggy's bed and get in beside her and the smell of her hair would numb his pain and they would sleep together till morning. This became their one mutual comfort and happiness in the first months of their life in the workhouse.

A year passed. After breakfast one morning, Frank and two other boys were taken to the Matron's office. She said, abruptly, "You are big boys now that you are seven, and you are going to the boys' section today. Wait in the hallway, and the van will come for you at nine o'clock."

The boys did not know what it meant, and the three of them sat on the bench, engaged in mock fights and ribaldry.

At nine o'clock a man entered the front door and enquired, "Are these three to go?"

They were taken outside to a green van and told to climb in the back. It was all very exciting. They had never been in a van before and they clambered in willingly, ready for adventure. The van started with a jerk, and they were thrown off the bench onto the floor. They shrieked with laughter. This was going to be a good day. A ride in a van! You wait till we get back and tell the others. The van stopped twice more, and other boys of their own age climbed in. Soon there were eight boys, all shouting with laughter and skidding around the floor of the van as they turned corners; or pressing each other to see out of the small back window in order to wave at people as they passed. Everyone turned to look, because motorised transport was comparatively unusual in those days. The boys felt very privileged, and infinitely superior to the people walking, or in horse-drawn carts and wagons.

Eventually the van stopped and the back door opened. Frank saw a very large grey-stone building in front of him that he did not much like the look of.

"Where am I?" he asked.

"This is the boys' section. You come here when you are seven until you are fourteen," said a tough looking man, who was a workhouse officer.

"And where's Peggy?" he demanded.

"I don't know who Peggy is, but she's not here."

"Peggy is my sister and I look after her. My dad told me to."

The officer laughed.

"Well, someone else will have to look after her. There's no girls allowed in here."

Still Frank did not understand. He was unsure, uncertain and he felt like crying, but he wasn't going to let the other boys see him in tears, so he squared his shoulders, clenched his fists and put on a swagger as they were taken to the Master's office.

The interview was brief. They were told that they must obey the rules, obey the officers at all times, and that if they did not do so they would be punished. The Master then said, "You will be given your duties, and lunch is at one o' clock. You will start school tomorrow."

Frank had wanted to ask about Peggy, but the Master so terrified him that he did not dare to speak. He followed the officer to the dining hall with a feeling of panic and terror in his heart that he had not known since the night when his mother had not returned, and the bed was empty.

Lunch in a huge refectory with about one hundred and fifty other boys, some of them very big, was awesome, and he could not eat. He ate half a potato and drank some water, but it nearly choked him, and he could not stop his tears from falling. Some of the bigger boys pointed at him and sniggered. None of the male officers showed any sympathy. The eight new boys who had come together were all considerably sobered now. The fun and high spirits of the van ride evaporated when the reality of the situation began to dawn upon them. They had left the small world and comparative kindness of the nursery, where there were women officers and nurses, for the harsh, often brutal world of the workhouse proper where, for the next seven years, they would encounter only male officers.

Back in the nursery, after breakfast, Peggy looked around for Frank, but could not find him. She looked in the lavatory and the washroom, but he was not there. She looked in the classroom and under the stairs, but he was not in those places either. Bewildered and frightened, she stood on the bottom stair hugging the banister, and stamping with temper. An officer came up to her, but she screamed and stamped her little feet even faster, and shook her off.

"Poor little thing," remarked the officer to a colleague, "she's going to miss her brother, they were very close. She'll just have to get over it in her own time. There's nothing we can do."

Peggy was three years old. Frank had been with her all her life. She had not noticed the loss of her father when she was eighteen months old and had only the vaguest memory of her mother. But Frank was her world, her life, her security and all the love in her heart was for him alone. She was utterly devastated. All day she stood on the bottom step, hugging the smooth, round balustrade. Sometimes she was silent, sometimes sobbing. Sometimes she kicked the stair and hurt her toe. Twice she wet herself, but she wouldn't move. Jane came up, and tried to talk to her, but she shook her shoulders and stamped and screamed, "Go away".

"Leave her alone," said an officer to Jane, "she'll get over it in a day or two."

Towards evening Peggy started to bang her head on the balustrade. It hurt, but she wanted it to. Perhaps Frank would come when he knew she had hurt herself. But when he didn't come she sobbed uncontrollably and slipped down onto the stairs in a deep sleep. A nurse picked her up, and carried her to the dormitory and put her to bed.

For the next three months Peggy hunted for Frank every day. She always expected to find him, but she never did. She asked everyone: "Where's Frank?" and was told that he had been transferred to the big boys' section — but she did not understand. She developed the habit of sitting alone in a corner and rocking herself. A nurse who knew that this was a particularly frightening development in a lonely, insecure child, tried to comfort her. But Peggy could not be comforted. Each lonely night, she sucked her thumb and rocked herself and cried for Frank to come to her. But he didn't come, and she cried herself to sleep.

As the months passed she stopped looking for Frank and asked for him less, until eventually she stopped asking. It was assumed that she had forgotten all about him.

It was to be nine years before brother and sister saw each other again, and by then they did not recognise each other.

Billingsgate

At the age of seven, Frank had entered an all-male world of petty rules, upheld by harsh, uncompromising discipline and gratuitous tyrannies. Many of the officers were men who, themselves, had been brought up in a workhouse during the nineteenth century when conditions for paupers were simply appalling. A child had to have a very strong constitution to survive the brutality, the work, the cold, and near-starvation. These men knew of no other way of life, and to them it was only natural to impose the same sort of regime on the boys in their charge.

Frank was immediately set to work on one of the numerous tasks assigned for paupers: cleaning potatoes, cutting cabbage, scrubbing out the huge cooking vats (only the smallest boys could get inside them), burnishing the stoves, cleaning the brass, and hosing down the vast stone floors of the kitchen — and woe betide any boy who got himself wet! The list was endless and the day long, starting as it did at 6 a.m. The boys also went to the local council school, so the work had to be done before or after school. Frank found that if his tasks were not finished in time for school, he got a beating from the officer in charge, and if he stayed behind to finish the job he got a beating from the schoolmaster for being late for school!

Small boys quickly learned to hide their tears. They learned that any sign of weakness could be seized upon by a bigger boy and mercilessly exploited. Bullying, constant intimidation, public jeering, would be the only sympathy a smaller boy could gain from tears. Once, and once only, Frank asked an officer where Peggy was. The man must have told one of the older boys, perhaps maliciously, knowing what would happen. The same day, in the washroom, a chorus went up.

"Peggy, Peggy, who's Peggy?"

"Peggy's his tart. What a fart!"

"Peg, Peg, peg your nose, what a pong!"

"Peggy's a stink."

"He has to put a clothes peg on his nose 'afore he can touch 'er."

Frank burst into tears, and a big boy came and pushed him over onto the slippery floor.

"Garn, you aint got no tart, yer titch," said this boy, squeezing Frank's testicles so hard that he screamed with pain.

The officer came in and the big boy swiftly merged into the crowd, looking innocent. The officer looked round and asked no questions.

"Get up," he said curtly to Frank, "and get washed and go to the dormitory."

In throbbing pain Frank crept into bed and cried, as he did every night, for his mother and his sister. He had learned to make no sound when crying, so as not to attract attention and to keep very still, so that he seemed to be asleep. But he often lay awake for many hours, his heart bursting.

During these wakeful hours he often — nearly always, in fact — heard movements and soft footsteps, and grunting and puffing and cursing sounds, as iron bedsteads rattled and straw mattresses squeaked. Each dormitory had an officer in charge who slept in a closed cubicle at the end of rows of beds, and each night a boy would slip quietly out of bed and go into the cubicle.

What can one expect if a crowd of men and boys are compulsorily thrown together, with no escape and no female influence? All the boys were lonely. All of them were motherless. They had only each other in whom to find comfort and, let us hope, a little happiness because for them, life would be short. From 1914-1918 the older boys in Frank's dormitory — those born in the 1890s — were destined to grow up to be sent straight from the workhouses of England to the trenches of France, to die as cannon-fodder in defence of King and Country.

It was September 1914. A costermonger by the name of Tip called at the workhouse and asked to speak to the Master. The Master was prim and pompous; the coster, flashy and talkative. He explained, in a husky voice, inclined to squeaks, that his lad had gone off to the war, and he was left without a boy, and a coster must have a boy, lest how was he going to do his trade, like, an' what he was lookin' for was a sharp little lad of about eleven or twelve, eleven being the preferential age, seeing as how they learns quickest, who was a good worker, an' quick, an' it didn't matter about no book learning, because he never could see no use for that in the trade, and them as had book learning never seemed to get on spectackiler like in the trade, and he, Tip, would edicate the boy himself an' make a right sharp coster out of him, as how he could earn his living honest-like, an' keep his head up with the best, an' he would supply his lodgins an' 'his victuals, least as to say his doxy would, an' had the Master got such a boy, who was hard-workin' an' willin'?

The coster delivered all this in his curious voice that growled and gurgled sometimes, and squeaked and whistled at others. The Master paused to think, and the coster, who never paused and could not conceive of anyone else doing so for any reason whatsoever, started again, "an' he's gotta be strong, 'cause its no place for a wimpish lad, an the doxy'll feed him well an keep his strength up, an' . . . .".

The Master held up his hand to silence the man.

"Just wait here, will you?" said he, as he left the office.

Workhouse masters were encouraged to off-load inmates in order to reduce expenses, but they were not allowed to turn them out onto the streets unless provision for their maintenance was assured. The apprentice system was the answer.

The Master thought carefully about the coster's request, and his mind fixed on Frank — he was eleven, he was strong, he was hard-working, he was obedient, and he was, by all reports from school, one of the "has ability but must try harder" type — the despair of every honest schoolmaster.

The boys were at tea, and Frank was called out.

"Now stand up straight, and look lively and don't answer back," said the Master as he cuffed him round the ear. "There's a man here wants to see you."

They entered the office, where the coster was whistling. He had a beautiful, mellow whistle that seemed a most unlikely adjunct to his peculiar speaking voice.

"This boy seems to answer your requirements. I give you my assurance that he is hard-working. All our boys are trained to work."

The coster looked Frank up and down and sucked his teeth. He had only two, one in the upper and one in the lower jaw, both at the front, so he was able to vary his sucking with singularly comic effect. He pinched Frank's ear.

"You're a skinny li'le sprog. Can you lift a box of herrings?"

Frank didn't dare to answer back in front of the Master, so he just nodded.

"Ain' chew got a tongue, ven?" demanded the coster.

Again Frank nodded.

"Yes he has and he can use it to good effect when he wants to," answered the Master.

"Vat's what I needs, a boy as can holler good and loud like, an' make 'em all sit up."

"This is the boy for you, then. He's got a voice like a foghorn," said the Master conclusively.

"I'll take 'im. An' if he don't come up to scratch, I'll bring him back next week."

Before Frank had time to say a word, he was whisked off to the clothes cupboards, his workhouse uniform removed, and ill-fitting street clothes put on him. The coster took him by the hand and they stepped out into the road together.

Tip was a flashy dresser. Not for him the drab greys and browns of working men. He wore green corduroy trousers and a shirt of vivid blue. His shoes were tied with enormous bows which bore no resemblance to the humble shoelace, and at his throat was tied a silk neckerchief of red and blue. His cap was not your ordinary cloth cap, as worn by the English, nor the beret favoured by the Frenchman, yet it had a closer similarity to the French style. Tip's cap could be described as a very large beret, manufactured out of the best velvet and the colour, neither blue nor green, seemed to change with the light and the movement. Tip considered himself a real swell, and his doxy admired him prodigiously.

He glanced down at Frank and his masculine vanity acknowledged that the boy was taking in his elegance.

"You've gotta look sharp in our trade, titch. No use lookin' like a bag 'o dirty washin'. The ladies don' like it. An' it's the ladies as wha' does the buyin', see? So you gotta please the ladies. That's rule number one. We'll 'ave to get you some new clobber. Can't 'ave you goin' round lookin' like vat, queering my pitch. The ladies would run away fritted, vey would. I knows of a Jew as what can fix you up cheap and natty like."

Tip had started the sentence in his baritone voice, but as he came to the end of it, the words came out in a series of high, unexpected squeaks. Aware that Frank was listening with puzzled attention, he explained.

"It's the toobs. The toobs, like what wears out with all that 'ollering. They gives out if you're a good coster, like what I am, 'cause they're too delicate to stand all that 'ollerin'. Vat's what I needs a boy for, to 'oller, along with other fings, lots of other fings, all of which I will teach you, but 'ollerin' will be one of your first jobs. Now let's 'ear you 'oller. See vat li'le lad over there, playing in vat puddle? Well, you call out, loud as you can, now, 'hey, mucky, your mum's comin'.'"

Frank caught the spirit of things, and bellowed it out with all his strength. The boy jumped up and ran round the corner like a greyhound.

Frank roared with laughter, and squeezed Tip's hand.

"Vat's what I needs," said Tip. "Reckons as how you'll suit me, an' if you can pick up the other tricks of the trade quick like, we'll get on famous. Now we're gettin' to my lodgings, an' my Doxy's Doll see, and Doll, she's a rare 'un, but she won' stand no lip from boys, see, so you don' give her no lip an' you won't feel the back of 'er 'and." Tip rubbed the side of his chin reflectively and muttered, "an' you don't wanna feel the back of 'er 'and, I can tell yer."

They climbed a dark and foul-smelling staircase to the fourth floor. A large and shapely woman ambled comfortably towards them. She wore a red skirt, frayed and dirty at the hem, and a purple blouse, high at the neck, with a row of jet buttons down the front, at which a full bosom pressed, screaming for release. Black jet beads hung to her waist, and heavy black hair hung around her shoulders. When she smiled, her teeth also were black, as though they had been painted to match her outfit. She looked at them both, then cried out in a strident voice, "Is vis the li'le workhouse kid, ven? Oh, look, he's fin, the pet," and she pressed Frank's head to her bosom, an experience which he found not unpleasant, though the smell could have been sweeter. "We'll 'ave to give 'im some pie dahn Dill's, eh Tip?"

"Let's ge' goin', ven," said Tip with a leer.

Doll twisted her hair up on the top of her head in a fashionable coil (Frank was watching, fascinated) and stuck several pins in. One of them had a bird on the end and this she settled on the top of her head.

"You bet, squire," she said with a wink. Then she leaned down to Frank.

"He's a nice-lookin' li'le lad, bu' fin like. Oh, I don' like 'a see 'em so fin. What's yer name an' all, eh? We'll ge'choo some pie, ven. How's va'?"

It was nearly 7 o'clock and the streets were filled with people. Apart from marching to school in a crocodile, Frank had not been outside the workhouse gates for years. He was filled with wonder. To linger was irresistible. Here, a family was fighting, the man and woman threatening each other with equal fury; there, some boys were playing skittles; yonder a woman was fetching water, whilst a crowd stood around with their buckets, gossiping as they waited. Frank had not seen women for years, and couldn't take his eyes off them, until he realised with alarm that Tip and Doll were almost out of sight, and he ran to catch up with them. They sauntered along, greeting people, chaffing children, Tip pinching the cheeks of young girls, Doll screaming across the street to another woman. The dress of both of them was more gaudy than any of their neighbours wore, and Frank felt proud to be with them, although neither looked round to see if he was still there.

They entered a beer shop, high ceilinged, bare walled, with a wooden floor. The serving counter was at one end next to a raised platform with a piano on it. The room was not particularly full, and Tip and Doll seemed to know everyone. Frank was all eyes and ears. This was high life indeed!

"You standin' a top o' reeb, Al?" (*pot of beer*)

"Sey, (*yes*), I done a doogheno flash (*good deal*) today. But kool 'im (*look at him*). Who's he?"

"My wen dal (*new lad*). Give 'im some reeb an' rater." (*beer and water*)

Frank took his beer and sipped it, puzzled. Conversation continued.

"Jack, 'e 'ad a regular tosseno tol (*bad luck*). Had a showful (*bad money*). Bigger loof (*fool*) 'im."

"He musta bin flash kurnard (*half drunk*) at ve time."

"On (*no*), just a dabeno." (bad debt)

Costers in those days spoke to each other almost entirely in back slang, incomprehensible to an outsider. This continued until well after the 1939-1945 war.

Frank's eyes rested on each of these big, confident men as he spoke, but none was as flamboyant or assured as Tip, and hero-worship entered his young heart.

He drank his beer. No one seemed to notice him. He was getting hungry and Doll, who was flirting with a man sporting a walrus moustache, appeared to have forgotten the pie she had promised.

The beer shop filled up, cards were brought out and men sat down to the serious business of gambling. A group of boys in a corner were engaged in the equally serious business of 'three ups'. A piano player started a tune, to which everyone sang, getting louder and louder at each chorus. A girl leaped onto the stage and started dancing with more energy and vigour than grace, accompanied by shouts and cat-calls from the audience. The beer flowed and the laughter grew louder. Exhausted, Frank fell asleep on the floor.

He was awakened by Doll, screaming,

"Oh, the poor li'le nipper. 'Ere, Tip, you'll 'ave to carry 'im."

"Take me for a monkey?" said Tip, scornfully. He shook Frank hard and pulled him to his feet.

"Come on; there's a day's work ahead."

Doll was the worse for wear and hung onto Tip's arm as they walked through the streets. Frank, more asleep than awake, kept close behind them. They climbed the endless steps to the fourth floor, and a straw mattress and a blanket were pulled out from behind the big feather bed and put on the floor under the table for Frank, who was only too thankful to lie down anywhere. He went to sleep to the comforting and familiar sounds of grunting and puffing and rhythmic bed rocking.

Frank was awakened by a flannel of cold water thrown on his face. He leaped up and banged his head on the table under which he was sleeping. Stunned, bewildered, he gasped: "What's up? Where am I?"

Tip spoke. But it was a very different Tip from the evening before. Gone the flashy clothes, gone the easy swagger and pleasant bonhomie. The morning showed Tip the coster, Tip the businessman, Tip of the calculating, clever, ruthless eye for a bargain.

"Out o' bed, sharp now. There's work 'a be done. Billingsgate opens at four, and it's three o' clock now, an' we've gotta get the barrow and the gear, an' be there. Get some clothes on, an' follow me."

Tip was already in his working trousers and was pulling on his heavy boots. Frank felt the urgency and leaped out of bed. He was still dressed from the night before and had only to find his boots. He pulled them on hastily and stood up straight.

"Good. Now take vat bag, an' we're off."

Out in the night air Tip was electric with energy. He kept doing little runs and skips and punching the air with his fists. He made several short, barking shouts. He took in great lungfuls of breath and blew out noisily. He was working himself up to a fever pitch of excitement.

Frank caught the energy. He sensed that something significant was happening. The adrenalin surging through the man's body stimulated the boy's, and he ran along the dark, quiet street, alert and alive to everything, tingling with excited anticipation.

They went to a tunnel under a bridge. Other men were there already. Each man had a boy. They greeted each other in their own lingo. A door was opened, revealing a pitch black cavern, and a flare was lit with a match. The flame leaped up, revealing a stack of barrows, trucks, hand carts, donkey carts, bridles, hooks, chains, ropes, tarpaulins — a medley of wood and metal.

Tip growled to Frank, "Watch wot I takes, and be sure you remembers it. If you don't ge' the right gear, you can't do yer job, an' the tally bloke there, he'll cheat you if he can."

He selected what would be needed for the day, and paid the rental to the man with the flare.

"Push this 'ere, an' let's get goin'"

A boy called out.

"Hey, yennun — you."

Frank took no notice. The boy kicked him hard.

"Don't you answer ven, yennun?"

Tip explained.

"He means 'new one'. That's you, see? Take no notice, we got work 'a do. You'll pick up ve lingo in no time."

In pain, and limping, Frank pushed the barrow. He had learned to hide all signs of weakness in the workhouse and it stood him in good stead.

"Now, we must get a move on."

Tip leaned his weight on the barrow and it sped over the cobbles, rattling on solid, iron-framed wheels.

Billingsgate was the fishmarket of London, lying on the north bank of the Thames, east of the Monument. Fishing boats came in throughout the night and the market stalls, laden with fresh fish, were ready for business when the market opened at 4 a.m.

Tip's electric excitement is, if anything, intensified and every nerve of his body seems to be quivering. A fishy, seaweedy smell hits his nostrils, and he inhales deeply. "Beautiful, beauooootiful," he murmurs appreciatively.

The noise all around is intense. Above the babble of voices Frank can hear the shouts of salesmen, standing on boxes or tables, roaring out their merchandise and their prices. A perfect Babel of competition.

"'Andsome cod, best in the market — all alive."

"Fine Yarmouth bloaters — oo's the buyer?"

"Eels O! Eels O! Alive O!"

"Wink, wink, winkles, best for tea."

"'ere you are, guvner, fine brill, come an' look at 'em, gov. You won't find better."

"Over here. Finney haddock. Had . . . had . . . had . . . hady haddock.

"Now or never — whelks, whelks, whelks, whelks, I say."

On all sides everyone is asking "what's the price?" whilst shouts of laughter from salesmen and customers, bargaining and bantering, burst out over the noise of the crowd.

Frank can see, in the semi-darkness of the sheds, the white bellies of turbot shining like mother-of-pearl; scarlet lobsters, their claws flailing helplessly in the air;

mounds of herrings with scales glittering like sequins; huge baskets piled with grey oysters, blue mussels, pink shrimps, sackfuls of whelks, their yellow shells piled up high; buckets of grey and white eels slithering and sliding all over each other.

Frank sees porters in queer-shaped leather helmets, rather like squashed pagodas, carrying fish baskets on their heads. Eight hundred tons of fish pour in and out of Billingsgate every day and all of it, down to the last herring, is unloaded and portered in this way. A man whose neck is 'set' can carry sixteen baskets, each weighing a stone, on his head. These powerful men are the backbone of the fish market, and their history is high romance. The Quinquereme of Nineveh, laden with spices and precious oils, was unloaded in exactly the same way in medieval London. Caesar's galleys, rowed up the Thames by chained men, were berthed here, London's most ancient port, and unloaded by men such as Frank sees. Nothing has changed.

Frank flattens himself against a wall as one of these awe-inspiring giants passes, shouting: "Move over — make way, please — gangway."

A thin man, trembling under the weight of his load, mutters, through clenched teeth: "Shove to one side, can' choo?"

Everywhere ragged, desperate-looking men and boys, are clamouring for the job of porterage, hoping to earn a shilling or two before the day's end.

Through the arches of the open end of the huge covered building, silhouetted against the grey sky of dawn, Frank can see the masts and tangled rigging of the oyster boats and the lobster trawlers. Sails, black against the skyline, shift and tremble. He sees the red caps of sailors as they draw in the sails. He hears the chug-chug of primitive engines as a throttle is opened. He hears the shouts of men as they unload their vessels.

"Keep close beside me," Tip growls, "an' listen to everyfink. Don't miss nuffink, see? You gotta learn how to buy."

He assumes a nonchalant air and saunters down the gangway, whistling as though he were on holiday. He passes through the arches onto the quayside, where the river glides black and secretive, and silver threads of light pierce the grey sky. They clamber over ropes and rigging to the long row of oyster boats moored close alongside the wharf — known as "Oyster Street" in the trade — where the fishermen sell direct from their boats.

"No middlemen here. Best prices," hisses Tip out of the corner of his mouth.

Each boat has its black signboard and the master, in his white apron, walks up and down calling his prices. The holds are filled with oysters and sand, which a man turns over with a spade, rattling the masses of shells.

Tip discusses price with the master, shakes his head and walks away, saying loudly to Frank, "I knows of better oysters dahn ve sewers."

The oyster merchant shouts after him. Tip ignores the shouts, and clambers over shrimp nets and weights to reach a fisherwoman, with huge muscular arms, shouting the price of shrimps. The master of the vessel is behind her, filling a jug with shrimps and letting them fall back like a shower of pink confection. Tip breaks the head off one, and sniffs it.

"I wouldn't give that to my dog," he says and hands it to Frank, who doesn't know what to do with it.

Clambering over ropes, rigging, sails, cans of engine oil, netting, lobster pots, gang planks, ladders, baskets, trays — all littered over the quayside in a seeming mass of confusion, Tip and Frank scramble the whole length of Oyster Street. Nothing is bought.

Six o' clock is approaching. Tip snaps into action, his nonchalance leaving him as fast as it had been assumed. He returns to the fisherwoman, and buys shrimps at half her asking price, oysters for a third. Brill and dab he buys, which he had earlier disdained as "poison", with a bucket of eels added, "to clear 'em".

Buying is over. The excitement is past.

Tip hired a porter — a half-starved looking man of sixty — and refused to pay the sixpence the man asked.

"Three pence, then," said the man, humbly.

"I'll gi' yer tuppence, take it or leave it. I can soon find another, stronger'n you, you miserable ol' skele'on, you."

The man took it, and staggered out of the gate to where Tip and Frank had left the barrow.

"An' now for breakfuss," said Tip.

A Coster Lad

The woods are lovely and dark and deep,
But I have promises to keep,
And miles to go before I sleep.

Robert Frost

"Betty, my dear, I say, Betty, why you look charming this mornin'. I'll draw up my chair here an' get close in by this nice, invitin' fire, like. An' you, Betty my love, can 'ave the infinite pleasure of supplyin' me with some good 'am an' heggs an', if you got some nice 'ot muffins an' butter, I'll 'ave 'em, an' some of yer best Rosie Lee good an' strong. Betty, my love, why you do look ravishin' this fine morning, you can look after vis young lad, like wot he was your own son. Bring him the same, cause 'e's new, an' there's a hard day's work ahead, an' likewise as a man can't go to work on an empty stomick, no more can a boy."

Tip leaned back in his chair, put his feet on the table, and placed his order, with an expansive wave of the hand. Frank sat down to the best breakfast he had ever had in his life. After years of workhouse bread and margarine it tasted like nectar. The muffins oozed butter down his chin as he sank his teeth into them; the yellow yolk of the egg ran across the pink ham and he dipped his bread into it. He ate with concentrated enjoyment. Men and boys came in and sat down. Betty

99

rushed around serving. The fire crackled; tobacco smoke filled the air. The sound of separate voices merged into a quiet hum, and Frank fell asleep, his head on the table.

A heavy hand hit his shoulder.

"Right now. It's eight o' clock, an' we gotter get a-goin' on the round."

Tip walked swiftly out into the yard and Frank staggered after him, rubbing the sleep from his eyes. They fixed the cart together, Tip instructing every move, securing the sides, the shafts, the step, placing the trays, the weights and measures, the knives, bags, and torn newspapers. At each move, he would say "Now don't forget this one".

They started the round. If Frank thought that life in the workhouse was hard, that was because he had not experienced life as a coster. From that day on he never stopped working and he never stopped loving every minute of it.

He hollered his way down the streets, bawling out the day's catch. Shrimps, mackerel, herrings, whelks — his high-pitched voice carried from one end of a street to the other. He learned quickly, and within a month he could gut a fish so fast you couldn't see him do it. He charmed the ladies with his appealing eyes, so that they bought what they didn't want. He flicked a mussel from its shell with a twist of the knife, faster even than Tip. He could worm a whelk before they knew what had hit 'em.

The round was about ten miles walking distance. Tip usually closed the barrow about three o' clock in the afternoon. Anything left over was Frank's to sell. A tray was suspended round his neck and he went out alone. Tip would size up the value of the fish on the tray and say what he wanted Frank to get for it. Anything over that amount was commonly known as a 'bunt', or 'bunce', and the boy could keep the money. This was regarded as a coster boy's pay, because they had no wages for their work, food and lodgings being regarded as quite sufficient recompense for a day's labour.

Frank quickly learned that this was to be the hardest part of his day's work. The tray was heavy and so were his legs. Buying was mostly over for the day. Customers were fewer and they had to be first attracted, and then persuaded to buy. The fish was getting stale and nothing can disguise the smell or the look of stale fish, especially in the summer. Frank often had to trudge several miles before he had sold his stock and gained the money Tip demanded for it. Frequently there was nothing at all left over for his bunt. But on other occasions there was, and Frank was ecstatic at having earned himself sixpence or a shilling — a fortune for a boy who had never had anything of his own. To earn his bunt became his one aim, and often he did not return to the lodgings before 9 or 10p.m. to crawl under the table dog-tired. He would then sleep until 3a.m., when he was wakened to go to the market.

He learned quickly and thoroughly. He picked up the lingo in a few weeks, and was talking fast and confidently in the incomprehensible doggerel costers proudly shared. He assumed the devil-may-care swagger of the other coster lads. He copied Tip's

101

easy-going banter with the ladies. He also copied Tip's flamboyant style of dress, achieved from a few cut-downs of the master-dresser and a few bits such as a neckerchief and shoelaces which he had bought himself from his bunts. His one aim and ambition in life was to buy himself a flashy cap.

He adopted the costers' attitude to money, "Spend it while you've got it, tomorrow you may die". He saw that costers worked very hard and that a good trader earned a lot of money. He saw this money being thrown around each evening in the pubs and taverns, with extravagant and careless ease. Any man who had had a good day wouldn't hesitate to spend his entire profit on drinks for his mates. If he'd had a bad day, another coster would buy for him. If any coster was in hard street, or turned in by the police, there would be an immediate whip-round for him. No coster ever saved a penny, nor yet a halfpenny, for the future.

Costers didn't live in homes. They lived in lodgings, where they dossed down for a bit, and then moved on. The lodgings were always unspeakably squalid and cheerless, because costers and their women were hardly ever in them. Life was lived in the streets, the markets, the pubs, the penny hops, the penny gaffs, the race tracks, the bawdy houses. Life, with all its richness, was lived outside. Costers went back to their lodgings only for a few hours' kip, before the next day dawned and the markets opened.

Above all, Frank learned the trade. Unless he had been trained from boyhood upwards, no man had the slightest chance of being a successful coster. The tricks and dodges, the graft and guile, were just as important to learn as the skills of buying and bartering, and a grown man was too old to learn the tricks of boyhood.

Frank learned all this lore from the other coster lads as they went around in the early evenings, selling off the day's 'left-overs' and trying to earn an honest bunt. He learned to cover his fish with parsley, to keep it smelling nice. He learned to squeeze a lemon over it, to improve the taste. He added a few nuts to his store, to increase his range. He learned to sell four pints of whelks as five, by taking a bit off the top of each. He learned where he could sell fish heads and tails, and the best times when he could find the buyer. He learned to mix dead eels with live ones, to increase his stock by five to one, and "they don't notice one's dead until vey gets vem 'ome". He made the acquaintance of an unscrupulous pieman who would take two-day-dead eels for ready money. He learned that herring and mackerel look fresher by candlelight, so he carried a candle stuck in a turnip for dark evenings. He learned to wheedle and whine, saying his master would knock him about if he didn't sell it all. He always sold.

By the age of twelve, Frank was as sharp as a terrier. He was up to every dodge in the business, and there were some that said he was as clever a man as Tip. He spent long hours in the markets, he knew the price of everything and forgot nothing. An expert in slang he conducted all his business in the lingo. He could chaff a peeler so uncommon curious that the only way to stop him was to let him off. He was a master of his trade.

At the age of thirteen Frank decided it was time to go it alone. He wasn't going to give the best years of his life to a master, not he. He'd be his own master, do his own buyin' and sellin, an' keep his own profits. He'd show 'em how it's done.

He left Tip and Doll and moved into a common lodging house for men. It was the back room of a public bar, open only to the water's edge. The floor was rough stone, the ceiling and walls unplastered. For twopence a night he could hire a straw mattress and a blanket on the floor. Any other lodgings would cost him tenpence a night. So Frank took it, reckoning that he would hardly be in it anyway, and why waste money on a place he only slept in?

The men were rough, obscene, vicious, and put the fear of God into the lad many times, but he was growing fast, was quick on his feet, and good with his fists. He coped, but only just. His one great terror was of being robbed. He had seen it happen more than once. A sobbing little lad, about twelve years old, stuck in his mind. The boy was skinny and pale and had lost all his stock money overnight. If a lad can't buy, he can't sell. Frank gave him a shilling to buy some walnuts for the theatre trade, and learned the lesson to keep his stock money safe. He kept it in his socks and slept each night with his socks and boots on with the boots tightly laced.

Most of the men in the lodging house were casual labourers, picking up a day's work if and when they could. All were unskilled. Frank considered himself an aristocrat, being skilled in the fish trade. He hired his own gear, bought his own stock, and sold in the streets, keeping all his own profits which he spent on flashy clothes, fancy foods, beer, girls, the penny hops, the penny gaffs and gambling . . . gambling.

By the age of fourteen, it would be safe to describe Frank as a desperate gambler. All the coster men and boys gambled, but none more seriously than Frank. The love of the game was first in his thoughts and dreams, and not a spare moment would pass, but he would toss a coin and invite a bet on it. He did not care what he played for, or who he played with, as long as he had a chance of winning. Every day he worked untiringly, spurred on by the thought of the money he would earn, which he could lay against the odds with the next gamester he met. Many a time he lost not only all his money, but also his neckerchief and jacket as well, but nothing could dampen his ardour for the game, a run of continual bad luck making him more reckless than ever.

The coster boys would meet at various points to pitch against each other. They met under railway arches, in pub yards, on the quayside of the river, or even on the shingle when the tide was out. If ever a group of boys' backs and heads were seen crouching in a circle, it would be safe to say that it was a group of gamblers, and ten to one Frank would be in the middle, calling the loudest, the quickest, the fiercest.

"Sixpence on Tol."

"Sixpence he loses."

"Done."

"Give 'im a gen." (*shilling*)

"Flash it then." (*show it*)

Tol wins and the loser bears his losses with a rueful grin. Now Frank goes into the ring and takes up a stance to toss his coins. His face is scornful.

"Sixpence on Frank."

"A gen he loses."

"I take that one."

"Owl on Frank." (*two shillings*)

"Kool Tol, he's fritted. Done." (*look at Tol, he's afraid*.)

Frank is cool and determined. He plays three up, and calls "Tails". The three coins fall, all tails up. Frank takes his winnings.

Betting starts again. Tol throws, calling "Heads". The coins fall, one head, and two tails. He throws again. The coins fall, showing three tails. Frank takes his winnings. Tol curses and spits, and throws again. "Heads." Again they come down tails. Frank wins. He stares hard at Tol.

"An half-counter (*half sovereign*) next throw."

A gasp goes up from the onlookers, and they bet among themselves for or against Frank.

"Done," says Tol defiantly.

Frank tosses. "Heads," he calls. The three coins fall, all heads up.

"You stinking fish," screams Tol, and pledges his jacket and his boots to honour the debt. He is getting aggressive, and the crowds press closer. He jerks his elbow savagely.

"I wish to Christ you'd stand back."

Tol's lips are compressed, his eyes anxious and watchful.

The tense atmosphere has attracted men to the scene, who start their own betting on the two gamesters.

Tol adopts new tactics to bring back his luck. He pushes aside the onlookers and shifts his position a quarter circle to the right before throwing.

"I'll have it off you. A half counter," he cries with bravado, knowing full well that he is pledging half his stock money.

"Done," said Frank, confidently.

Betting amongst the onlookers continues and Frank and Tol know that sovereigns are being placed on one or other of them.

Tol spits on the coins, then takes a halfpenny and tosses it on his hand to see what he should call. He then spits again on the three coins and shifts his feet defiantly on the cobbles. He tosses his three coins, calling out "Tails". The coins fall, all tails up. His features relax, and he looks round the circle with a triumphant grin. He puts on his jacket and boots with the air of a winning man. Money changes hands among the spectators.

That throw marked the end of Frank's luck for the day. He tossed again and again and, four times out of five, he lost. He could hear the bets of the men going against him, and he ground his teeth in fury. If it were an accepted part of gambling to murder your opponent, he would have done so. Tol called again and again. Every time Frank accepted and challenged in return. He lost all his winnings, all his earnings, his neckerchief, his jacket, he even pledged his magnificent velvet cap, vowing it would bring him luck. It didn't, and he lost it.

With the cap in his hands, Tol stood up. He cast a contemptuous look at Frank, spat on the cap and threw it in the river.

"I'm off now to get a liner." (*dinner*).

He swaggered off to the admiring gasps of the boys and the amused shrugs of the men.

Seething with fury Frank vowed revenge.

"You wait, you scab, I'll have you to rights. I'll muck you, you scurf, you," he screamed.

The men laughed and sauntered off. The boys lost interest. A new game started up.

Frank tried to strike a jaunty pose as he stood up, but with no jacket, no neckerchief and no cap, he didn't feel like the cold, calculating gamester any more. He turned quickly and walked in the opposite direction from Tol.

He walked for hours, not feeling the keen wind blowing off the Thames, his mind full of the next game, when he would get even. He'd show 'em. He'd 'ave the houses (*trousers*) off that lousy skunk. He'd get 'is money back, an' more. Hatred filled his heart when he remembered the insult to himself and his trade. Being called a stinking fish was more than a man could stand. He'd get even. His luck'd be in next week. Not for an instant did it occur to him that he had been a fool. The passion for gambling had him in its obsessive grip.

108

In anger and resentment Frank trudged on, unaware of his surroundings, hating everyone, scowling at those who passed. Ahead of him was a two-bit jerk of a little nipper in baggy trousers, and shoes down on the uppers, leading by the hand a little girl, not yet out of nappies. He hated them both. The little girl was laughing as she toddled along on unsteady legs. Suddenly she fell and let out an exaggerated howl of pain. The boy bent down and helped her up. He wiped her eyes with his sleeve, and rubbed her knees, spitting on his fingers in order to do so. He laughed and said: "All better now", but the little girl wouldn't be consoled. She rested her blonde head on his shoulder and put her arms around his neck. He picked her up and carried her into a court, and Frank saw them no more.

Life turns on little things. The momentous events in history can leave us untouched, while the small events shape our destinies.

Frank stood quite still in the street, feeling suddenly cold. The heat of revenge left him, and the cold draught of uncertainty entered his heart. He shivered and leaned against the wall, feeling unexpectedly dizzy. What was it? Everything seemed so cloudy, so misty. What could it be? He didn't seem to be real any more. He touched his face and felt tiny soft arms around his neck. He breathed in and could smell the lovely scent of a baby's hair. Stunned, he wanted to run after the boy and the little girl, to find out who they were. But they had gone. Had he really seen them — a boy in baggy trousers and a tiny girl with blonde hair — or were they ghosts? He shivered and rubbed his eyes, trying desperately to recall something. But the mists of forgetfulness swirled around, and he could not remember what it was.

He made his way back to the lodging house, his mind in turmoil. He was Frank the coster; Frank the rising man; Frank the desperate gambler, feared by all. What did these kids in baggy trousers and nappies mean to him? Nothing! He tried to shake off the image. All right, he had a sister and she was in the workhouse. So what? That wasn't his fault, was it? Let her look after herself, like what he'd done. Anyway, he hadn't thought of her for years, an' likely as not she'd forgotten all about him. He hadn't asked his father and mother to die, that was their lookout, bigger fools them, he'd got on all right without them. He shook off the thought of the boy and girl, and whistled his way back to his lodgings. He'd had nothing to eat all day, because he had lost his money, but he wrapped himself up in his blanket in defiance of hunger, and lay down on his palliasse. But sleep evaded him.

He heard the other men coming into the lodging room. He heard their cursing and swearing, their belching and farting, and he hated them. How could they be like that? A ghost of a man crept up to his bed, a big man who was strong and gentle. This man looked after his wife who was frail and coughing. The ghost merged into the farmyard sounds and smells of the men around him, and Frank fell into a light sleep. For the first time in years he dreamed of his mother whom he had loved so passionately. She was leaving him to go to work. With a cry of anguish he sat up in bed. He felt all over the bed for her, but she wasn't there and then he remembered where he was and wept bitterly. He remembered now that terrible night when she had not returned, and he remembered holding little Peggy in his arms until the next day when they had been taken to the workhouse.

Memories came flooding back to him as he lay staring into the darkness: the court where they lived, the room they shared, his mother laughing and singing to him, or his mother coughing, and his father anxious. The big ghost was hovering all around the place, but never quite materialising. He remembered the tiny baby born no bigger than a teacup. He thought of the times they had washed her, he and his mother, and put baby clothes on the little creature that were far too big for her. He remembered his mother feeding her, and he wept afresh at this strange and beautiful memory. He buried his face in the straw palliasse, as he had done so often in the workhouse, to muffle the sounds of his sobs. The ghost came nearer to him and seemed to want to speak, but did not do so.

Frank woke at the sound of the other costers getting ready to go to market. What a crazy night! What had been going on? This was the real world. He threw a boot at his mate, and asked him for a loan of stock money for the day. Costers always help each other out when one of them faces hard times.

At Billingsgate he was the cool, hard, professional buyer again. His eyes never missed a trick. His ears didn't miss a sound. He hollered his way through his round with double the usual energy and was sold out by 2p.m. He found his mate to repay the loan. It was a point of honour for costers to repay a debt.

He counted his earnings. There was enough for stock money for tomorrow, and a tightener (*dinner*) today. He went to Betty's and ordered the best Kate and Sidney (*steak and kidney*) she'd got, with spuds and two doorsteps (*thick lumps of bread*), followed by spotted dick (*currant pudding*) and custard and a pint o' reeb (*beer*). No. He thought again. Make that two pints o' reeb.

That's what a man needed inside 'im, some good grub. He hadn't eaten since breakfuss yesterday, what with the game, an' queer goin's on, an' one thing an' another. No wonder he'd felt funny yes'day. A man can't keep goin' without a good lining to his stomach. He sat down with his back to the door. Betty brought his food and chaffed him, and pinched his ear, but somehow he didn't feel like responding and she retired, offended.

A big man came into the caff. He had hired a boy to hold the bridle of his horse, and called out to the boy as he entered, "You look after her, lad, while I'm away."

Frank heard the words, and the ghost came back and sat down beside him, though there was no chair. He remembered, at first dimly, and then as clearly as though it were yesterday, that he had promised his father that he, Frank, would look after his mother and his sister.

The spotted dick nearly choked him, and he could eat no more. Did Betty hear him mutter, "I'm sorry,

Dad, I'm sorry," as he glanced sideways, or was she imagining it? She certainly saw him brush a tear from his eye with his sleeve, and she said to Marge, the cook, in her motherly way, "Vere's somefink up with vat young 'un. Can't eat 'is spotted dick, an' all. Sumfing's up, I tells yer."

Frank sat at the table for a long time, unable to move. The ghost left him, but the memories remained. His mother was dead but his sister, as far as he knew, was alive and in the workhouse. He thumped his fists on the table and dug his nails into his hands as he remembered the tyranny and cruelties he had endured. He prayed that it had not been as bad for his sister in the girls' section. Perhaps they were kinder to little girls. He remembered the time they were together in the infants' section, and carrying her to his bed when she cried at night. He recalled fighting a bully-boy who had called her "baldy" and he grinned with satisfaction. He remembered a little girl called Jane, who was a friend of them both, and he prayed that Jane had looked after Peggy when he had been transferred to the boys' section. He had never prayed before, but now he did and he vowed to Heaven, his teeth and his fists clenched, that if his sister were still alive he would find her and get her out of the workhouse, and look after her as he had promised his father.

Betty came up, concerned and motherly, and cleared the table.

"How about a nice cup o' Rosie Lee, luv, good an' sweet? On the 'ouse, o' course."

Peggy

Frank was again in the workhouse. This time he was waiting in the Master's office. He had smartened himself up, as best he could in a communal lodging house, and was waiting with sick dread in his heart. Was she still alive? Children died in workhouses. He had seen it himself, and had heard stories from people that he had met. If Peggy had died, he'd kill someone and swing for it. Footsteps came along the corridor, and he stood up.

Frank's first surprise at meeting the Master after nearly four years, was how little he was! He had a childhood memory of a big, terrifying man, whose word was absolute law and who had the power to beat and flog for the slightest misdemeanour. Yet here was this flabby looking little man, about a head shorter than himself, who looked as if he hadn't the strength to lift a bit of cod off a plate, never mind a box of them off a slippery quayside. Frank looked at his puny muscles and compared them in his mind with the lean and muscular men he had worked with for years, and nearly laughed out loud. Was this the terror of the workhouse, this pathetic looking jellyfish?

114

But he had come for a purpose, and must be polite. He enquired about his sister — was she still alive? Yes, the Master replied, without giving anything away, she was. Frank gave a huge, shuddering sigh of relief. Where was she, then? The Master replied, guardedly, that she was in the girls' section, where she was well cared for. Frank's joy was unconfined. Here, in this very building? Could he see her, then? His eyes were eager. The Master was prim. No. Boys were not allowed in the girls' section.

Frank was nonplussed.

"But I can't help bein' a boy," he blurted out. "If I was 'er big sister you'd let me see 'er, wouldn't you?"

The Master smiled, and agreed, but rules were rules, he said with such finality that the interview ended.

Frank's joy at knowing she was alive was greater than his disappointment at not being allowed to see her. But he would see her — damn the Master — and he changed his round so that he would be near to the workhouse gate at 4p.m. when the girls returned from school. He hung around, shouting "whelks and eels", as the crocodile of girls marched past him. But he couldn't pick her out. There were a couple of dozen little girls with blonde hair, about the age that she would be, but even though he went every day for a fortnight and looked carefully at them, he couldn't recognise his sister. Several of the bigger girls giggled and nudged each other and winked at him as they marched past. At another time he would have flirted back, but he had no heart for flirting now. He changed his round again.

He sought another interview with the Master. On this occasion he had carefully prepared his questions. If he couldn't see his sister because of the rules, what were the rules about taking her away altogether? The Master was surprised at the boy's persistence and explained, condescendingly, that any relative could apply for the discharge of an inmate and, provided the applicant could prove that he could provide adequately for the said inmate, the application would be considered favourably. Frank's quick brain translated.

"You means, if I can support my sister, I can get her out of here?"

The Master nodded.

"An' what would you means by 'support'?"

The Master looked at the eager fourteen-year-old sitting before him, and smiled at the impossibility of his hopes.

"I would say, firstly, that the applicant must be of good character and must have decent accommodation to offer. He must prove himself able to support the inmate for whose discharge he is applying, and that he should have a reasonable sum of money saved against illness or loss of work."

"An' how much would you call a 'reasonable sum'?"

The Master tapped his pencil, and smiled archly.

"Oh, I would say £25. That is a fair sum."

Frank swallowed. Twenty-five pounds! Ask a working boy today to save £25,000 and he might swallow and turn pale, just as Frank did.

The Master concluded the interview and assumed that he would see no more of Frank.

Frank dragged his feet miserably back to the lodging house. The obstacles seemed insurmountable. Why couldn't he just take her? When he entered the squalid room, in which about twenty men slept and ate, he realised the Master was right. He couldn't possibly bring a girl here. He would have to be able to provide for her decently.

Frank then worked as he had never worked before, spurred on by necessity. He did his fish round as ever, but instead of knocking off when he had sold it all, he looked into the fruit and nut trade, and hawked them around the pubs and theatres and music halls until ten or eleven at night. He doubled his income.

He changed his habits and became something of an outcast from his old mates, because he never gambled, never flashed his money around by joining them in the taverns, and they resented it and ridiculed him. He opened a Post Office National Savings Account. No coster ever saved. Conspicuous spending each evening in the pubs and taverns was their invariable habit. But Frank wasn't interested in what the others did. Let them do what they liked. He had opened the account because he knew that in a communal lodging house he would be robbed. When he learned that he would earn four per cent on his investments he was thrilled and carefully worked out how many pennies that would be to every pound saved. By the age of fifteen he had saved eight pounds.

There is no doubt about it, Frank was a brilliant and imaginative coster. He went into the fried fish market, arranging for the fish to be cooked at a baker's, and employing a lad to hawk it around at a fixed rate, plus the bunting system. He looked into the roast chestnut market and worked out that the hire of the gear would pay for itself around Christmas time. He was right, and by the age of sixteen he had twenty-five pounds in his Post Office account.

He then looked round for a room to rent for himself and Peggy. It had to be a decent room, on that point he was determined. His sister was not going to be dumped in any old hole. She would be twelve years old now, quite a young lady. He had not seen her since she was little more than a baby, but he visualised her as petite and pretty, and felt sure she looked like his mother, whom he could not visualise either. Mother and sister merged into each other in his imagination, a numinous female ideal, the guardians of all his hopes and dreams and longings.

He found a room on the top floor of a house at eight shillings a week, plus two shillings for the rent of furniture. It was an upper-class house, he considered. There was a gas stove on the middle landing for everybody's use, and a tap in the basement. There was even a lavatory in the yard. Frank was well satisfied.

Frank was again in the Master's office. He had on his best clothes and his Post Office book was in his pocket. The Master had not expected him, and was astonished when he saw the proof of twenty-five pounds saved in two years. How had a boy of sixteen achieved it? He looked at him with new respect. He said: "Your request will have to be considered by the Board of Guardians. They meet in three weeks' time."

He gave the date and time of the Guardians' meeting and told Frank to come back on that evening.

Frank asked if he could see his sister, and was told curtly that he would see her in three weeks' time. Seething with frustrated fury, he looked at his powerful fist and nearly knocked the man down. But he remembered he had to be 'of good character' and thrust his hands behind his back. He would never get Peggy out if he hit the workhouse Master!

The Guardians debated the application. It was unusual, but they agreed to release the girl, if she herself wished to go with her brother. Frank was called into the boardroom and interrogated. They seemed satisfied and were especially impressed by the Post Office book. They told him to stand by the window, and Peggy was called away from her evening duties.

Peggy was in the washhouse, helping to prepare the younger girls for bed. It was a duty that she loved — better than scrubbing the greasy old kitchen floors, or putting out smelly old dustbins. She could play with the little girls, and there was always laughter when Peggy was putting them to bed. They had to laugh very quietly, so as not to get into trouble but, somehow, a bar of soap slithering across a stone floor seems even funnier if you have to stuff a towel into your mouth to stop shrieks of laughter. Suppressed giggles double the fun for young girls.

Peggy was pink and flushed with the steam and the laughter. Her blonde hair was damp and the wispy bits around her forehead curled upwards. Her apron was wet and her arms soapy. An officer came in.

"The Guardians want to see you. Come with me."

She didn't know what it meant and had no time to feel alarm. She was shown into the big boardroom where a group of gentlemen sat around an oval table.

Frank, standing inconspicuously by the window, watched her every step. She was taller than he had expected. He had imagined a tiny creature, because he remembered a tiny baby. But this was a full-grown girl in early puberty. He liked her dishevelled hair and laughing features, still damp from the washhouse. He saw, with a stab of pity, the fear and uncertainty as she stepped towards the oval table.

The Chairman said, not unkindly,

"Your brother has made an application to remove you from the workhouse."

"My brother?" Peggy looked bewildered.

"Yes, you have a brother. Didn't you know?"

She shook her head. The anguish inside Frank made his legs turn to jelly. He leaned against the wall.

"Well, you have, and he asks permission to take you out of our care and to look after you himself. Do you wish to go with him, or do you prefer to stay here with your friends?"

Peggy didn't say anything, and a member of the Board said sharply.

"Speak up, child, and answer the Chairman when he is good enough to speak to you."

Peggy's lip trembled and she began to cry. She still said nothing. Frank's anguish had turned to a horrible dread. What if she did not want to come? It was a possibility he had not even considered.

The Chairman who was kindly, with daughters of his own, said gently, pointing to Frank: "This is your brother Frank. It is to be regretted that you have not seen him since you were three years old, but now he has applied for your discharge and we, your guardians, are satisfied that he can provide for you. Do you wish to go with him?"

Peggy looked over towards the window, and saw a tall stranger. He did not mean a thing to her. Insecure children are terrified of change. She thought of the happy laughter in the washhouse, and her friends at school and in the dormitory. She stared at this unknown, unknowable young man, and her heart was set on her friends and the routine she had always known.

Frank saw cold rejection in her eyes and panic spurred his movements. Before she could speak, he stepped swiftly across the room.

"Stay where you are, you have no right . . ." shouted the Master.

Frank took no notice. He walked straight up to Peggy and stood looking down at her. Everyone in the room was hushed as brother and sister looked at each other for the first time in nine years. Then, slowly, he extended the little finger of his right hand and curled it round the little finger of her right hand. He held it close and grinned.

"Hello, Peg."

The action stirred her memory as nothing else could have done. Holding little fingers was an old childhood sign of special intimacy. No one else had ever done that to her. She had forgotten all about it, but now she remembered. A dim, faint, far-off memory of loss and longing stirred within her. She looked at this tall young lad and the love that she had not known for years flooded her warm young heart.

She squeezed his little finger in return, and smiled a smile of secret understanding. He saw the dimples in her cheeks, and knew that he had seen them somewhere before. Then with sudden, impetuous warmth, she threw her arms about his neck and leaned her head on his shoulder. The guardians watched with breathless wonder. Even the Master was silent. The intoxicating smell of her hair sent a thrill through Frank's tense body and he relaxed, knowing that she was his sister, and that all would be well.

She did not hold him for long, but turned to the Chairman and curtsied.

"I will go with my brother if you please, sir."

Memories of early childhood dwell in a limbo sphere which is neither forgetting nor quite remembering. As Peggy danced along the pavement, looking up at Frank, she tried desperately to recall him, but could not. She looked up at his face, his hair, his smile, and tried to persuade herself that she knew him and could remember him when they were little, but she had to admit to herself that he was a stranger. Yet he wasn't. His big, rough hand grasping her own felt familiar, his arm round her shoulders as he led her down a dark street was familiar too. Something in his touch struck a chord within her that she knew and responded to.

Frank was jubilant. He felt a king. None of his mates could have done what he'd done. He had got her out of that place, his little sister, and he would never let her go back. She did not look as he had imagined, but that did not matter; she was better than he had imagined. He greeted several of his friends, who nudged each other and shouted, "Who's yer tart? Where didja find 'er? Any more like 'er fer us?"

Frank replied, good humouredly, "She's my sister, and there's no-one in the whole world like her."

He took her back to the lodgings — in a respectable street, he pointed out. He was proud to show her the facilities of the house. He led her up to the second floor and showed her the last word in luxury — the gas stove on the landing, where she could cook. They climbed two more flights of wooden stairs, and he proudly flung open the door.

It was a small attic room with a sloping roof and a garret window, of which a broken pane had been patched up with cardboard. The walls were unpainted and bits of plaster were falling off. The ceiling was yellow and stained with damp. The furniture, rented for two shillings a week, consisted of a rough wooden table and chair, a narrow iron bedstead with coarse grey army blankets, a wooden box, a candle stuck in a milk bottle, a jug and washbowl and a chamber pot. It looked pretty bleak, but children like small rooms, and to Peggy it looked like heaven. She threw her arms around Frank.

"It's lovely, lovely. Are we really going to live here?"
Her eyes filled with uncertainty,

"Will I have to go back? Don't let me go back. I want to stay here with you."

He folded her in his arms protectively and said fiercely,

"You'll never go back. Didja hear me? Never. Not as long as I can see to it. We'll be together, always. Vat's a promise, an' all. Now, let's see vat smile o' your'n, so I can see them dimples."

She smiled with trusting confidence, and he put his little fingers into the dimples.

"You'll 'ave to smile a lo' more offen, yer know."

He had brought in some wood and lit a fire in the narrow grate. Red and yellow flames leaped up, filling the little room with dancing colour. He had bought some muffins and some real butter, and they sat on the floor by the fire, toasting the muffins stuck on the end of a knife. They were so delicious she couldn't stop eating them and the butter ran down her chin. He chuckled and wiped it off with his finger. She took hold of his hand and licked the butter off his finger, looking up at him with big melting eyes. A thrill ran through him, and he did not know what to say. She murmured,

"Muffins. Muffins and butter. What heaven. Better than nasty stale old bread and margarine. Can I eat muffins for evermore, Frank?"

"'Course you can. Thousands of 'em. I'll see to va', you'll see. Muffins every day, if you wants 'em. An' candy, an chocolate, an' cakes an' all."

"And can I have jam and honey and cream?"

"Wha' ever you wants, my li'l sister, you can 'ave. You'll see."

"And pretty dresses?"

"Loads of 'em."

"And a carriage to ride in, with four horses?"

"'Course. Six 'orses, and a coachman, an' all."

Peggy sighed with happiness. But something inside her stirred, and she clung to him with desperate appeal.

"But you won't go away? You won't let them take me away from you again, will you?"

Her eyes were wide with terror. His eyes were serious and his voice was firm.

"No-one can take you away from me, not no-one, never. I've promised, haven't I? We'll be together always."

Satiated with muffins and warmth and the emotion of the day, her eyes began to close. He was watching her closely and thinking he had never seen such a pretty face. She was so much prettier than the coster girls most of his mates had. They were rough-looking girls with loud voices and dirty hair. He leaned forward and touched her hair, flame-lit and golden. It was like silk, and so fine he had to blow it, just to watch it move. She felt his breath on her face, and opened her eyes dreamily.

"Come on, little girl, it's time for you to go to bed."

Frank used the words he had used when he was six and she was two. The joy of remembering the love they had shared shaped his words and actions. She giggled, and leaned back against the wall, kicking her heels against the floor.

"Shan't."

He leaned towards her and took off her boots and socks, saying as he did so, "This little piggy goes to market, This little piggy stays at home."

She caught the rhyme and finished, "And this little piggy goes wee, wee, wee, all the way home."

"Home, Frank, home. Not the workhouse but home, with you."

He undressed the sleepy young girl just as he had done nearly ten years before. He put her into the bed and she fell asleep straight away, snuggled into the warm blanket that he pulled around her.

He put another log on the fire. He did not feel sleepy. He felt wide-awake, alight with teeming emotions that tumbled into his conscious and subconscious mind.

He had done it! He'd got her out. Out of that prison house! Out for good an' all. Hadn't that stinking workhouse master sat up when he showed him the Post Office book, and told him there was respectable lodgings to take her to? He looked proudly round the little room. This was real swell, this was.

He stroked the hair of the sleeping child, and a wave of tenderness swept over him. This was his sister. Was she like their mother? He couldn't say. Already the shadow of his mother was fading, as the reality of Peggy grew more distinct. How soft and pretty girls were. He stroked the smooth white skin of her arm and compared it with his own, all covered with black hairs! How did girls get to look like that? He took up her hand, then noticed with fury, that it was all red and rough, her nails short and broken, with little cracks at the finger tips. The brutes! They had got her scrubbing and heavy washing already! They'd better not come his way again, or he'd murder someone! No — that was too good for them. He'd get the Master and the lousy officers onto hard scrubbing. They could scrub for years. That'd learn 'em! He swore angrily to himself and vowed that she would never again have to work hard.

He got up and turned the log with his boot. Sparks shot up the chimney and the embers glowed fiercely red. It made the meagre little attic look cosy and intimate with a glowing redness that reflected the inner glow of his secret pride and happiness. He looked around, and thought of the squalid mens' lodging house on the water front where he had lodged for two years. Ugh, disgusting! Men were always coughin' an' spittin'. Men were always fartin' and belchin' an' swearin'. Always fightin' over nuffink, they were. 'Orrible. It wasn't jus' Peggy who'd bin rescued. Rescuing her had rescued him from that lousy, flea-ridden dump, an' he'd never go back there. Not 'im. Never.

He sat down again beside her and listened to her quiet breathing. Men snored! Leastwise as saying, all the men he'd ever known snored like elephants. Enough to keep anyone awake all night. Peggy let out a tiny puff as she moved in her sleep, and he held his breath in delight. Was that how girls snored? What a lovely sound. Perhaps she would do it again. The workhouse dormitory with seventy boys and an officer came into his mind, and he shut the thought out quickly. He didn't ever again want to think of it. It was too awful. They were both out of it now and they'd stay out. They belonged together, and he'd see to it that they stayed together. His jaw was set with determination as he looked into the future. The future . . .

She would have to go to school. His sister was going to have a good edication, an' grow up to be a lady. He'd see to it, he would. His sister wasn't goin' to be a common coster girl, like them poor li'le kids. Half starved, half froze, unwanted li'le bits of kids, sent out for hours an' hours to sell a few lousy apples or rotting pears that no-one'd buy an' then gettin' beaten because they hadn't sold nuffink. His sister'd be a lady with book-learnin' an' a posh accent.

His sister would go to a decent school, a good school. That's as saying, not the workhouse school. He didn't know much about schools, but he was set on that one. He'd find out where there was a good school as would take her. They'd be lucky to get her an' she'd be top of the class every time.

The log shifted on the fire, and the sound broke his train of thought. Perhaps he'd better get some shut-eye an' all. He'd have to be up at three to go to the market. It was more important than ever that his trading showed a profit. He could think about schools tomorrow. But he didn't want to disturb the magic of the moment. The firelight was fast fading, but he could see the dark curve of her lashes shadowing her pale skin. He could see the slender white shoulder against the grey blanket. He leaned over and kissed it, very gently, so as not to disturb her. This was the best day of his life. He'd been planning it for two years, and now, now . . . .

Quite suddenly he felt really tired. The excitement of the day had caught up with him at last. He pressed the log down into the ashes and the firelight was almost extinguished, except for a faint orange flicker on the ceiling. He could not see her anymore, so he undressed and crept into bed, hoping not to disturb her. But the bed was so small that he had to push her over to make room for himself. She sighed, and stretched out a sleep-warmed arm which, feeling his body, curled around his neck and drew him towards her. She murmured: "Is that Frank? Is that really Frank, my lovely brother? Oh, I love you so much."

He kissed her eyes, her hair, her face, her mouth. He passed his hands down her slender body, and fire ran through him as he felt the circle of her tiny firm breasts and buttocks. She was neither asleep nor awake, but she loved him with all her heart and mind, with all her soul and body. Their union was as inevitable as it was innocent.

'Til Death Us do Part

Peggy was singing her way through her scrubbing and polishing at Nonnatus House. It was always nice to hear her. Sister Julienne casually remarked, "You sound happy. How's Frank these days?"

"Frank? Well, he's had a bit of a stomach ache recently, but a dose of Epsom Salts will soon see that off."

A few weeks later she confided to Sister,

"Frank's still got the stomach ache, Sister. Salts don't seem to do him any good. What else can I give him?"

Questioning revealed that Frank's stomach ache had lasted for six weeks. Sister advised seeing the doctor. But Frank would not go to the doctor. Men like Frank never do.

"I've never bin to a sawbones in me life an' I'm not startin' now. I'll work it off, you'll see."

But he couldn't work it off, and a couple of weeks later he had to shut up his stall in Chrisp Street Market at 11a.m. with half the fish unsold — an unheard of precedent. He took a couple of codeine and slept when he got home, and felt sufficiently well to go to Billingsgate at 4a.m. next morning.

"There, I said I'd work it off, didn' I?" he said as he kissed Peggy goodbye.

But some of his mates brought him home at 7 a.m. The pain had got so bad that he couldn't continue. Peggy put him to bed and called the doctor, who examined him and advised hospital. Frank refused. The doctor assured him it would be for only a few days for tests. Peggy insisted and Frank acquiesced. Tests revealed the early stages of carcinoma of the pancreas. They were told it was inflammation of the pancreas. Radium treatment was advised.

At Nonnatus House Peggy sought reassurance.

"It's only inflammation, and what's the pancreas, anyway? It's only a tiny organ in the body, they tell me; it's not like the liver or the stomach, a big important organ. The radium treatment will get rid of it in no time, I guess. After all, the pancreas is not much bigger than your appendix, and thousands of people have their appendix out, don't they?"

We reassured her. What else can you do? We did not say that no one had ever been known to recover from cancer of the pancreas. And to this day, in the twenty-first century, this is still the case. A tiny, obscure organ it may be, but the pancreas is utterly essential to life and nothing can replace its functions.

Frank was given the choice of hospitalisation for the radium therapy, or an out-patient visit twice a week. He stayed at home. He handed over the lease of his stall for three months to a mate of his, saying he would want it back when he had had a good rest and was better. He told Peggy not to give up any of her work, because he didn't want to be fussed. However, Peggy did give up most of her work, arguing that this would be the only time in their lives when he was not working six days a week, and they were going to enjoy it as a holiday. A bit of radium therapy would hardly signify and they could go out and about on the other days and have a good time.

However, Peggy continued her work at Nonnatus House. Perhaps she needed the proximity of the Sisters for reassurance and advice. She did not appear anxious, saying things like, "He's getting on nicely now, thank you, Sister," or, "We haven't been out anywhere, really. The radium seems to make him tired, so we stay in, and he likes to hear me reading to him. It's better than going out, we reckon."

One day she said, "He seems to get pain at night, but they've given him some tablets, and that'll do the trick, eh, Sister?"

Another time she said, "He's lost a bit of weight. Good thing too, I tell him. 'You were beginning to get quite a paunch on you,' I said, and he laughs and says 'you're right there, Peg,' he says."

Within a few weeks we were requested to take Frank for home nursing. Sister Julienne and I went to assess him.

Peggy and Frank lived in a prefab on the Isle of Dogs. These were small, ready-made buildings erected in huge numbers after the war, to house some of the thousands of people whose homes had been destroyed. They were put up as an emergency measure, intended to last four to five years. Many of them lasted forty to fifty years. They were very pleasant, very cosy and greatly preferred to the terraces that had gone up in smoke. As we approached the prefab estate in the morning sunlight, it looked charming, with the low buildings, leafy trees full of sparrows and the river lapping in the background. It always surprised me that only a short distance from one of the biggest commercial ports in the world such quietness and peace could prevail.

Their tiny garden, about six to ten feet of space all around the house, was well tended, with flowers and cabbages and runner beans growing well. A vine was trained up the south wall and I wondered if they ever got any grapes worth eating. The front door opened straight into the sitting room, which was comfortable and pretty. It was also spotlessly clean. Peggy was obviously very house-proud.

She greeted us with her usual happy smile.

"It's good of you to come," she said as she took Sister's cloak and hung it up. "He's in bed at the moment, but he's going along nicely. He's had two weeks of the radium treatment now and he's getting stronger all the time. He says he'll be back on the market in no time."

We went into the bedroom and I was thankful that Sister Julienne was with me. Had I been alone, my reaction at seeing Frank for the first time in about three months would probably have betrayed my shock. He looked ghastly. He lay listlessly in the middle of the big double bed, his eyes sunken, his skin grey. He had lost so much weight that his flesh hung in wrinkles and he had lost most of his hair. I doubt if any of his mates at the market would have recognised him.

Sister went straight up to him, with her gentle warmth.

"Hello Frank, how nice to see you again. We miss you at Nonnatus House, and look forward to you returning to work. The other man's good, we've no complaints, but he's not the same as you."

Frank smiled, and the skin pulled tightly across his nose and cheek bones. His eyes, sunk deep into their bony sockets, gleamed with pleasure.

"I'll be back right enough, Sister. It's only a matter of a few more weeks of this radium, an' I'll be on me feet again."

"Are you sure you won't go into hospital for the remainder of your treatment? It would be more restful, you know. The ambulance journey back and forward can be very tiring, especially after the treatment."

They were both adamant that he should remain at home.

Sister examined him. She carefully moved his emaciated body, the arms and legs that seemed to have insufficient muscle to lift their own weight. Was this the man who had lifted a hundredweight box of cod only a few short weeks ago? I went to the other side of the bed and caught in my nostrils the smell of death as I leaned over him.

Strangely enough Peggy did not seem to notice how desperately ill he was. She seemed perfectly happy, and kept saying things like "He's getting on fine", "He's getting stronger each day", or "He ate all the milk pudding I made for him. That shows he's getting on well, doesn't it?" I was struck by the fact that we all see what we want to see. Peggy appeared to have closed her mind to the reality of Frank's condition, to the extent that she literally couldn't see it. To her, Frank was exactly the same as he had always been, her brother and lover. He was the beat of her heart, the blood in her veins. He was the meaning of her life, and the physical changes, obvious to anyone else, she just did not see.

It was arranged that I should call for home nursing twice a day, and that Sister would come any time that Peggy requested.

I do not know whether or not Sister Julienne noticed the sleeping arrangements in the little house. The prefabs were constructed in a rectangle with a single large room and two small rooms leading off. These were intended as bedrooms. But one of the rooms in Frank's house was a dining room, which we could see through the open door. The only room used for sleeping had a double bed in it. If Sister Julienne noticed these things and put two and two together at no time did she say so. The Sisters had seen it all before many, many times. In cramped living conditions where a family of ten, twelve, fifteen or more lived in one or two rooms, what else can one expect but incest? Families kept their secrets and the Sisters did not comment or judge. I felt that there was nothing in human life that they had not witnessed in the seventy years that they had worked in Poplar.

Later Sister said to me, "We will have to keep up this pretence that he is going to get better. The charade has to go on — treatments that will do no good, drugs that are useless — just to give the impression of medical competence and nursing care. 'Hope' lies in all the treatments and, without hope for the future, most of our patients would endure an agony of terror and torment at the end."

One day when I called they were studying travel brochures received from Thomas Cook. Frank was very alert in his mind. His speech was slower and quieter, but his eyes were bright, and he seemed almost animated.

"Peg an' me, we thinks we'll go to Canada for a good holiday when the treatment's done an' I'm on me feet again. She's never bin abroad a'fore. I was in France and Germany in Hitler's war, an' I never wants 'a go near Europe agen. But Canada, now — big clean open spaces. Look a' this 'ere, nurse. Lovely pictures, aren't they? We reckons Canada's just the place for us, don't we, Peg? Who knows, we might stop there if we likes it enough, eh, Peg?"

She was sitting on the edge of the bed, her eyes glowing with love and happy anticipation.

"We'll go on the Queen Mary," she agreed. "First Class, like a couple of swells."

They both laughed and squeezed hands.

Together Peggy and I helped him to the bathroom. It was difficult, but he still had the strength to get there. She washed him all over, because although he could get into the bath, he did not have the strength to get out. In clean pyjamas he sat in the sitting room looking at the plaster ducks flying across the wall, whilst Peggy and I changed the bed with the text over it, executed in big, childish embroidery stitches, 'God is Love'.

We had taught Peggy many essentials in the art of nursing, such as treating pressure points, dealing with pain or nausea, and many others. She was quick to acquire any small skill to make him more comfortable. I enquired about appetite, pain, bowels, vomiting, headaches and fluid intake, and left them happy with their plans for Canada. Should it be Vancouver or the Rockies? They couldn't decide.

The air was sweet as I left the little house, and the sounds of the huge cargo vessels, the cranes, the lorries, seemed far off. I thought of the thousands of powerful men working ceaselessly in that great port, and the fragility of life. Health is the greatest of God's gifts which we take for granted, and in fact almost expect as though it were a right, yet it hangs on a thread as fine as a spider's web which the tiniest thing can snap, leaving the strongest of us helpless in an instant.

Frank received a six-week course of radium therapy, being taken twice a week by ambulance to the hospital. They both expressed wonder and a touching appreciation that all this was free. "It's lucky I got ill now, an' not a few years ago. I could never have paid for all this expensive treatment." They seemed completely confident that it would be effective, probably because it was so elaborate. That he was getting weaker every day was put down to the temporary effects of the radium, which would pass when the treatment was completed. Everyone, that is, all the medical and paramedical staff (who must have totalled at least thirty people) kept the illusion going, though there was no corporate decision to do so.

Nausea is an unpleasant side effect of radium treatment which Frank had been warned about in advance. He attributed his weakness and weight loss to the fact that he could not eat much. "'Cos a man's gonna get thin like, if he's not eatin' like what I'm not. Once I get some good grub inside me, an' keep it down, I'll pack the old weight on, you'll see."

Pain was another matter. The control of pain is the first responsibility of anyone involved in the care of the dying. Pain is a mystery that we cannot fathom, because there is no measure. Everyone's tolerance level of pain differs, therefore the correct dose of analgesic will differ. One must balance the strength of analgesic to the level of pain perceived and not allow the pain to develop beyond the patient's tolerance level.

Frank was having half a grain of morphine three times a day. Later this was increased to four, then six times daily. It was sufficient to dull his pain to an acceptable level, but did not impair his faculties. He was interested in everything.

He said once: "Every mornin' I hear the fishin' boats come up the river. Can't get out of the habit of wakin'. In my mind I can see the sails, dark against the red sun, like wot' they used to be like, comin' quietly out of the morning mist. Boo'iful they was, just boo'iful. You've gotta have seen it to know wot' a lovely sight it was. Now I listen to the sounds of the engines. I can tell you by the sound if it's an oyster smack or a mackerel trawler. I can even tell you how many deep sea vessels from the Atlantic come in. It'll be good to be back at Billingsgate."

Peggy and I agreed that it wouldn't be long. He was getting on famously.

Peggy had given up all work now and never left his side, except for essential household duties. She spent hours reading to him. Frank had never learned to read fluently, and could barely write.

"Book-learnin's never been my strong point — but Peg, she's the scholar. I love to hear her read. She's got a lovely voice."

Peggy read about half a dozen of Dickens' novels in this way, sitting close to him, outwardly reading but inwardly attentive to every mood and movement. She was conscious of every shade or shadow in her loved one, ready to close the book if she sensed tiredness, or a change of position if she saw discomfort. Peggy knew before he knew himself what his needs were going to be.

Love permeated every nook and cranny, every corner and crevice of that little house. You could feel it as you entered the front door, like a presence so tangible you could almost reach out and touch it. If there is one thing that a dying person needs more than relief from pain, it is love. I have seen, later in my career when I was a ward sister at the Marie Curie Hospital in Hampstead, unloved, unwanted people dying alone. Nothing can be more tragic or pitiful. And nothing is more hopeless or intractable for the nursing staff to deal with.

Love prompted Peggy to sing to Frank every evening, the old songs, the folk songs and hymns that they had both learned in childhood. Love prompted her to move the bed so that he could see the masts and funnels of the boats as they approached the docks. Love told her which visitors to admit and which to turn away from their front door. They grew even closer together. They had always been one flesh. Now they were one spirit, one soul. And all the time she kept up the pretending game that he was going to recover. If she cried alone in the kitchen, he never saw it.

It was Frank who first startled me. We had just finished a blanket bath (he no longer had the strength to get to the bathroom) and he asked Peggy for a hot drink and a hot water bottle. As soon as he heard the kitchen door close, he said, "Nurse, you must promise me you won't let on to Peggy. It'll break her heart. Promise, now."

I was putting things away in my bag and my back was towards him. I didn't move, or breathe. I had to respond in some way, but I couldn't find my voice.

"I want you to promise, now."

"What do you mean?" I said, eventually.

I had to turn round, and he was looking straight at me, his sunken eyes bright in their dark sockets.

"I mean I'm not gonna get better an' I don't want Peg to know until she has to."

"But Frank, what makes you think you won't recover? The radium treatment ends next week and then you will begin to feel stronger."

140

I hated myself for this pathetic falsehood. I felt degraded by it. Why do we have to be like this? In India, apparently, a man predicts his own death, says farewell to his family, goes to a holy place, and dies. Yet for us, we cannot admit to someone that he is dying, so we have to play false, and I have been as big a deceiver as anyone.

He didn't say a word, but closed his heavy eyes. We heard the kitchen door. He hissed fiercely, "Promise. Promise you won't tell her."

"I promise, Frank," I whispered.

He sighed with relief and closed his eyes.

"Thank you." His voice was husky. "Thank you, now I can rest easy."

The radium treatment had halted the malignant growth for a while, but could not be continued beyond six weeks, as it would destroy other organs. Frank's deterioration was rapid when treatment stopped. The pain became more intense, and the morphine was increased to one grain, then two grains every four hours. He could barely eat, and Peggy sat beside him feeding semi-solids into his unwilling mouth.

"There, Frank love, just another little spoonful, put some strength into you."

He would nod, and try to swallow. She washed and shaved him, turned him, cleaned his mouth and his eyes. She dealt with his urine and his bowels, and kept him clean and comfortable, all the while humming the songs he liked. He no longer looked at travel brochures, nor had the mental strength or interest to listen to Dickens, but he seemed to like to hear her singing. He

141

rarely spoke and was drifting in and out of consciousness.

Frank was quietly slipping away into that mysterious border land between life and death where peace and rest and gentle sounds are the only needs. One day, in my presence, he gazed at Peggy for a long time as though he did not recognise her and then said, quite clearly:

"Peggy my first love, my only love, always there, always when I need you." He smiled and drifted away again where no one can follow.

More than anything else a dying person needs to have someone with them. This used to be recognised in hospitals, and when I trained no one ever died alone. However busy the wards, or however short of staff, a nurse was always assigned to sit with a dying person, to hold the hand, stroke the forehead, whisper a few words. Peace and quietness, even reverence for the dying, were expected and assured in hospitals.

I disagree wholly with the notion that there is no point in staying with an unconscious patient, because he or she does not know you are there. I am perfectly certain, through years of experience and observation, that unconsciousness, as we define it, is not a state of unknowing. Rather, it is a state of knowing and understanding on a different level that is beyond our immediate experience.

Peggy was aware of this and, in ways that neither she could explain nor anyone understand, she entered into Frank's mental state in the last few weeks and days of his life.

One day, as I was leaving, she said,

"It won't be long now. I shall be glad for us both when it's all over."

She did not look unhappy. In fact she looked as serene and as confident as ever. But all pretence was gone.

I asked her, "How long have you known that he was going to die?"

"How long? Well, I can't say exactly. A long time, anyway. From the time the doctor first said he should go into hospital for tests, I suppose."

"So you've known all the time, and never let on?"

She did not reply, but stood on the doorstep, smiling.

"How did you guess?" I asked, intrigued.

"It wasn't a question of guessing. I just knew, quite suddenly, as though someone had told me. I've had so much happiness in life with Frank, more happiness than anyone can expect. We're more than brother and sister, more than husband and wife. How could I fail to know that he was going to die?"

She smiled, and waved to a neighbour who was passing, and replied to the enquiry, "Yes, he's getting on nicely thank you, he'll be up and about soon, you'll see."

The last evening of his life came surprisingly quickly. Rash is the professional who will predict death. The young can die while your back is turned, yet the old and frail, who you think will die in the night, live on for weeks. I recall just such an old lady when I was a night sister. She looked on the point of death at 1 a.m. so I took all my notes and paperwork into her cubicle to write the report, and sat with her all night. At 4a.m. she opened one eye and said, "You think I'm going to snuff it, don't you? Well I'm not. I'll have a boiled egg for breakfast."

But I digress.

The late summer evening was beautiful as I approached the prefab estate. The long shafts of sunlight glimmered on the river and made the little buildings glow like pink marble.

Peggy greeted me at the door with the words, "He's changed, nurse. About an hour ago he just changed. Something's different."

She was right. A deep motionless stupor had come over Frank. He did not appear in any discomfort or distress. In fact I have never in all my experience known anyone to die in a state of distress. 'Death agony' is a common idea, but I have never seen it.

Frank's breathing had changed. It was very slow and deep. I counted the breaths and there were only six per minute. He was cyanosed around the mouth, nose and ears. His eyes were open but unseeing. Peggy took his hand and grasped it firmly. She stroked his forehead with her other hand and leaned over him whispering, "I'm here, Frank. It's all right, my love, I'm here."

He appeared quite unconscious, but I saw his hand move as he gripped hers more firmly. What is this mystery we call the unconscious? I felt sure he knew she was there. Perhaps he could even hear her and understand her words. I felt his nose, his ears, his feet. They were quite cold. I felt his pulse; it was only twenty beats per minute. I whispered, "I'll stay here quietly. I'll sit over by the window."

She nodded. I sat down to contemplate them both. She was completely calm and relaxed. She did not look unhappy or even anxious. Every nerve of her concentration was focused on the dying man. She was with him in death as she had been in life.

His breathing dropped to four per minute and his hand holding Peggy's fell limp. I felt his pulse again, but could not locate it, and when I did it was a feeble eight or ten beats per minute. I sat down again, and Peggy continued to stroke his face and his hands. The clock ticked steadily, and quarter of an hour passed. Frank gave a deep, deep breath which made a rasping sound as it passed through the collapsed throat muscles. A little fluid oozed out of his mouth and trickled down the pillow. His eyes were still open, but a white film was collecting over them. Peggy whispered,

"I think he's gone."

"I think so. But wait quietly for a minute."

She sat unmoving by the inert body for about two minutes. Then, to our surprise, he took another huge, rasping breath. Would there be another? We waited for a full five minutes, but he did not breathe again. There was no pulse or heart beat.

Spontaneously Peggy said, "Into Thy hands, oh Lord, I commend his spirit."

Then she recited the Lord's prayer, in which I joined her.

Together we straightened and laid out the dead man's body. We closed his eyes. We could not keep his mouth shut so I tied the chin with a bandage to keep the lower jaw in place. We could take it off when rigor mortis had set in. We had to change the bed linen completely, because at the time of dying his bowels and bladder had emptied.

We washed him all over, and I said, "We will leave him in a shirt, put on back to front. The undertakers will bring a shroud."

She replied, "I've got one. I got it several weeks ago. I couldn't have left him not decent like, could I?"

She fetched a chair and climbed up to a small cupboard high above the gas meter. There was a box in it from which she extracted a shroud. We put it on him. I asked her if she would like me to contact the undertakers. She thanked me, and said she would be grateful.

"But tell them not to come till tomorrow morning, will you please?"

That was perfectly normal. In those days the deceased often lay in the house for a day or two as a mark of respect for the dead. Family and neighbours would come in to 'pay their respects'.

Throughout, Peggy was completely calm and tranquil. Her face and voice betrayed no sign of sorrow or loss. In fact I would have said she had an ethereal quality about her. I left her with a feeling of admiration.

At the door, she said, "If you see anyone, any neighbours like, don't tell them Frank's died, will you? I'll tell them tomorrow. I want to tell them myself."

Of course not, I reassured her. But I would have to report it at Nonnatus House. Her anxiety relaxed.

"That's all right. It's just the neighbours I don't want to know yet. They can come tomorrow to pay their respects. But not tonight."

We smiled at each other, and I squeezed her hand. No one would come barging in tonight, not the undertakers, nor the neighbours, nor anyone. She could be alone with her thoughts and her memories. Would she like a couple of sleeping tablets?

She thought for a second. Yes, that might be a very good idea. I opened my bag and handed her a couple of Soneryl.

Peggy shut and locked the door when I left. She sat for many hours on the edge of the bed, unable to take her eyes off Frank, their life together tumbling through her mind. Her happiness had been perfect and complete, she had always known that, and now she was not going to be parted from him.

She pulled up a chair and climbed again to the cupboard above the gas meter and took out two boxes, one very small, the other larger. She undressed and brushed her hair. She opened the larger of the two boxes and took out a white shroud, which she put on, tying the ribbons carefully at the back. She opened the small box and tipped out fifteen grains of morphine, to which she added the two Soneryl. She took a bottle of brandy and a glass from the bedside cabinet, and swallowed all the tablets in two or three gulps. She continued drinking brandy until she could no longer sit up.

When the undertakers arrived the next morning they could not get in. They broke the window and saw her dead, her arms around her brother.

And the Meek shall Inherit the Earth

The Reverend Thornton Applebee-Thornton had been a missionary in Sierra Leone for twenty-five years. He was enjoying a six-month furlough home in England, which he tried to spend mostly at the Applebee-Thorntons' country house in Herefordshire. This was not always easy because his father, a widower of ninety who was looked after by two ladies from the village, was a retired Indian Army colonel who had never been able to understand his only son's priestly instincts. In fact he despised them and despised his wet and wimpish ways, and felt secretly aggrieved that he should be afflicted with such offspring. His only son, he grumbled to himself, might have had the decency to turn out to be more of a man than that poor thing with his dog-collar and his sermons, now a missionary pandering to the blasted natives.

"Bah!", he would shout, "kick hell out of the blasted wogs. That's the only way they will respect you. It's the only language they understand."

At which point his reverend son decided that perhaps it was time to visit his cousin Jack at his farm in Dorset;

149

but cousin Jack had just retired to the South of France, leaving his son Courtney in charge of the farm and yes, of course, (the letter read) cousin Thornton would be more than welcome to stay if he could accommodate Fiona's busy programme at the riding school which they had just opened. A week at the farm convinced the Reverend Mr Applebee-Thornton that all this horsey stuff was not for him. Equally, the young couple decided between themselves that the poor old boy was really a frightful bore and they couldn't be expected to introduce him to their circle, and perhaps Africa was the best place for him.

So he visited old school friends and students from his theological college days. They were delighted to see him but sadly, after they had exhausted shared experiences of thirty to forty years before, found they had little to say to each other.

Perhaps a couple of weeks in Brightlingsea — or did they call it Brighton these days? — would be pleasant. The Metropole was comfortable and he enjoyed the sea breezes but, as he sat on the front watching life pass by, he was forced to conclude that he had spent so long in Africa and given so much of his mind and energy to the Mission, that he had lost touch with changing England. Expecting the customs and manners, dress and behaviour of the 1920s, he was a little shocked, and more than a little pained by what he saw.

The Reverend Mr Applebee-Thornton was a bachelor, not, he was quick to assure his friends, by choice. He greatly admired, indeed revered, the fair and gentle sex, and would very much have wished the

150

solace and companionship of a loving wife, joined in the felicity of holy matrimony as vouchsafed to his more fortunate friends and colleagues; but the fair ideal had just not come his way. The truth is that the reverend gentleman was essentially a one-woman man, and the only woman he had ever fancied was, unfortunately, a nun. He had never spoken to her, beyond the sacramental words: "this is the body of Christ, take this . . . . . ." as he gave her the consecrated bread, but she was enshrined in his heart and when he was moved to another mission her memory went with him, never to be effaced. But it was all a long time ago, he mused, as he watched the boys and girls flaunting themselves half-naked on Brighton beach, and times have changed. Perhaps one was out of touch.

He pulled a letter from his pocket. One of his old friends from theological college was the Rector of St Augustine's, Poplar. The Rector would be delighted to see him, the letter read, and to show him around the parish. Would a couple of weeks be sufficient?

This was how the Reverend Thornton Applebee-Thornton came to be in Poplar at the time of which I write. As the mission in Sierra Leone was planning to introduce a midwifery service, the Rector suggested that his old friend might like to study the work of the Sisters of St Raymond Nonnatus.

It seemed an invitation not to be missed. Accordingly, the Rector contacted Sister Julienne, and arranged that conducted tours of our domiciliary practice should start the following day, with visits, by arrangement, to some of our patients.

The Reverend Mr Applebee-Thornton came to lunch at Nonnatus House. We were about twelve at table that day. We were accustomed to luncheon visitors, who were mostly clergymen and sometimes retired missionaries, and it was always a pleasant change. He was a tall, distinguished man of around fifty. He was good-looking, with fine, slightly sharp features and a sensitive mouth. He had a full head of pure white hair and sun-weathered skin. He was very thin and I thought this was due, probably, to repeated bouts of dysentery and other intestinal infections. He ate very heartily of the lamb stew provided by Mrs B, our cook, complimenting her with loquacious courtesy upon its excellence. He had a deep, kindly voice and kindly eyes that looked at each person around the table with intelligent understanding. If he spoke directly to anyone his attention was so focused and so penetrating, that he seemed to read the mind and character of the person he was speaking to.

Conversation was general. Sister Julienne asked him to tell us about the mission at Sierra Leone and he expanded on the size of the Christian community, the dire poverty of the natives in their primitive huts and the work being done to found schools and hospitals. He spoke with fluency and charm, with not a trace of self-aggrandisement, to which he would have been entitled, having been a pioneer in a primitive and hostile environment.

He was fascinating. We all hung on his words, especially Chummy, our nursing colleague, whose burning ambition, in fact her only reason for training as a nurse, was in order to be a missionary. Eagerly she asked him about the plans to start a midwifery service, to which he smilingly replied that he hoped she would honour the mission by being their first trained midwife. Chummy's huge shoulders expanded with pride and joy. She closed her eyes and exclaimed, with a shuddering sigh, "Oh, I will, I will. You can rely on me."

He looked at her quietly and carefully, his pleasant eyes taking in her youthful enthusiasm. Many people reacted to Chummy's massive size and awkward gestures with ill-concealed humour, but not this gentleman. He leaned towards her and said, softly, "I am quite, quite sure that we can rely on you."

Chummy's breath quivered out of her in a series of happy gasps and she could bring herself to say no more.

The Reverend Mr Applebee-Thornton turned to Sister Julienne.

"Which brings me to the purpose of my being here today. What with the charm of the company and the excellence of the luncheon, I had almost forgotten that my purpose is to be shown around your district nursing and midwifery practice."

Was it an accident? Was it coincidence? Was it a mistake? Or was it devilish cunning? With a perfectly straight face, saucy little Sister Julienne, whose eyes never missed a trick and whose mind was everywhere, without so much as a blush, looked coolly at him and lied through her teeth.

"I very much regret that none of the Sisters will be available to escort you on a tour of the district. I cannot express my regret too strongly, but we all have other duties this afternoon."

He looked disappointed and everyone else looked surprised. She continued, "It is a busy time for us and therefore, unfortunately, none of my trained nurses can be spared for the purpose either."

The poor man looked uncomfortable, as though he was superfluous to requirements, and ought to be going.

"However, Jane is available this afternoon . . ."

At this poor Jane nearly fell off her chair, knocking over a salt pot and a dish of mint sauce which slid greenly across the table; neither of which accidents Sister Julienne appeared to notice.

". . . . . . and Jane, who knows the district well, perhaps better than any of us, will be delighted to accompany you."

She rose to her feet, and we all got up with her and stood behind our chairs as she said grace. My eyes were lowered, but by lifting my eyebrows I was able to look across the table at Jane. Her hands were not folded; they were clinging to the back of her chair and she was panting. Little beads of perspiration had broken out on her forehead and all in all she looked on the point of collapse. What on earth was Sister about, I wondered. This was sheer cruelty.

In the hallway I heard Sister making suggestions to Jane about taking the Manchester Road and the Dockland areas first. Then they could look at Bow, Limehouse and the other parts of the district another day.

Jane went to fetch her coat and her legs were shaking. I saw the Reverend Mr Applebee-Thornton watch her closely as she walked in front of him. His face was very thoughtful. Jane reached to take down her coat, but her hands twitched so convulsively that she could not take it off the peg.

"Allow me," he said courteously, and helped her to put it on. He put his hand on her arm and led her to the door. He turned and thanked Sister for allowing him such an excellent guide, who he was quite sure would be most helpful and informative. He opened the door for Jane with a slightly old-fashioned bow and murmured: "After you, madam".

They returned at tea-time and he was full of praise, saying how informative Jane had been, and how greatly he valued the time she had so graciously spared him. Asked if he would like more conducted tours of the district, he said that there was no limit to his thirst for knowledge. Asked if he was quite happy with Jane as his escort, would he prefer a trained midwife on another occasion, he became profuse in stating his preference for Jane who, he declared, was the perfect guide and mentor. Her erudition and encyclopaedic knowledge of the topography and sociology of the area was more than he had dared hope for.

Jane appeared to accept her new role as guide for the Reverend Mr Applebee-Thornton, and carried out her duties with her customary attention to detail. Sister Julienne advised her to take a map, and to keep notes of what they had seen.

A week or two later at lunch, Sister enquired how things were going. Jane replied eagerly, "Well, Pippin wants . . . ."

She turned a deep red and gasped. Her hands flew to her mouth. Stuttering, she tried to excuse herself.

"I don't mean to be impertinent, Sister, but he asked me to call him Pippin. I said I couldn't presume to be so familiar, but he said that all his friends call him Pippin, and he would be hurt if I didn't."

To this Sister replied, with exaggerated solemnity, that Jane had done quite rightly, and must certainly call him Pippin, if that was his wish.

That same evening we were in the bicycle shed. Sister Julienne was mending a puncture, and I was tightening my brakes. To my great surprise, she said "Where do you get your clothes from, Jennifer?"

With the tyre lever grasped firmly in her small hand, Sister ripped off the outer tube.

"Well, I have a dressmaker. I don't usually go for the off-the-peg stuff."

"But what store would you recommend for good clothes?"

I thought a bit. Sister plunged the inner tube into a bowl of water.

"Liberty's, I suppose, in Regent Street."

"Ah yes, Liberty's. That sounds most suitable."

She was turning the inner tube thoughtfully in the water, looking for bubbles.

"Jane needs some new clothes. I am going to tell her to get some. I wonder Jenny, would it be too much to ask you to go with her? I'm sure she would value your

156

advice. You need spare no expense, because Jane earns money but she never spends it."

No one could ever resist an appeal from Sister Julienne — certainly not me.

More surprises were in store.

"And who is your hairdresser?"

"I always go to Chez Jacques in Regent Street, which just happens to be opposite Liberty's."

Her eyes lit up. She had found the puncture, the water was bubbling. But her real interest and excitement seemed to be in my hairdresser.

"Just opposite! Now, that's marvellous. It couldn't be more convenient. If you are in the area, could you make it convenient to take Jane to the hairdresser? She always cuts her hair herself, but I am sure she would look prettier if a good hairdresser would attend to her."

Now, none of my nearest and dearest would suggest that I am quick off the mark when it comes to match-making or pairing-off. My poor mind doesn't work that way. Slow, they call me. But on that occasion the penny dropped.

"It will be a pleasure, Sister. Just leave Jane in my hands."

Jane was dingy, drab and plain. Her clothes were about the worst I have ever seen. Her shoes were heavy, black lace-ups. Her stockings — tea-coloured lisle — were baggy. Her hair always looked a mess. And her skin was grey and deeply lined. To smarten her up would be quite a job.

After breakfast next morning Sister Julienne said: "Jane, you need some new clothes. Go with Jennifer this afternoon and she will choose some for you. You also need a haircut."

Jane meekly said: "Yes, Sister."

It may seem extraordinary to speak to an adult in such a manner, but there was no other way of dealing with Jane. She was incapable of making even the smallest decision for herself and had to be directed in everything. I took my cue from Sister. I had thought carefully, and decided that a new look for Jane would have to be subtle. If I tried to dress her up like a fashion plate, the result might be disastrous.

But first, the hairdresser.

Jane had never before been inside a West End hairdresser's and she hung back timidly at the door. But I only had to say, "I've made an appointment for you; you've got to come in," and she obeyed meekly.

I had a quiet word with Monsieur Jacques: ". . . a gentle style, to frame the face, nothing exaggerated, no backcombing, something to suit a mature lady of quiet habits."

Monsieur Jacques nodded gravely, and took up his scissors.

As every woman knows, it's the cut that counts, and Jacques was a master cutter. Had he ever achieved anything as spectacular as his reinvention of Jane? Perhaps the enormity of the challenge inspired him. The result was little short of a miracle. Her natural curls moved in all the right places, her dingy greyness was now a confident iron-grey, with a softening of white

158

at the temples. Jane looked at herself with astonishment in the huge mirrors, and as he flicked a wayward curl with his tail-comb, she actually smiled. Some of the worry left her face and she giggled.

"Ooh, is that me?"

At Liberty's I looked out for a sales assistant who would not intimidate Jane. Some of them can be so smart and sharp they set the teeth on edge. A languid young woman with a drainpipe figure and a contemptuous eye shimmied across the carpet, but I steered Jane towards a homely-looking soul with a tape-measure round her neck. I explained the requirements, and she murmured reassuringly. "The unconscious elegance of a Hebe-Sports, with a little blouse or two. Leave everything to me." And she deftly applied the tape measure to Jane's bony frame.

As promised Jane emerged from the changing room transformed by a tailored suit in elegant grey. The tape-measure breathed, "The iconic statement of the suit is in keeping with modom's splendid height. The subtle moulding of the skirt lends softness to the hips. Observe the detail of the pockets, rounding and moulding the line of the hips. Notice how the curve of the collar flatters modom's superb shoulders."

All of which was another way of saying that Jane's gaunt figure and prominent bones had somehow been concealed by the cut of the suit. She stood, meek and silent, passively allowing the collar to be adjusted a fraction of an inch.

One would have thought that the tape-measure had by now exhausted her repertoire, but not at all. She was just winding up for a virtuoso performance.

"The slender figure and sublime height of modom is perfection for the timeless beauty of the true suit. Observe the effortless grace of modom's posture." (Jane was drooping as usual). "Good clothes reflect the creativity of their creator, striving for the zenith of creation. The true suit is visionary, in a restrained and dignified mode. Modom's intuitive understanding of the truly chic speaks volumes for her ineffable vision."

Jane was looking utterly bewildered, and I felt myself sinking out of my depth.

The tape measure cast a swift, professional eye over us both, absorbed the fact that we were floundering and came in swiftly on the attack again.

"Observe how the silken threads pick out a million dancing lights, and enhance the flickering shades in modom's beautiful hair."

I had to agree that the colour certainly matched Jane's hair, whilst she stood silent, having no opinion on the subject.

The tape-measure turned to the drainpipe.

"And now we must consider the passive and perfect necessity of the little blouse. Quintessentially, Tara lawn is the first essential, wouldn't you agree?"

"Oh, quintessentially essential," the drainpipe gushed as we crossed the floor to a room filled with blouses.

"The colour at the throat is all important. Modom requires the understatement. The bold gesture is not for modom. The impalpable discrimination of the subtle is what we now seek. Dusty pink, I think."

She pulled from the rail a pink blouse and held it against Jane's scrawny throat. The result was undeniably pleasing.

"Whilst the blue — muted, of course — draws attention to modom's fine eyes."

A second blouse was held up. It was true. I had never before noticed how blue Jane's eyes were.

The tape-measure drew forth yet another.

". . . .and what does modom say to mellow yellow?"

Jane had nothing to say, but the drainpipe ventured to suggest that perhaps mellow yellow was a little over-emphatic in its proclamation, and would not the merest whisper of lilac speak with quiet authority?

The tape-measure raised her manicured hands.

"Lilac! Heavenly lilac! How could I forget?"

She signalled to the drainpipe, who trickled away and returned with a third blouse, of perfect fit and colour. Jane looked charming in all of them. The tape-measure was rhapsodic.

"Ah! the lilac, the perfection of lilac. Queen Mary's favourite colour, and modom's truest friend. Lilac is a poem, a fragrance, a hint of nothingness. Modom cannot possibly miss heavenly lilac from her wardrobe."

These women certainly give value for money; we took the lot.

Shoes, gloves, handbag and some decent stockings were all chosen by the same strategy, and we were on our way east of Aldgate, and back to Poplar.

Was Pippin likely to be aware of all the intense female activity that had been going on for his delight and diversion? Was he likely to see any difference? The sad answer to these questions was probably 'no' to both of them. I have yet to meet a man who can give you even the vaguest description of what a woman was wearing ten minutes after she left his company. He would probably say, with an airy wave of the hand, "Oh, she was looking lovely in a green floaty thing," whereas she was wearing tight-fitting blue.

Jane changed for lunch and therefore it was for an all-female audience that she created her sensation. Cries of "lovely," "transformed," "fab hair-do," went up all around, and Jane looked pink and surprised, and was quietly gratified by all the compliments. Sister Julienne allowed herself a meaningful wink as she whispered to me, "Well done."

Pippin came at 2p.m. promptly and exhibited no surprise at Jane's appearance. Perhaps he saw no change! They left together for Mile End, the most northerly border of our district.

Let us not enquire too closely into these guided walking tours, conceived and executed with a view to benefiting the native people of Sierra Leone. To do so would be a lapse of good taste. Sufficient to say that the two-week stay at the Rectory was lengthened to six and that, day by day, bit by bit, Jane looked more relaxed and happy, and less chronically nervous.

Pippin came to lunch one Sunday a few weeks later, and towards the end of the meal he said, "I will have to be leaving you all soon. My six month furlough draws to its close, and I must return to the duties God has been pleased to entrust to me in Sierra Leone. Before I leave England I must spend a few weeks with my aged father in Herefordshire. These visits are not always easy for me, because we do not always see eye to eye, especially over the treatment of the native African. My father, now aged ninety, was an army officer in the African wars of the 1880s, and his principles I regard as harsh, whereas he regards mine as weak and mollycoddling. It can be very difficult."

He turned to Sister Julienne.

"I was wondering Sister, if you could possibly spare Jane for a couple of weeks to come with me? I feel that a feminine influence would ease the tension in an all-male household. With her charm and tact, and her gentle disposition, I feel that she could mollify and soften my father in ways that I never could with my blunderings. Jane has already agreed to come if you can spare her. And I, for my part, would be eternally grateful if you could."

Jane's hand was resting on the table, he touched it lightly, and gave it a little squeeze.

She blushed and murmured: "Oh! Pip."

The visit started badly because the old colonel called Jane "a raw-boned horse" and Pippin was furious and would have walked out of the house without even unpacking. But Jane laughed and said she had been called worse than that in her time. Pippin raged on about "that impossible old man" until Jane went up to him, placed her fingers on his lips, and whispered: "Just be thankful that you have a father at all, dear."

163

In an agony of self-reproach he caught hold of her wrists and drew her to him.

"May God forgive me. I am not worthy of you."

He kissed her gently.

"All my sins will be redeemed by your suffering, my wise and perfect love."

Later that evening the colonel returned to horses when he referred to "that little filly of yours . . ." Pippin stiffened, but his father carried on, "she's got good legs. Always a sign of pedigree in a horse or a woman. You can tell the breeding by the shape of the ankle."

The weeks passed well and the colonel took to Jane. Her quietness appealed to him and her self-effacing habits were what he liked. He barked at his son one evening.

"Well, there's one thing to say. That little filly of yours is not going to drive you mad with a lot of silly chatter. Never could abide those magpie women, m'self; yakety-yakety-yak, all day long."

His son smiled and said, "I can take it that we have your blessing, then sir?"

"Whether you have my blessing or not, my boy, I can see you are set on the filly and nothing will make any difference. Go ahead, go ahead, your mother would have been pleased, God rest her soul."

The Reverend Mr and Mrs Applebee-Thornton returned to Poplar for a few days, before they sailed for Sierra Leone. I have never in my life seen a woman so changed. She was tall and regal, her eyes were smiling, and calm confidence seemed to spring from deep within her. Pippin hardly took his eyes off her, and always referred to her as "my dear wife", or "my beloved Jane".

Of course, we had to have a party. Nuns love a party. They are very sedate affairs, ending at 9p.m., in time for Compline and the Greater Silence, but they are fun while they last. Mrs B provided excellent cakes and sandwiches, to which was added a little sweet sherry, compliments of the Rector. The invitation was open to anyone who had known Jane and wanted to wish the happy couple well in their new life. About fifty people came, and some boys from the SPY (South Poplar Youth) club provided music with their guitars and drums, which was considered to be very risqué. Pippin gave a delightful speech. The length of the phrases and the extravagance of the language, about pearls of great price, and the best wine being served last, was lost on many people, but the gist of the message was that he was the luckiest man alive, and everyone cheered.

Dancing had just begun when the telephone rang. I was first on call.

"Yes . . . yes . . . this is Nonnatus House . . . Mrs Smith . . . what address, please? How frequent are the contractions? Have the waters broken? Keep her in bed, please. I'll come straight away."

Part II

Sister Monica Joan

Sister Monica Joan did not die. She developed severe pneumonia after wandering down the East India Dock Road wearing only her nightie one cold November morning, but she did not die. In fact, the incident seemed to rejuvenate her. Perhaps she enjoyed all the extra pampering and cosseting supplied by her Sisters and Mrs B, the cook. No doubt she enjoyed being the centre of attention. Perhaps penicillin, the new wonder drug, had pumped fire into her old heart. Whatever the reason, Sister Monica Joan, at the age of ninety, enjoyed a new lease of life, and was soon to be seen trotting all over Poplar, to the great rejoicing of everyone who knew her.

The Sisters of St Raymund Nonnatus were a nursing order of fully professed nuns, bound by the monastic vows of poverty, chastity and obedience. The Sisters were all trained nurses and midwives, and their vocation was to work amongst the poorest of the poor. They had maintained a house in the London Docklands since the 1870s, when their work was revolutionary. Poor women in those days had no medical care during pregnancy and childbirth, and in the middle of the nineteenth century maternal deaths amongst poor women living in the worst slum conditions were around thirty per cent. Infant deaths were not even recorded, but were possibly in the region of sixty per cent.

Midwifery as a profession did not exist. In each community local women, with a sort of folk-lore tradition passed on from mother to daughter, went around delivering babies. Such a woman was called 'the handy woman' and her practice usually consisted of 'lying-in and laying-out' (i.e. lying-in after childbirth and laying-out of the dead). Some of these women were quite good at their trade, better than nothing one might say, but others were ignorant, illiterate, slatternly drunkards. The portrait of Sairey Gamp in Martin Chuzzlewit was not merely a caricature figure — she was real.

Against relentless parliamentary ridicule and opposition, many inspired women, including the Sisters of St Raymund Nonnatus, fought to have midwifery recognized as a profession, and midwives to be trained and registered. Eventually, after a series of Bills were defeated in the House, the women won, and the first Midwives Act became law in 1902. The Royal College of Midwives was born, and from that moment maternal and infant deaths began to fall.

The Sisters were true heroines. They had entered slum areas of the London Docks at a time when no-one else would go near them, except perhaps the police. They had worked through epidemics of cholera, typhoid, tuberculosis, scarlet fever and smallpox, careless of themselves being infected. They had worked through two world wars and endured the intensive bombing of the Blitz, careless of their own lives. They were inspired and sustained by their dual vocation — service to God and service to mankind.

But do not imagine for a moment that the Sisters were trapped by their bells and their rosaries, and that life had passed them by. The nuns, collectively and individually, had experienced more of the world and its ways, more of heroism and degradation, of sin and salvation than most people will experience in a lifetime. No indeed, the nuns were not remote goodie-goodies. They were a bunch of feisty women who had seen it all, lived and loved and suffered throughout, and remained true to their vocation.

Nonnatus House was situated just off the East India Dock Road, near to Poplar High Street and the Blackwall Tunnel. It was a large Victorian building next to a bomb site. A third of all Dockland dwellings had been destroyed by the Blitz, and most of the derelict buildings and rubble had not been cleared away. Bomb sites were children's playgrounds during the day and the dormitories for meths drinkers overnight.

Overcrowding had always been chronic in Poplar, and it had been said that Poplar housed 50,000 people per square mile. After the Second World War it was even worse, because houses and flats had been destroyed and re-building had not yet commenced. So people just moved in with each other. It was not unusual to find three or four generations of one family living in a small house, or fifteen people living in two or three small rooms in the tenements — the Canada Buildings or the Peabody Buildings and the notorious Blackwall Tenements. These were Victorian buildings constructed on four sides around a central courtyard, with inner facing balconies which were the arteries of the tenement. There was no privacy. Everyone knew everyone else's business, and terrible fights could occur when the tensions of overcrowded family life erupted into violence. The tenements were bug-infested and insanitary. Some of the better ones had an indoor lavatory and running water, but most of the buildings had neither. Infections spread like wildfire through the tenements.

Most of the men worked in the Docks. It is difficult to remember today that London used to be the biggest trading port in the world. Thousands of men daily poured through the gates when they opened. Hours were long, the work was heavy, and life was hard, but the Cockney men knew no other, and they were tough. The Thames was the background of Poplar, and the boats, the cranes, the sound of the sirens, the whisper of the water was the backcloth upon which the tapestry of life had been woven for generations past. The river had been their constant companion, their friend and enemy, their employer, their playground and frequently, for the destitute, their grave.

Cockney life, for all its poverty, squalor and deprivation, was rich. Rich in humanity and humour, rich in drama and melodrama, rich in pathos and poignancy, and rich, unhappily rich, in tragedy.

The Sisters of St Raymund Nonnatus had served the people of Poplar for several generations. The Cockneys did not forget, and the nuns were loved, respected, even revered by the whole community.

During the time of which I write, an incident occurred that shook the foundations of Nonnatus House. In fact it shook the whole of Poplar, because everyone got to hear about it and for a time the local people could talk of little else.

Sister Monica Joan was accused of shoplifting.

My first intimation that something was wrong occurred when I returned from my evening visits, wet and hungry, and wondering why anyone was ever fool enough to be a district midwife. What about a nice cushy little office job, I thought to myself, as I pulled the bag from the carrier of my bike, knowing it would take me an hour to clean and sterilize all my instruments and repack the bag ready for use the following morning. Yes, that's it, I thought for the umpteenth time, a nice cushy little office job, with regular hours and central heating, sitting behind a nice smooth desk, tapping my Olivetti, and thinking about my evening date; a job in which the maximum responsibility would be to find the minutes of the last meeting, and the biggest disaster would be a broken fingernail.

I entered the front door of Nonnatus House, and the first thing I saw were a great number of large wet dirty footprints all over the fine Victorian tiles of the hallway. Large, dirty footprints in a convent? They were certainly very large, far too large to be those of a nun. Could it be that men had recently entered? It seemed unlikely at seven o' clock in the evening. If the rector or any of the curates had called they were unlikely to leave dirty footmarks. If any tradesman had called in the morning, leaving such an unseemly visiting card, the mess would have been cleared up before lunch. But there they were — large dirty footprints all over the hall. It was inexplicable.

Then I heard Sister Julienne's voice coming from the direction of her office. Sister's voice was usually quiet and well modulated, but now it had a slight edge to it, either of anxiety or nervousness, it was hard to tell. This was followed by men's voices. It all seemed very strange, but I didn't want to linger, knowing that I had my bag to prepare before I could get anything to eat, so I made my way to the clinical room, where I found Cynthia and Trixie and Chummy in deep and earnest conversation.

Chummy had opened the door, apparently, to a sergeant and a constable who had asked to see the Sister-in-Charge. Chummy was all of a flutter and tremble, because she always went to pieces when any man entered the room, but chiefly because the constable was the policeman she had knocked over when she was learning to ride her bicycle. Intense mortification and embarrassment at the sight of him had rendered her speechless. The men had entered the hallway, and in her awkward confusion she had banged the front door so hard that it sounded like a gun shot. Then she had tripped over the doormat and fallen into the arms of the policeman she had injured the year before.

Chummy was still in such a state of nervous distress that it was hard to get a word out of her, but Cynthia, apparently, hearing the bang of the front door and the noise of poor Chummy falling over, had come to see what it was all about. It was she, apparently, who had taken the policeman to the office and called Sister Julienne.

None of us knew much more than that, but female speculation can make a great deal out of very little. Whilst we boiled our instruments and cut and folded our gauze swabs and filled our pots and bottles, our imaginations ranged over everything from arson to murder. Chummy was convinced the visit of the law had something to do with her assault on a policeman — or why should he have come? she asked. But Cynthia gently calmed her down, saying that there was no way a charge would be brought a year after the event, and his coming to Nonnatus House was a coincidence.

We went to the kitchen for supper, deliberately leaving the door open, of course. We heard the office door open and heavy footsteps, and we all pricked up our ears, but we heard only a quiet: "Good night, Sister. Thank you for your time, and you will be hearing from us in the morning." The front door quietly closed, and four inquisitive girls were left in unrequited curiosity.

It was after lunch the following day that Sister Julienne asked us all to remain in our seats as she had something to say to us. Fred the boilerman and Mrs B the cook were also asked to come into the dining room, because the matter had to come out into the open, and Sister did not want rumours flying around, which would undoubtedly get exaggerated.

Apparently, Sister Julienne told us, Sister Monica Joan had been in Chrisp Street Market and the owner of a jewellery stall had seen her fingering several items. He had heard from other stall holders that one of the Sisters was 'light-fingered' so he watched her, but pretended not to be doing so. He saw her pick up a child's bracelet, look around her and then deftly tuck it under her scapular. Then she had assumed her usual haughty aspect, head held high, and attempted to walk away. But the stall holder stopped her. When he asked to see what she was holding beneath her scapular, she was at first extremely rude to him, telling him not to be so impertinent, and calling him a "boorish fellow". A crowd, of course, had gathered. The man got cross, and called her a "scraggy old God-botherer" and she'd better hand it over, or he'd get a peeler. Whereupon Sister Monica Joan had flung the gold bracelet across the stall with a contemptuous gesture, crying: "You can keep your tawdry trinkets, you loutish lump. What do I want with them?" and stalked off with an expression of offended dignity on her fine features.

Mrs B exploded: "I don't believe a word of it. Not a word. He's a liar, vat bloke. I knows him, an' I knows as what he's a liar, I do. You won't get me believing a story like vat about Sister Monica Joan, you won't, love 'er."

Sister Julienne silenced her.

"I'm afraid there is not a shadow of doubt about the truth of it. Several people are ready to testify that they saw Sister Monica Joan throw the bangle across the stall before she stalked off. But I'm afraid that is not all. There is worse to come."

She looked sadly around at us all, and we held our breath as we listened in silence.

The costermonger, probably enraged at having been called a "boorish fellow" and a "loutish lump" went round other stallholders who had talked about a "light-fingered Sister" and collected eight men and women who claimed that they had strong suspicions, or who had positively seen Sister Monica Joan take something small and hide it under her scapular. Collectively they had gone to the police.

Sister Julienne continued, "The police have been here yesterday and this morning. I felt bound to confront Sister Monica Joan with their report, but she wouldn't say a word to me. Not a single word. She just looked out of the window as though she had not even heard me. I told her I was going to look in her chest of drawers, and she just shrugged her shoulders dismissively, and pursed her lips and said 'poo to you' with something like contempt. I must say her attitude was extremely annoying, and if she behaved in that way to the coster, whom she had just robbed, it is not surprising that he was enraged."

Sister Julienne produced a suitcase from under the table, saying: "This is what I found in Sister Monica's chest of drawers," and she withdrew several pairs of silk stockings, three egg cups, a great quantity of coloured ribbons, a lady's silk blouse, four children's colouring books, an ornate hair-piece, a corkscrew, several small wooden animals, a tin whistle, a quantity of teaspoons, three ornamental china birds, a bundle of knitting wool all tangled up, a necklace of gaudy beads, about a dozen fine lawn handkerchiefs, a needle case, a shoe horn and a dog collar. All of the items were unused, and some of them still had a label attached.

There was really no need for Sister Julienne to say, "I'm afraid this has been going on for quite a long time". It was painfully obvious to all of us and Mrs B burst into tears.

"Oh, the love, bless 'er, oh the poor lamb, she don't know what she's doin', she don't, love 'er. Wha's going to 'appen to 'er, Sister? Vey wouldn't lock 'er up, not at 'er age?"

Sister Julienne said she didn't know. Prison seemed an unlikely outcome, but the costermonger was definitely bringing a charge, and Sister Monica Joan would be prosecuted.

At this point in my narrative a few words of explanation are necessary.

Sister Monica Joan was a very old nun born into an aristocratic family in the 1860s. She had obviously been a strong-willed girl who had rebelled against the restrictions and narrow self-interest of her social class, because she had broken away from her family (a shocking thing to do!) around 1890 in order to train as a nurse. In 1902, when the first Midwives Act was passed, the young Monica Joan trained as a midwife and shortly after joined the Sisters of St Raymund

Nonnatus. Her profession to a monastic order was the last straw, and the family disowned her. But the Novice Monica Joan didn't care a hoot and carried on doing her own thing. When I knew Sister Monica Joan she had lived and worked in Poplar for fifty years and was known by virtually everyone.

To say that by the age of ninety she was eccentric would be an understatement. Sister Monica Joan was wildly eccentric to the point of being outrageous. There was no telling what she would say or do next, and she frequently gave offence. Sometimes she could be sweet and gentle but at other times gratuitously spiteful. Poor Sister Evangelina, large and heavy, and not gifted with verbal brilliance, suffered most dreadfully from the astringent sarcasm of her Sister-in-God. Sister Monica Joan had a powerful intellect and was poetic and artistic, yet she was quite insensitive to music, as I witnessed once on the occasion of her shocking behaviour at a cello recital. She was very clever. Cunning, some would say. She manipulated others unscrupulously in order to get her own way. She was haughty and aristocratic in her demeanour, yet she had spent fifty years working in the slums of the London Docklands amid poverty and squalor. How can one account for such contradictions?

Whilst being a professed nun and a devout Christian, in her old age Sister Monica Joan had become fascinated by esoteric spirituality, ranging from astrology and fortune-telling to cosmology and centric forces. She loved to expiate on these subjects, but I doubted if she knew what she was talking about!

179

At the time I knew her she was verging on senility. The focus of her mind seemed to come and go, to shift and change. Sometimes she was perfectly focused and rational, while at other times it was as though she was seeing the world through a mist and was trying to grasp things half-seen. Yet I suspected she knew her mind was going, and used the fact to get what she wanted! Somehow she had a magnetic quality about her. She fascinated me. I loved her dearly and loved to spend time in her company.

When Sister Julienne solemnly told the group in the dining room that Sister Monica Joan would be prosecuted for theft, a wave of shock rippled around the dining table. Novice Ruth cried quietly. Mrs B protested vociferously that she wouldn't believe it. Trixie said she wasn't surprised. Sister Evangelina snapped "Be quiet, we'll have none of that," and sat very still, staring down at her plate, but her temples were twitching, and her knuckles went white as she gripped her hands together. Sister Julienne said: "We must all commit Sister Monica Joan to our prayers. We must seek God's help. But I will also engage a good lawyer."

I asked if I might visit Sister Monica Joan in her room that afternoon, and permission was readily given.

As I mounted the stairs, my mind was in a turmoil. How would I be received by a lady who had been visited by the police, from whose chest of drawers numerous stolen items had been extracted, and who had been told that she would have to face prosecution?

Sister Monica Joan's room was not the customary cell of a nun, bare and plain. Hers was an elegant bed sitting-room with all the comforts due to a distinguished old lady, and these were probably a great deal more than any other nun could expect, but Sister Monica Joan had a knack of always getting her own way. Since the pneumonia she had spent more time in her room, and I had been a frequent and happy visitor. But on this occasion, as I mounted the stairs, my heart was pounding with anxiety. What would be my reception?

I knocked, and heard a sharp: "Enter. Come in, don't just stand there. Come in."

I entered, and found her at her desk, notebooks and pencils all around her. She was scribbling away furiously and chuckling to herself. She was alight with excitement.

"Ah, it's you, my dear. Sit down, sit down. Did you know that the astral permanent atom is equivalent to the etheric permanent atom and that they both function within the parallel universe?"

She seemed to have no recollection of what had been going on, for which I was profoundly relieved. If she had been in a state of remorse it would have been hard to know what to say. I grinned and sat down.

"No, Sister. I didn't know about the parallel universe, nor the permanent atoms. Do tell me."

She started to draw a diagram for my benefit.

"See here, child, this is the point within the circle, and these bands are the seven parallels that are the unifying stability within the atoms that are the essence of the parallel universe wherein men and angels and beasts and others . . . I think."

Her voice trailed away, as she scribbled furiously, her mind obviously racing ahead of her pencil. Suddenly she cried out, her voice squeaking with excitement:

"I have it. Eureka! All has been revealed. There are eleven parallels. Not seven. Ah, the perfection of eleven. The beauty of eleven. All is revealed in eleven."

Her voice dropped to a trilling whisper, and she raised her eyes to heaven, her features irradiated by her thoughts. I felt again the magnetism of this woman who could hold me in a spell just by moving her fingers or lifting an eyebrow. Her skin was so fine and white that it seemed barely sufficient to cover the fragile bones and the blue veins that meandered up her hands and arms. She sat perfectly still, a pencil poised between two fingertips, the first digit of which she could bend independent of the rest of the finger. With eyes closed she was murmuring, "Eleven parallels, eleven stars . . . eleven crowns" and I was bewitched all over again. I knew that many people could not stand her. They found her arrogant, haughty, supercilious and too clever by half and, I had to admit, with some justification. Many thought she was an affected poseur, playing some sort of role, but I could not agree with that. I thought she was absolutely sincere in whatever she said. That she was utterly unpredictable was agreed by all and now, it seemed, she was a shoplifter! I felt quite sure that she had no recollection of what she had been doing, and could not be held accountable for her actions. She was murmuring "Eleven stars . . . .eleven spheres . . . .eleven teaspoons." Suddenly she opened her eyes and snapped, "Two policemen were here this morning. Two great big clomping fellows with their boots and their notebooks, going through my drawers, as though I were a common criminal. And Sister Julienne took it all away. All my pretty things. My colouring things, my ribbons, eleven teaspoons. I had been collecting them — eleven — just think, and I needed them, every one."

Grief seemed to overcome her. She didn't cry, but she seemed frozen with terror, and murmured: "What is going to happen to me? What will they do to me? Why do elderly, respectable women do this sort of thing? Are we tempted, or is it a sickness? I don't understand . . . .I can't know myself . . . ."

Her voice faltered, and the pencil dropped from her trembling fingers. She knew all right. Oh yes, she knew.

Fossie-Jaw

Nonnatus House was subdued and saddened pending the prosecution of Sister Monica Joan for shoplifting. Even we young girls, always ready to giggle and joke about almost everything, felt restrained. We somehow felt it unseemly to laugh when the Sisters were suffering collectively. Sister Monica Joan spent more of her time than formerly in her room. She did not go out of the house at all, seldom came down to the dining room, and really left her room only for mass and the five monastic offices each day. I saw her sometimes entering or leaving the chapel, and she hardly spoke to her Sisters. They treated her with much gentleness and kindness, but she returned their smiles and kindly glances with a toss of her proud head as she went to her pew to kneel in prayer. We are all complex creatures, but prayer and downright rudeness seemed incompatible.

The only people she consistently spoke to were Mrs B and myself. Dear Mrs B, whose love of Sister Monica Joan was unconditional and unreserved, and who still didn't believe a word of it, was up and down stairs all day, pandering to her every wish. Sister Monica Joan at this time treated Mrs B more like a personal lady's maid than she had any right to, but Mrs B seemed perfectly happy with her new role, and nothing seemed to be too much trouble. She was heard muttering to herself in the kitchen one day: "China tea. I though' as 'ow tea was just tea. But no. She wants China tea. Now where am I goin' to get vat?" None of the grocers in Poplar seemed to stock China tea, so Mrs B went all the way up West to get it. When she proudly and happily presented a cup to Sister Monica Joan, Sister sniffed it and sipped it, then declared that she didn't like it. Anyone else would have been furious, but Mrs B took no offence and murmured, "Not 'a worry, my luvvy. You just 'ave a slice o' vis honey-cake I made this mornin', while I run along and make you a nice pot o' tea, jus' as 'ow you likes it."

Sister Monica Joan could out-Queen the Queen Mother when she chose. Her attitude was serenely gracious as she inclined her head. "So kind, so kind." Mrs B glowed with pleasure. Sister broke a piece of honey-cake with her long fingers and delicately raised it to her lips.

"Delicious, quite delicious. Another slice, if it's not too much trouble."

Mrs B, fairly bursting with happiness, ran downstairs for the umpteenth time that day.

Sister Monica Joan fascinated and bewitched me as she did most people. But she never treated me as a lady's maid. No doubt her instinct told her that it just would not work. We understood each other as equals and found endless pleasure in each other's company.

During the uncertain weeks of waiting we had many conversations in her pretty room just after lunch, or before Compline. We talked for hours. Her short-term memory was faulty. Often she did not know what day or month it was, but on the other hand her long-term memory was excellent. She could recall clearly and vividly facts, incidents and impressions from her Victorian childhood and her working life in the Edwardian era and the First World War. She was highly intelligent and articulate and could express herself vividly, often in beautiful language which seemed to come naturally to her. As I wanted to learn more about old Poplar I tried questioning her. But this did not work. She was not easy to pin down, and often took no notice of what I had said or asked. She had a habit of making statements unrelated to anything that had been said beforehand, like: "That rapacious old mongrel!" And then no more! The old mongrel had obviously come into her mind unbidden and then slunk away, his tail between his legs. The memory was forever lost.

Sometimes she really developed her thoughts and her words flowed easily. She would make a dramatic statement: "Women are the cohesive force in society."

She picked up a pencil and balanced it delicately between her two fingertips, those astonishing fingers that she could bend at the first digit. Would she continue? To say a word might break her thoughts.

"And 'woman' in the slums is capable of taking on almost superhuman responsibility, from a very young age, that would crush most of us. Today they live in luxury — look at all the giddy young girls around us —

they have no memory of how their mothers and grandmothers lived and died. They have no understanding of what it took to raise a family twenty or thirty years ago."

She glanced at the pencil and twisted it round with her thumbs. Privately I questioned the "luxury" in the tenements, but said nothing for fear of chasing away her memories. She continued, to my great enrichment, "There was no work, no food, no shoes for the children. If the rent was not paid the family would be evicted. Thrown onto the streets by the law of the land."

She paused, and a memory flashed through my mind of something that I had seen only a few weeks earlier, when I was cycling back from a night delivery.

It had been about three o'clock in the morning, and I saw a group of people, a man and woman and several children, coming towards me, keeping close to the wall. The woman was carrying a baby and a suitcase. The man was carrying a mattress on his head, and a rucksack and several bags. Each of the children, none of them over ten, was carrying a bag. They saw the headlights of my bike and turned their faces to the wall. The man said, his voice quite distinct in the quiet darkness: "Don' chew worry. It's only a nurse," and I cycled past, not realizing at the time that a dramatic and tragic event was taking place; an event that used to be referred to light-heartedly as a 'moonlight flit'. The family were anticipating eviction and fleeing unpaid debts. God only knows where they ended up.

Sister Monica Joan was staring at me, hard, and then she narrowed her eyes.

"You remind me of Queenie — turn your head."

I did so.

"Yes, you look just like her. I was so fond of Queenie. I delivered her three children and I was with her when she died. She was no more than your age, but she died in trying to avoid eviction."

"What happened?" I whispered.

"She went into the Bryant and May factory making matches. They were a lovely family, and I knew them well. No fights in that family. Her husband was no more than a boy when he was killed in a riverboat accident. What could Queenie do with three little children? The Parish would have taken them from her, but she wouldn't have it. She went into the match factory because they offered higher pay than anywhere else. Danger money, they called it, and wriggled out of any responsibility by saying the women accepted the danger when they accepted the pay. Wicked it was. Wicked. Death money it should have been called. Queenie worked there for three years and kept a roof over their heads and just enough to eat. We thought she would escape fossie-jaw. But it got her, yes, it got her, and she died a terrible death. I was with her at the end. She died in my arms."

Sister Monica Joan said no more. Could I risk a question?

"What is fossie-jaw?"

"There you go. What did I say? Young girls have no idea how women had to live and work. The matches

188

were made from raw phosphorus. The women inhaled the vapour, and the fumes got into the mucous membrane of the mouth and nose. The phosphorus penetrated the bones of the upper and lower jaw. The bones literally sloughed away. In the dark you could see the woman's jaw glowing with a bluish light. There was nothing that could be done for these women. They would die a slow and agonizing death. Don't ask me again what fossie-jaw is, you ignorant girl. It's what Queenie died of, trying to provide for her children, trying to avoid eviction."

She glanced at me, and clamped her teeth together.

"That's what we fought for. Girls like Queenie, hard working, loving, young and full of life who were driven to their deaths by the system. I was with her when she died. It was ghastly. The bones of her lower face crumbled away, and she suffered weeks of agony. There was nothing we could do. Her children went to the Workhouse. There was nothing else for them."

The rain fell quietly on the window, and she sat quite still. I could see the pulse beating sluggishly in her long neck carrying the life-giving blood to her brain. "Draw the curtains, please, dear." I did so, hoping she would continue, but she only murmured, "It seems like yesterday, no time at all." And there was no more.

The memories of people like Sister Monica Joan should be cherished above price. I sat on the edge of her bed, my legs drawn up underneath me, and tried to interpret from her sensitive intelligent features what was in her mind. I did not want Queenie to fade from her memory, so I asked about the children going to the Workhouse, but she became irritable and snappy.

"Questions. Always questions. You give me no peace, child. Can I not expect a little repose in my old age?"

She threw her head to one side with an affected sigh. At that moment the bell sounded for Compline.

"There now. See what you have done. You make me late for my religious duties."

She swept past me without a further glance and made her way to the chapel.

That evening I attended Compline. The lay staff at Nonnatus House were not bound to do so — we were not professed religious — but we could attend any Offices if we wished to do so. I particularly loved the words of Compline, the last Office of the day, and had been very affected by the story of Queenie, so I followed Sister Monica Joan into the chapel. Her behaviour was atrocious! She entered without so much as looking at anyone else, and did not take her usual pew, but went straight to the visitors' seats, took a chair and sat with her back to her Sisters and the altar. Sister Julienne quietly came up to her and gently, with smiles, tried to draw her into the group around the altar, but Sister Monica Joan rudely pushed her aside and even drew her chair further away so that she was looking directly at the wall, her insolent back conspicuously addressed to her Sisters. Compline proceeded in this fashion.

Sister Julienne was obviously saddened, and the love and pity in her eyes showed that she knew something strange and unapproachable was going on in the mind of the old lady, which she was trying to understand. Perhaps it was advancing senility, or perhaps one of those mental illnesses that make people turn away from, and become aggressive towards, the people who have been closest and most dear in former years. Quietly the Sisters left the chapel. The Greater Silence had begun. After that evening Sister Monica Joan always sat with her back to her Sisters, even at Mass.

The following afternoon I went to her room after lunch, hoping that she would not turn against me as she had turned against her Sisters. She had enriched my life so much by her friendship, and I knew it would be greatly impoverished if her friendship were suddenly withdrawn and replaced by cold hostility. She was sitting at her desk, alert and busy with her notebooks and pencil. She turned.

"Come in, my dear, come in. This will interest you. The hexagon meets the parallel," (she was drawing a diagram again) "and the rays combine here . . . .oh bother!" Her pencil broke. "Fetch me my pencil sharpener, will you, dear? The second drawer down in my bedside cabinet." She continued tracing the lines across the paper with her forefinger.

I went across the room to her bedside cabinet, happy that she was not excluding me from her affection. What made me pull open the third drawer down? It was not intentional, but it almost paralysed me, and for several seconds I thought I would choke. The open drawer revealed several gold bangles, two or three rings (one looked like a sapphire), a small diamond watch, a pearl necklace, a ruby pendant on a gold chain, a gold cigarette case, a couple of gold cigarette holders studded with stones, and several tiny gold or platinum charms. The drawer was only about two inches deep and no more than ten inches wide, but it must have contained a small fortune in jewellery.

Silence can attract immediate attention. She turned round and saw me transfixed, looking into the drawer. At first she did not say anything, and the silence developed an ominous quality, broken by her hissing, "You wicked girl, prying into my affairs. How dare you. Leave the room immediately. Do you hear? Withdraw, at once."

It was so shocking. I had to sit down on the edge of the bed. Our eyes met, mine full of grief and hers flashing with anger. Gradually the defiance crumbled away though, and her old, old face assumed a tired and pathetic quality. She whimpered, "All my pretty things. Don't take them away. Don't tell anyone. They will take them all. Then they'll take me away, like they took Aunt Anne. All my pretty things. No-one knows about them. Why shouldn't I have them? Don't tell anyone, will you, child?"

Her beautiful hooded eyes filled with tears, her lips trembled, and the toll of ninety years descended on her as she crumpled into a sobbing wreck.

It took only a second to cross the room and take her in my arms.

"Of course I won't tell anyone. No one will ever know. It's a secret, and we won't tell anyone, I promise."

Gradually her tears dried, and she blew her nose and gave me one of her saucy winks.

"Those great clod-hopping policemen. They'll never know, will they?"

She raised one eyebrow and chuckled conspiratorially. "I think I will take my tea now. Go, child, and tell Mrs B that I will have some of that delicious China tea."

"But you didn't like the China tea."

"Of course I like it. Don't be silly. You are getting muddled up, I fear!"

Laughing, I kissed her goodbye and made my way down to the kitchen to deliver the message to Mrs B.

It was not until later that same evening that the awfulness of the dilemma hit me. What on earth was I going to do?

Monopoly

A promise is a promise, but theft is a criminal offence, and my pledge to Sister Monica Joan that I would not tell anyone about the stolen jewellery weighed upon me so heavily that I could hardly keep my mind on my work. Purloining a few pairs of silk stockings and handkerchiefs was naughty, but stealing jewels, some of them very valuable, is a serious offence. Normally nothing disturbs my sleep — but this did. If I told Sister Julienne she would call the police again, and they would search Sister Monica Joan's room a second time, more thoroughly than before. Perhaps there would be other things hidden away, in a box maybe, or in the bottom drawer of the bedside cabinet. The gravity of the offence could be more than doubled. They might arrest her on the spot, old as she was. I blocked out such a thought. Sister Monica Joan must be protected at all costs. I would not tell anyone.

Antenatal clinic was particularly trying that week. There were too many women, it was too hot, and there were too many small children running around. I felt like screaming. We were clearing up afterwards. Cynthia was cleaning the urine testing equipment, I was scrubbing the work surfaces. She said: "What's up? You've not been yourself lately."

Relief swept over me. Her deep slow voice with a hint of laughter in the tone acted like a balm to my troubled spirits.

"How do you know? Is it all that obvious?"

"Of course it is. I can read you like a book. Now come on, out with it. What's up?"

Two of the Sisters were still in the clinic packing up the antenatal notes and filing them away. I whispered, "I'll tell you later."

After Compline, when the Sisters had gone to bed, Cynthia and I sat in her room with an extra helping of pudding left over from lunch.

Briefly I told her of the jewellery. She whistled.

"Phew! No wonder you have been quiet recently. What are you going to do?"

"I'm not going to tell anyone in authority. I'm only telling you because you guessed something was up."

"But you can't keep it to yourself. You've got to tell Sister Julienne."

"If I do she'll tell the police and they might arrest Sister Monica."

"You're not being rational. They won't arrest her. She's too old."

"How do you know? This is big stuff, I tell you. It's not just pinching a few crayoning books."

Cynthia was quiet for a while.

"Well, I don't think they will arrest her."

"There you are, you don't know. You only think, and you might be wrong. If they arrested her it would kill her."

There was a bang on the door.

"I say, you chaps, how about a game of Monopoly, what? No-one in labour. All the babies tucked up in bed. What say you, eh?"

"Come in, Chummy."

Camilla Fortescue-Cholmeley-Browne. Descended from generations of High Commissioners of India, educated at Roedean and polished by finishing school, Chummy represented the upper-crust in our small circle. She had a voice that sounded like something straight out of a comic film and she was, unfortunately, excessively tall, which affliction caused her to suffer much ragging. But she took it all with sweet good nature.

Chummy tried the handle.

"But the door's locked, old bean. What's going on? Something rummy's afoot, or I'm a brass monkey."

Cynthia laughed and opened the door.

"We've got some pudding in here. If you want some go and get a dish and while you're about it, tell Trixie."

When she had gone, Cynthia said to me, "I think we had better tell the girls. They are neither of them in authority so the police won't be called, and they might help. Chummy's father was a District Commissioner or something in India and Trixie's cousin is a solicitor, so both of them might know something about the law."

I agreed. It was a relief to be sharing the responsibility after all my silent anguish.

Both girls came in with a dish and a spoon, Chummy bearing the Monopoly board. We shared out the pudding. Cynthia sat on the only chair and three of us sat on the bed. The Monopoly board was laid out on the bed, supported by books to stop it sagging. I had been against playing Monopoly, but Cynthia said it would help relieve the tension, and she was right. It did.

We sorted out our money and tucked it in piles under our knees and Cynthia told them the story.

Trixie burst out laughing.

"What a scream! So the old girl's been pinching things left, right and centre. Tucking them under her scapular and no one would ever suspect. The cunning old vixen." She roared with laughter.

"You cat. Don't you call Sister Monica Joan names or I'll . . . .'

Cynthia intervened. "I won't have you two squabbling in my room. If you want to start a row you can go somewhere else."

"Sorry," I muttered reluctantly.

"I'll be good," added Trixie, "I won't even call her a female fox. But you must admit it's a scream. I can just see the headlines: 'The Secret Life of a Naughty Nun'."

Trixie threw the dice. "Two sixes. I start."

"That's just the sort of thing I'm not going to allow to happen," I snarled. "The police are not going to be told."

I moved my piece. "Liverpool Street. I'll buy that." I laid down my money with determination and took the card.

Chummy threw her dice. "This is a Council of War, and I go along with you, old horse. The important thing is to protect Sister Monica Joan from the machinations of the Constabulary, what? Mum's the word, I say. What ho!, not a syllable. Lips sealed."

Cynthia shook the cup slowly and thoughtfully, and the dice rattled ominously. "Well, someone's going to find out, even if we don't say anything. The police are going to be in her room again; they are not fools, you know."

"I've thought of that," I said, "and thought perhaps we could take the jewels secretly out of her room and hide them."

"Don't be a fool," Trixie was always too sharp for my liking, "then you'd be an accessory."

"What's that? I thought accessories were things like gloves and handbags and scarves."

"Accessories are the law. You can be an accessory before the fact, or an accessory after the fact. It doesn't matter if it's before or after; either way you'd be in for it." Trixie pushed the dice to her neighbour as she spoke.

Chummy shook the dice slowly and thoughtfully.

"I'd say she's got to the root of the matter. If the jewels were in your possession, the Robert Peelers would say you egged the old lady on. Bally awkward situation, and you'd be as sore as a gum-boil. No. We've got to prove that she didn't know what she was doing."

Chummy moved her piece, but decided not to buy.

Trixie jumped on it in a flash.

"I'll buy that. Come off it. That old girl's as sharp as a razor. She's got it all weighed up. No one suspects a nun, so she's in the clear, she thinks."

"I'm not so sure." Cynthia moved her piece. "Islington. I'll buy that. I like the blue properties. I think her mind is definitely disturbed."

"Don't give me that one," Trixie snapped. "She's as crafty as they come. Look how she manipulates everyone to get her own way. She knows exactly what she's doing. Another visit from the police would do her good. I'll put a house on each of my properties please, Bank."

Chummy was Bank and sorted out the high finance.

"Well, I can't agree, old sport. I think another visit from the police would give her a stroke."

"Of course it would." I threw the dice so hard they overshot the board and landed on the floor. "The police will never know. I'll see to that."

Cynthia, who as the room-owner, had the right to sit on the only chair, retrieved the dice. "I have a feeling it's not as easy as that. You have to tell 'the whole truth and nothing but the truth'."

"That's only in court," I said, "and we're not in court . . . .yet. Park Lane — I'll buy that."

"You're not thinking straight, idiot, I've already got Mayfair. It won't do you any good. Anyway, if you're in court giving evidence, you've got to speak the whole truth."

I decided not to buy Park Lane and Trixie gleefully snapped it up.

"If you don't it's called 'obstructing the course of justice'. I've heard my cousin talk about that."

It was Chummy's throw.

"I've heard of that one, too. It's the same sort of thing as 'withholding evidence' and it's a serious offence. I say, this pudding's no end good. Is there any more, Madam Hostess?"

"No, but I've got some biscuits here in my wardrobe. Just let me move the chair and we'll get them. How about a coffee?"

Trixie shook her head. "I've got a much better idea. My brother bought a couple of bottles of sherry for Christmas; he thought I needed cheering up, stuck in a dreary hole like a convent. We'll have them. It will help us in the discussion. We've got to come to a sensible decision about this. Get your tooth-mugs, girls."

Trixie slid off the bed and Chummy remembered some chocolates and chrystalized ginger left over from a previous occasion. I ran down the passage to get my tooth-mug and some figs and dates to which I was partial.

We settled down again around the Monopoly board which had wobbled with all the movement on and off the bed. After some little argument about whose piece was where, and which houses were on whose properties, we poured the sherry, took handfuls of food, and continued the game.

Trixie was clearly winning. She had houses on Park Lane and Mayfair, and the dice fell in her favour. Everyone seemed to stop there and had to pay rent.

Groans all round. The sherry slid down nicely, assisted by all the sweet foods. Chummy made a general point that had been in all of our minds.

"Where do you think the old lady got all those sparklers from? I say, this sherry's going down nicely. I always say sherry tastes so much better out of a tooth-mug than one of those bally little glasses, what? Perhaps the dregs of toothpaste in the bottom of the mug give it that special flavour. I did a Cordon Bleu course, you know, but they never mentioned that. If I ever go back there, I'll recommend it. Hell's bells! Go back five places — that puts me in jail!"

Trixie giggled.

"We'll get Sister Monica Joan in jail before the night's out. Sorry! Sorry! Don't take on so. Just stirring it up. Have another sherry!"

Cynthia filled my mug. "Yes, where did she get it from? There's no-where in Poplar that sells expensive jewellery."

Trixie had the answer — inevitably.

"I reckon she's been going to Hatton Garden. It's not far from here. Only a short bus ride. A pious looking old nun going around the shops and warehouses. Easy. No one would think to suspect her, the wicked old thing."

"She's not wicked," I shouted. "Don't you dare. She's . . . ."

"Now, now, you two. My turn and I collect £200 for passing Go. Come on, Bank. Wake up. I want my money."

Chummy jerked herself upright. "I'm beginning to think the police have got to be told because of this business of withholding the course."

"The what?"

"Holding the course."

"Course of what?"

"The course of evidence, of course."

"You're not making sense."

"Yes I am. You're not listening."

Cynthia was carefully tucking her £200 down her bra. "I think you mean the course of justice."

"That's what I said."

"No you didn't. You said the course of evidence."

"Well, same thing, and it's an offence."

"What is?"

"Holding the evidence, old bean. And it's not allowed."

"You mean withholding the evidence."

"That's what I said."

"No you didn't. You said holding it."

"Holding what?"

"Look here, this is going round in circles. Anyway it's my turn." Trixie picked up a card from the pack. "So you reckon we've got to get the police in again?"

"Yes, because of obstructing, old thing."

"No you don't. You want to get the police again because you fancy that policeman."

"I don't. Don't you dare." Chummy gulped down her sherry and went bright red.

"Yes you do. You're sweet on him. I've seen you go all coy and giggly when he comes to the house. So you want him to come again."

"You're a regular shower. You've no right to come out with whoppers like that, you gum-boil, you."

Poor Chummy looked on the verge of tears, so Cynthia came to her rescue.

"You're just stirring it up again, Trixie. You haven't looked at your card yet. Turn it over."

Trixie did so, and gave a howl of anguish.

"I'm ruined. I'm bankrupt. This isn't fair. Make repairs on all your houses, I shall have to sell. Give me another drink. I've got to think about this one."

She took another mug of sherry and another chocolate.

"I'll take Mayfair and Park Lane off you at half price," I said magnanimously.

"No you won't. I'm not selling at half price."

"You've no option."

"That's what it is — obtion." Chummy was obviously thinking deeply, as she gazed into her mug. "Obtion — the course of justice. And it's an obtion, I mean an offence."

"There's no such thing as an obtion."

"Yes there is, and it's an offence to obtion the justice of the course. I know it is. My father told me. Someone he knew obtioned the justice course, and I can't remember what happened, but it happened."

"Well thanks for nothing. A lot of help I'm sure. Look, I'm going to auction these. Does anyone want these priceless properties? I'll take eighty per cent. You won't get a better chance. All right then, seventy per cent, I'm not going to sink to half price, I'll have to do something else."

At that moment Chummy's legs got the cramp. They were too long to be kept in a confined space, and with a groan she stretched out, knocking the board for six.

"Well, that's that," said Trixie with satisfaction. "I'm the clear winner."

"No you're not. You haven't made repairs to your houses."

"I don't have to."

"Yes you do."

"Now don't you two start that again. Help me to clear up the board and the pieces. Chummy doesn't look as if she's going to be much help. There's a drop left in the bottom of this second bottle. Do you want it between you? I've had enough."

We did. Cynthia was shaking Chummy.

"Look, this is my bed. You go to your own bed."

Suddenly Trixie grabbed Cynthia's arm.

"Oh my God! I've just had a dreadful thought."

"What?" we said in chorus.

"Chummy's on first call tonight."

"Never! Oh no! What's to be done?"

The three of us gazed at Chummy stretched full length, smiling sweetly and deeply asleep on Cynthia's bed. We looked at each other, and looked again at the sleeping form. Cynthia spoke.

"I'll take first call tonight. There's nothing else for it. Trixie was out last night, so I'll take it if a call comes in. I've had less than you two anyway. We might as well leave Chummy here, and I'll sleep in her room. We must throw away these bottles and open the windows to let some fresh air blow in, just in case one of the Sisters comes up here tomorrow. Go and open the windows on the landing, at both ends, and the bathroom. We've got to get a good draught blowing through to clear the air."

Thankful for Cynthia's common sense I went to open the windows. The cold air hit me like a pain, and my head began to reel. The window flew out of my grasp and struck the brickwork. Cynthia came up and secured the window.

"I'm going to wash up these mugs and wash out the bottles too, to get rid of the smell. You had better go to bed. You'll be on duty at 8a.m. Don't listen for the telephone. I'll take any calls."

She went to Chummy's room and I to mine. For several nights I had lain awake, but that night I slept like a baby.

Aunt Anne

As I entered Sister Monica Joan's room she glared at me.

"I'll murder that fellow one of these days. You see if I don't. The dirty old goat!"

Strong language for a reverend Sister. It was intriguing, but I knew from experience that straight questions seldom got straight answers. However, if I entered Sister Monica Joan's world and, as far as possible, relived it with her, she would recall whole scenes of life and people of long ago. So I said, "He's always up to something. What is it this time?"

"You've seen him at it?" I nodded, and waited.

"He's always there. Lah-di-dahing around the factory gates in all his finery — silk shirt, bow tie and gold watch chain. I'll give him a silk shirt, I'll strangle him with his silk shirt, the old rascal."

This was going to be rich. She needed no prompting to continue.

"Those poor girls in the shirt-making factories. They are the lowest paid of all the workers, and they work the longest hours, too. There's a grass bank outside the factory gate — you know the one I mean?" I nodded.

"Well, he stands there in all his finery, twirling his moustache and as the girls come out of the gate he throws coins, mostly copper, some silver, up the bank towards the wall, shouting 'scramble girls, scramble for it'. And up the grass the girls go, shouting and pushing and laughing. There might be a fight to get at a silver sixpence. The dirty old man."

I was beginning to wonder why such a philanthropic act should provoke such vitriol. Sister Monica continued even more angrily.

"It's degrading them. Those girls wear no knickers, you know. How can they afford such a luxury? That's what he's after, the debauched old satyr. And when they are menstruating they have no protection. The blood just runs down their legs. The smell is supposed to be enticing. I don't know, perhaps it is. But it's degrading for those poor girls who scramble for a penny which will buy them a bun or a drop of milk. I can't bear to see women used and exploited in that way."

I understood what she was on about. "But women have always been exploited for their sexuality."

"Yes, I suppose so, and always will be, I fear. And some of them no doubt want to be. I daresay half the girls scrambling up the bank and sliding down with their skirts around their necks know what they are doing. But it pains me to see them degraded."

Angrily, she continued knitting. She did not continue with her thoughts, but asked me to go and see Mrs B about tea, which I did. When I returned to the room Sister Monica Joan was not there.

The jewels had been uppermost in my mind for days, so quietly I looked into the bedside cabinet. The drawer was empty.

As she had made no reference to my earlier discovery, I had assumed that she had forgotten all about it. Perhaps I had fondly imagined that she had forgotten about the jewels. But now I knew she had not forgotten anything and had taken the precaution of hiding them somewhere else. But where? Had she tucked them into her mattress? She was quite capable of cutting a small hole, stuffing them in and sewing it up neatly. No one would ever know.

Trixie's definition of a crafty old vixen came to mind. Perhaps she was. Perhaps she was piling up wealth for some hidden purpose of her own. But at the age of ninety? It was hardly likely.

She swept back into the room in high spirits. No remorse, no shame that she had been caught stealing, or fears of future discoveries. Perhaps she had hidden them in the lavatory cistern or behind the bath!

Her opening comment was, as usual, quite baffling.

"Twenty-seven dinner services, each with ninety-six pieces. I ask you, my dear, what sensible family can possibly need twenty-seven dinner services?"

Such a question requires a little thought before it can be answered.

Whilst I hesitated, she continued, "And fourteen sets of plates. Would you believe it, every single piece, every fish fork or sugar tong, had to be counted and checked before it could be put away. Have you ever heard such nonsense? And they thought I would be content to spend my life counting fish forks."

I was beginning to understand. One had to get used to following sideways the many strands of Sister Monica Joan's thoughts. Perhaps the dinner services and the fish forks related to her family and her young girlhood in the 1870s and 80s. Her next statement confirmed this.

"My poor mother was a slave to such possessions. For all her finery and 'Your Ladyship' she was more of a servant than her own servants. I doubt if she knew a day of real freedom in her whole life. Poor woman. I loved her, and pitied her, but we never understood each other."

Some things never change, I thought, remembering the mutual incomprehension which was about the only thing that my mother and I shared.

"My father ruled her life. Every move. Do you know, my dear, he had all her hair cut off and all her teeth pulled out when she was less than 35?"

I gasped: "How? Why?"

"She was never strong, always ailing. I don't know what was wrong with her, except perhaps her corsets were too tight." Corsets. The accepted torture instrument of women!

"I remember it quite well. I was only a little girl but I remember my mother lying in bed, with doctors present. One of them told my father that all her strength was going to her hair and her teeth and that they would have to go. She was never consulted in the matter, she told me many years later. Her head was shaved and all her teeth extracted. I was in the nursery and heard her screaming. It was barbaric my dear, and ignorant. I was frightened when I saw her later; her face swollen; blood all over her pillow and sheets; a bald head. She was crying, poor woman. I was about twelve years old and something happened to me in that moment. Something revolted inside me and I knew that women suffered through man's ignorance. As I stood by her bed, I changed from a carefree little girl into a thinking woman. I vowed I would not follow the pattern of my mother, my aunts and their friends. I would not become a wife whose husband could order her teeth to be pulled out, or who could be locked up like poor Aunt Anne. I would not spend my life counting fish forks. I would not be dominated by any man."

Sister Monica Joan's face assumed an expression of haughty independence and defiance. The young can be very lovely, but the faces of the old can be truly beautiful. Every line and fold, every contour and wrinkle of Sister Monica Joan's fine white skin revealed her character, strength, courage, humanity and irrepressible humour. I said, "Several times you have mentioned Aunt Anne who was locked up. Why was this?"

"Oh my dear, it was iniquitous. Aunt Anne, my mother's sister, was put into a lunatic asylum because her husband got fed up with her!"

"What! You are joking," I retorted

"Don't you accuse me of joking, you saucy girl. If you are going to be rude to me you can leave the room."

She turned her head and arched her eyebrows, slightly dilating her nostrils, the epitome of offended dignity, but I had a feeling it was put on just for effect.

"Oh, come off it, Sister. You know that was just an expression of shocked astonishment. What happened to Aunt Anne? That's what is important."

She turned to me and giggled like a child caught doing something naughty. But her expression quickly changed.

"Aunt Anne, dear Aunt Anne. She was my favourite aunt. Always pretty, always sweet and gentle with a soft laugh. When she came to the house she always came up to the nursery to spend time with us children, to tell stories and play games with us. We all loved her. Then suddenly she came no more. No more."

Sister Monica Joan sat as still as a statue, gazing out of the window. The sun was shining and she murmured, "It's too bright, it hurts my eyes. Draw the curtain across, will you child?"

I did so and when I returned she had her handkerchief to her eyes. "We never saw her again. When we asked our mother she just said, 'Hush dears, we don't talk about Aunt Anne.' We kept thinking she would come back with her games and her stories; but she never came."

She sighed deeply and balanced her chin on her long fingers, lost in thought, "Poor woman, poor dear woman. She was defenceless."

"Did you ever find out what had happened?" I enquired.

"Yes, years later I found out. Her husband tired of her and wanted another woman. So he quite simply spread the story around that she was weak in the head and going mad. Perhaps he ill-treated her; perhaps his repeated insinuations really did unbalance her mind, so that she began to doubt her own sanity. We don't know, but it is not difficult to drive someone mad. Eventually her husband got two doctors to certify that she was incurably insane. It would not have been difficult in those days. Perhaps the two doctors were cronies of his. Perhaps they were paid to certify. I do not suppose she was ever examined properly by an independent and impartial psychiatrist, as she would be today. It would have been very easy for him to choose his own doctors and the certificate was irreversible. Aunt Anne was taken away, taken from her children, who from then on were motherless. She was locked up in an asylum where she remained for the rest of her life. She died in 1907."

"That is one of the most shocking stories I have ever heard," I said.

"It was not uncommon. It was a very clever way for a rich man to get rid of an unwanted wife. He had to pay for the asylum care, of course, for the rest of her days, but that would not trouble a rich man. After a period of years, I don't know how many, he could get a divorce, with no scandal. Easy!"

"And did the woman have no-one to speak for her?"

"Oh yes, her father or a brother could, and probably would. It was not always plain sailing for an unscrupulous husband. But my grandfather, Anne's father, was dead, and there were no brothers, only four daughters in the family. So poor Anne had no-one to protect her."

"Could not her mother or sisters speak for her?"

"Women had no voice in any matter whatsoever. It had been the same for centuries. That is what we fought for." Her eyes flashed and she banged the desk. "Independence for Women. Freedom from male dominance."

"Were you a Suffragette?" I asked.

"Bah! Suffragettes. I've no time for Suffragettes. They made the biggest mistake in history. They went for equality. They should have gone for power!"

With a dramatic gesture she swept her arm across the desk scattering pencils, papers and notebooks to the floor.

"But I broke the mould in my family when I announced that I was going to be a nurse. Oh, you should have heard the rumpus. It would have been fun if it had not been so deadly serious. My father locked me in my room and threatened to keep me there indefinitely. Then he tried to insinuate that I was mad and should be confined to an asylum like poor Aunt Anne. But times were changing. Women were beginning to break the chains of their bondage. Florence Nightingale led the way and many others followed her. I wrote to Miss Nightingale from my prison in my father's house. She was quite an old lady then, but she was very powerful. She spoke to Queen Victoria on my behalf. I don't know what they said, but the result was that I was released from captivity. My poor docile mother never really recovered from the shock of having a rebel daughter. Nonetheless I was thirty-two before I could break away from my father's domination and start nursing. That was when my life began."

The Chapel bell rang for Vespers. Sister Monica Joan took up her black veil and adjusted it over her white coif. She turned to me with a naughty wink.

"If my father had seen me as a nun, he would have had a stroke. But mercifully he was spared, because he died the same year that the old Queen died. Hand me my prayer book, child."

It was on the floor, whence she had swept it from her desk. I retrieved everything that was scattered around, placed them on the desk and handed her the prayer book.

"Now for it," she said, her head held high, her eyebrows arched in a slightly supercilious curve, and her white skin, fragile and soft, draped in folds over her high cheekbones. A mischievous grin crinkled the corners of her mouth and eyes. "Now for it," she said again as she swept out.

There was nothing cringing and pathetic about Sister Monica Joan. She was going to battle it out to the end. If she couldn't face her Sisters in Chapel, she would sit with her back to them, and if they didn't like it they could lump it.

After the evening visits we were taking supper in the kitchen. This was a meal prepared by ourselves, because we all came in at different times. We were looking the worse for wear, particularly Chummy who couldn't hold her drink but did not want to admit it, and had been protesting all day that she thought she had a touch of 'flu. Chummy was, in addition, torn by a feeling of guilt because she had been on first call that night and it had been Cynthia who had gone out at the bleakest hour before dawn, 3a.m. We sat down around the kitchen table, eating our peanut butter sandwiches.

"They've gone," I whispered, in case any of the sisters were in the hallway.

"What's gone?"

"The jewels, they've gone. They are not in the drawer."

Trixie eyed me dubiously.

"Are you sure they were there in the first place? After all, we've only got your word for it. Perhaps you dreamed the whole thing. Sister Evangelina calls you Dolly-daydream, and not without reason."

"I did not dream it. I tell you, I saw them and now they've gone."

"Well she must have hidden them somewhere else, the cunning old . . .". Cynthia stopped her. "Don't you two start on that again. I'm too tired to put up with you two squabbling like a couple of children. Pack it up."

Chummy groaned and spoke in a weary voice. "I second that motion, Chairman. My poor bally head feels like a suet pudding that's gone cold and been warmed up again for the servants. Did I hear you say that the jewels have gone?"

"Yes."

"Well strike me pink."

Trixie was quick off the mark. "She's hidden them. It's as clear as daylight. She knows she's been rumbled, so she's hidden them again. You can't tell me she doesn't know what she's doing. Of course she does." Trixie cut another slice of bread and dug her knife in the jar.

Cynthia was less emphatic. "Well, this does throw rather a different light on things. I still don't think she knows what she's doing."

"Oh, go on with you. She pulls the wool over everyone's eyes. But she doesn't fool me for a moment," said cynical Trixie.

Chummy was licking the peanut butter off the knife. "Premeditated. That's what the constabulary will be after. Were her actions premeditated or were they not? If we're going to protect Sister Monica Joan, Counsel for the Defence, that's what we've got to prove. But at the moment, my poor bally head aches so much I can't think straight. I'm going to bed. Who's on first call?"

"You are."

"Groan, groan and thrice groan. That settles it. I must get in a bit of the old sweet slumber before that accursed bell pitches me out on to the floor. Nighty-night all. Sweet dreams."

Cynthia stood up. "And I'm going to bed too. Don't you two start quarrelling as soon as you're alone."

Trixie looked at me when they had gone.

"I reckon there's not much more to say. Chummy hit the nail on the head. Was it, or was it not premeditated? Come on, let's do the washing up."

Recreation Hour

Recreation in a convent is a time when nuns can let their hair down, metaphorically speaking of course. Usually the 'recreation hour' lasts from 2p.m. to 3p.m. With the morning work completed, lunch taken and no religious duties to perform until Vespers at 4.30p.m., the nuns are free. But 'free' only within the discipline of the Order. At Nonnatus House, for the 'recreation hour', the nuns withdrew collectively to their sitting-room, where they would engage in needlework and polite conversation.

How these reverend ladies found time for it, to this day, defeats me. Each of the nuns seemed capable of packing about forty-eight hours of work into every twenty-four hours and each of them did it with serenity and grace, with not a trace of hurry or rush. Sister Julienne, for example, who was Sister-in-Charge, was not only the senior nurse and midwife with overall responsibility for the practice, but she was in charge of the smooth running of the house. She was also accountable for maintaining the monastic tradition of religious observance, instructing the novices, teaching the student midwives, acting as hostess to numerous house guests, handling convent finances and keeping the accounts. She took her fair share of district visits, including night calls, as well as finding time to engage in needlework and polite conversation during her brief hours of 'recreation', when most people would want to lie horizontal with their feet up.

It was their practice, as I have said, for the nuns to retire to their sitting-room after lunch. But on some occasions Sister Julienne would say at lunchtime, "I think we will take Recreation in the nurses' sitting-room today," whereupon the Sisters would look with a particular benevolence upon we girls, who were not really known for our piety, as though they were granting us some very special favour. The nuns would then go to their cells (nuns sleep in cells, not bedrooms) to collect their work, and we would rush to our sitting-room to clear away dirty plates, mugs, ash-trays, magazines, glasses, empty chocolate boxes, biscuit tins, hair brushes, medical books (yes, occasionally, we put in a bit of study) and all the paraphernalia essential to the life of the average young girl.

The Sisters entered and we smiled sweetly, as though we hadn't been frantically clearing things away for the past five minutes. Sister Evangelina, not famous for tact, glared around her, growling, "Well, Nurse Browne, I believe your mother is coming to visit you at the weekend. You had better tidy the place up before she comes."

"Oh, but we have just had a thumping good tidy up for you, Sister." Chummy was not offended, simply puzzled.

Trixie gave a shrill laugh and was about to speak but Cynthia, the peacemaker, retorted, "We'll get out the Hoover, the polish and the dusters before the weekend, Sister."

Sister Evangelina snorted a few words of disapproval and opened her workbox. Everyone did the same except Trixie and me. Neither of us owned a workbox, and did not sew or knit for recreation. Sister Julienne was concerned.

"Oh, my dears, perhaps you could each make a little tea cosy for the Christmas Fayre. Tea cosies always go down well. People buy them for Christmas presents."

Material, stuffing, scissors, needles and cotton were provided and conversation centred on the desirability of a large number of tea cosies to boost the Convent's finances for the coming year. As well as everything else, the Sisters not only organised and ran a sale each year but made a large number of the items to be sold. For many decades the finance for supporting the midwifery practice had, to some extent, depended on the monies collected at the Christmas Fayre.

The Sisters were making many small items considered to be useful and necessary in those days, such as handkerchief sachets, glove folders, pin cushions, cushion covers, tray cloths, table cloths, pillow cases and virtually anything else onto which a bird or a daisy-chain could be embroidered. Conversation centred on the saleability of each item for the

Christmas Fayre. The need for a large number of chair-back covers puzzled me and, even more, the name by which they were called — 'antimacassars' — until I learned that they were intended to protect the back of a chair from the grease on men's hair. Many men plastered their hair with Brylcream in those days and the oil used in Victorian times was Macassar.

I looked around me with pleasure. It was all very genteel and sweet; it could have been a scene from any period in history when ladies had nothing much else to do. Sister Julienne was making rag dolls with great speed and efficiency, creating tiny waistcoats and shoes, fixing button eyes and snipping wool hair. Sister Bernadette was an expert in golliwogs. Children are not allowed to have such toys today, nor even to use the word, but in those days they were all the fashion. Sister Evangelina was hemming handkerchiefs, and Novice Ruth — what on earth was she doing? Novice Ruth had a wooden object rather like a large cotton reel. Four nails, without heads, had been hammered into the top. The Novice was plying heavy linen thread round and round the nails with a small blunt instrument and pulling the thread over the nails at each turn. Through the centre of the wooden reel a woven band emerged. It was already about a yard or two long but still Novice Ruth continued plying the thread and weaving.

What on earth was it? I watched fascinated. She must have read my mind because she laughed and said, "You wonder what I am doing. This will be my girdle. I am approaching the time of my first profession, when I shall take my first vows. A Sister wears a woven girdle three times around her waist and, at the end, we tie three knots. This is to be a constant reminder of our three vows of poverty, chastity and obedience."

She had such a beautiful face and such a radiant smile. Her vocation filled her with joy.

Conversation continued about the Christmas Fayre and who should attend the stalls. Mrs B, as usual, was in charge of the cake stall, and Fred the boilerman always managed a very good stall in second-hand tools, which attracted men to the Fayre. It was Fred's proud boast that he could sell anything. Give him a bag of bent and rusty nails and he would sell them for you.

The doorbell rang.

"Now who can that be?" said Sister. "We're not expecting anyone and no-one is likely to go into labour. Would you answer it, please Nurse Browne."

Chummy laid down her embroidery at which she was expert and left the room. We continued talking about the Christmas Fayre, speculating if the band from the SPY Club (South Poplar Youth) could be asked to provide some entertainment. Should they be paid and, if so, what? "How about tea and cakes?" someone ventured. "Wouldn't that be sufficient payment?"

"What on earth has happened to Nurse Browne?" Sister Evangelina grunted. "She's been gone at least five minutes. It doesn't take that long to answer the door-bell."

At that moment Chummy re-entered the room. She was bright red and twitching slightly. She took a step forward and kicked a waste-paper basket, which shot into the air spilling its contents as it flew. It hit Sister

Evangelina on the side of the head, knocking her veil and wimple sideways. The shock caused her to prick her finger and blood spurted all over the handkerchief she was hemming.

"You fool, clumsy fool," she shouted. "Look what you have made me do." She sucked her finger and waved the ruined handkerchief at Chummy.

Sister Julienne took charge.

"Never mind Sister, use the handkerchief to bind the finger or we shall have blood all over the other work. Better to spoil one item than half a dozen."

"Now, Nurse Browne, what on earth is the matter?"

Chummy opened her mouth and her lips moved but no sound was emitted.

She tried again with no success. The Sisters were looking seriously concerned.

"My poor child, do sit down and try to tell us."

Chummy sat down and again tried to speak. Her vocal chords finally responded and the words came out in a rush.

"Please Sister, the policeman is at the door and he wants to see you."

Trixie gave a scream of laughter.

"Didn't I tell you! There, look, Chummy's sweet on the policeman!"

Cynthia kicked her hard.

Sister Julienne looked troubled.

"Oh dear, oh bother. I'll go at once."

We all looked at one another. Sister Julienne would only use such an extreme expression as "oh bother" in an extreme situation.

The knowledge that the policeman was at the door again gave me a nasty jolt. I had managed to lay aside the awful dilemma of the jewels found in Sister Monica Joan's room. I looked anxiously at Cynthia, who was embroidering a cushion cover and who refused to look up. All the Sisters were silently bent over their work. Chummy was seated and took up her sewing again but her hands shook so much that she could not control the needle. Only Trixie spoke.

"Well, now for it. They've come to take her away. There'll be a right old rumpus now."

Sister Evangelina turned on her. "Hold your tongue you thoughtless, loud-mouthed girl. Just keep quiet for once."

"Sorry, I'm sure." Trixie didn't look at all sorry.

I managed to catch Cynthia's eye and we exchanged a look of shocked alarm. Novice Ruth stifled a tear and worked furiously at the girdle she was making. Sister Bernadette was stuffing a golliwog and poking the stuffing down hard into the legs. The clock ticked and no-one spoke except for the occasional "pass the scissors please", or "have you got the light blue over there?"

The soft footsteps of Sister Julienne were heard and we all looked up expectantly, but they passed the door and went upstairs. Glances of real anguish were exchanged between the Sisters. All the muscles around my chest and stomach seemed to tighten at once and I felt hot all over.

"Could we open a window, do you think?" I enquired.

"I was about to suggest the same thing," said Sister Bernadette, and Cynthia, who was nearest to the window, stood up and opened it. The clock ticked on and we continued sewing. No one spoke.

Again footsteps were heard — descending the stairs this time. We all looked up, each with the same thought in our heart. What were they going to do with her?

The door burst open and Sister Julienne stood there, her features alight with joy.

"They are dropping all charges and taking no further action! Oh, the relief. I can't tell you the relief. I have just been up to see Sister Monica Joan to convey the news, although I am not sure that she understood what I was saying because she just looked at me in complete silence, nor did she show any expression at all."

"Praise the Lord," said Sister Evangelina, sniffing hard. She blew her nose loudly into the blood stained handkerchief, which had bound her injured hand, and wiped the corner of her eye. "Let us just praise the Lord for his mercy."

We were all overjoyed at the news but Sister Evangelina displayed more emotion and relief from pent-up sorrow than anyone else in the room. Her reaction brought home to me the genuine goodness and charity of the woman who had suffered so much from Sister Monica Joan's verbal cruelties. The apparent dislike between the two women was not of her making, and a less loving soul might have been indifferent, if not secretly glad, to see her Sister's downfall.

Sister Julienne sat down and continued, "This calls for a celebration so I have asked Mrs B to bring up an early tea and we will have jam with our scones today."

Mrs B came bouncing in with a large tray. "There, din' I tell yer? As innocen' as a newborn babe, she is. An' them police, they wants their bleedin' 'eads (beggin' yer pardon, Sisters) bangin' together, vey do. An' I'd like to ge' my 'ands on vat lyin' coster I would."

Sister Julienne burst out laughing. "You'll do no such thing. We don't want you had up for assault. We don't want any more trouble. Perhaps you would pour the tea, Novice Ruth, and pass the scones."

Mrs B withdrew. The tea and scones were passed round, not forgetting the jam. Everyone was in festive mood. Sister Julienne continued her story.

"Apparently the legal adviser to the police has suggested that due to the age of the suspect and the triviality of the items found in her room, the police might find themselves in a position of ridicule if they were to proceed with prosecution. The costers involved have been informed that a charge will not be brought by the Public Prosecutor but that they would be within their rights to bring a civil action. Due to the fact that a civil case costs so much money and that they would be unlikely to get compensation or damages or costs, the costers have decided not to proceed."

Sister Julienne gave a huge sigh of relief, caressing her cup as she raised it to her lips.

We four girls did not match the happiness of the Sisters. We knew something of which they were completely unaware. The knowledge of the jewels in Sister Monica Joan's possession was weighing heavily upon us. I was terrified that Trixie would blurt out something ill-considered which would give the game away. Cynthia and I exchanged glances and clearly the same thought was going through her mind also. She was sitting near to Trixie so she nudged her and, by lip-reading, I was grateful to see her mouth the words, "We'll talk later." A plan was forming in my mind to remove the jewels from Sister Monica Joan's room, take them to Hatton Garden and just leave them somewhere. My mind was racing — yes, that would be the answer — or perhaps leave them outside a police station a long way away, so no-one would suspect. But where should I find them? The beastly things had gone from Sister's bedside cabinet. Perhaps I could talk to her about it. Would she see reason? It would be good to talk to Cynthia later; she was always so sensible.

Sister Julienne said, "I knew our prayers would be answered. I do so believe in the power of prayer. No need for a lawyer, eh?" and she giggled happily. I squirmed — if only she knew — and was firmer in my resolve to take the wretched jewels and leave them somewhere.

Tea was being cleared away, the sewing brought out again, and we all settled down to work.

The door opened. Sister Monica Joan stood at the threshold. She did not enter the room immediately but just stood quite still, with one hand resting on the door. She was wearing her full outdoor habit, with the long black veil falling over her, perfectly adjusted, white coif; her long habit touched her toes. She looked magnificent. Everyone stopped talking, laid down their sewing and looked up at her. Yet she did not move, her hand remained motionless on the door handle, her hooded eyes were half closed, her eyebrows raised and a slightly supercilious smile played around the corners of her mouth. No one spoke. She had a magnetic quality about her, which forbade speech.

Then she moved for the first time; slowly and deliberately she turned her head, beautifully poised on its long neck, and scrutinised each person in the room with a level and unfaltering gaze. She looked each person straight in the eye for a few seconds without blinking then, turning her head very slightly, looked at the next person in the same manner. No one dared to speak or move, each person being magnetised by her impressive appearance and her compelling eyes. I have never seen a more riveting performance in my life.

It was Sister Monica Joan herself who first broke the silence. She tilted her head slightly to one side and raised an eyebrow. A naughty little grin lit her features.

"Greetings all. Did I ever tell you about the Thief of Baghdad? They boiled him in oil don't you know; or perhaps they drowned him in a butt of Malmsey wine. One or the other, I'm not sure which; but they did him in, I'm sure enough of that."

Sister Julienne rose, both arms outstretched.

"Oh my dear, say no more of that dreadful business. Not another word. It was all a misunderstanding and we have put it behind us. But come in and join our happy circle. I see you have your knitting bag with you."

Sister Monica Joan graciously consented to be led into the room. Sister Evangelina rose from her seat.

"Have this chair my dear, it is the most comfortable." Sister Monica Joan sat down.

The jewels! They flashed and glistened, stolen and sparkling, into my mind. They had got to be disposed of. Now was the perfect time. Sister Monica Joan was quietly knitting and everyone else was sewing and chatting. There might never again be such an opportunity.

I excused myself and left the room. At the bottom of the stairs I removed my shoes, so that no one would hear footsteps. It was the work of a moment to reach Sister Monica Joan's room. Quietly I entered and wedged a chair under the handle, in case anyone tried to enter. The search started. I scrutinised every inch of that room, every drawer, every shelf or cupboard; I felt all over the mattress, the pillows, the cushions; the tops and the hems of the curtains. I rummaged through her underwear and her habits — it wasn't seemly to pry into a nun's private things, but it had to be done. Nothing! Nowhere! My earlier thought about the lavatory cistern returned, and I raced along the corridor to the bathroom. Nothing to be found. I began to feel panic grip me; recreation hour surely must be drawing to a close. If one of the sisters found me on their private landing or in their bathroom, there would be a lot of explaining to do. Running downstairs and replacing my shoes took only a few seconds, and I was back in the sitting room just as the ladies were folding up their sewing and talking about the evening visits.

I muttered my excuses: "I'm sorry, Sister, I don't seem to have got on very well with the tea cosy. I don't think I'm much good at sewing."

Sister Julienne smiled. "That's perfectly all right, we can't all be good at the same things."

She turned to Sister Monica Joan. "Can I help you dear? That is a lovely baby's shawl you are knitting, can I help you put it away?"

She took the handle of the knitting bag. Sister Monica Joan grabbed the bag. "Don't touch it, leave it to me." She pulled the side nearest to her, but the handle of the other side was caught over Sister Julienne's wrist. The seam burst and a shower of rings, watches, gold chains and bracelets were flung across the floor.

The Trial

Total silence followed the moment when the jewels were scattered across the floor. The two halves of the torn knitting bag were held by Sister Julienne and Sister Monica Joan, who looked at each other in silence. Sister Monica Joan was the first to speak.

"Inanimate objects have a life of their own, independent of the creature, have you not noticed?" She glanced round at each of us in turn, "And whenever an atom gets excited it creates magnetic fields."

"Are you suggesting, Sister, that these inanimate objects were somehow magnetised into your knitting bag, independent of human activity?" Sister Julienne's voice was sarcastic.

"Most certainly. 'There are stranger things in heaven and earth than are dreamed of in your philosophy, Horatio'."

"Don't call me Horatio."

"Poof, hoity-toity," Sister Monica Joan was aloof and haughty. "The difficulty of comparative study is the incomprehension in lesser minds. But keep the trinkets. Use them well. In the latter day they will be interpreted

230

in a mystery play, a drama, an allegory. Use them well I say, they have their own life, their own force, their own destiny." And with that she swept out of the room.

Trixie's suppressed giggles exploded. She turned to me. "I believe you now. I thought your fevered imagination was working overtime, but now I believe you. The cunning old — Sorry Sister."

Sister Julienne looked at me.

"How long have you known about this?"

"About two weeks." I was feeling very uncomfortable.

"And you said nothing to me?"

I could only mutter a feeble "I'm sorry, Sister".

"Come to my office after supper and before Compline. We must gather up these things." She bent down and started picking them up. We all helped in silence.

It was difficult to concentrate on my evening round and babies that would not feed seemed perverse and irritating. Part of me was glad that the secret, which had oppressed me for days, was at last out in the open. On the other hand I was furious with myself that I had not managed to dispose of the jewels before Sister Julienne found them. The knowledge that she required me in her office later gave me an uneasy feeling, and my legs reluctantly turned the pedals as I cycled back to Nonnatus House.

As soon as I entered the clinical room I knew, from the atmosphere, that the police were in the house. Usually, after a day's work, a group of young girls made quite a lot of noise chattering and giggling as they packed their bags and cleared up; but not on that occasion. Novice Ruth looked up. Her eyes were red and her voice subdued. "You are to go to Sister Julienne's office at once," she said.

A sick feeling grabbed at my stomach. Cynthia said: "I'll do your bag. Leave it here and don't worry".

I knocked on the office door and entered. The same sergeant and constable who had been assigned to the case earlier were present. The jewels were spread out on the desk. Sister Julienne spoke.

"Here is the nurse who has known of the existence of this . . . ." she hesitated, "this . . . this little haul, for more than a fortnight." My face was burning and I felt like a criminal. The sergeant was speaking, the constable taking notes the while. They required my name, my age, home address, next of kin, father's occupation and many more details beside.

"When did you first see these jewels?"

"On a Monday afternoon two weeks ago."

"Can you identify them?"

"Not really, I did not look closely enough."

"But are they substantially the same?"

"Yes."

"Where did you find them?"

"In the third drawer down of the bedside cabinet."

The constable looked back through his notebook. "We looked in the bedside cabinet, sir, and there was nothing there. They must have been placed there after our search."

"Just what I was thinking. And what did you do, nurse?"

"Nothing."

"Were you aware that these jewels are of considerable value?"

"I guessed they might be, but I didn't know."

Sister Julienne intervened. "Why did you not tell me?"

"I promised I wouldn't."

Sister Julienne was about to speak, but the sergeant silenced her.

"Who did you promise?"

"Sister Monica Joan."

"So she knew you had seen them?"

"Yes."

"And she made you promise not to tell?"

"Yes — no. She didn't make me promise. I just did."

"Why?"

"Because she was so upset."

"What was she upset about?"

"The jewels."

"Upset that you had found them?"

"I suppose so."

"Upset that she had been found out?"

"I don't know."

"Was she upset before you found them?"

"No. She was happy."

"And she was happy when you left her?"

"Yes."

"Why?"

I didn't want to answer. But he repeated "Why?"

"I suppose she was happy because I had promised not to tell."

The sergeant looked at the constable. "Sister Monica Joan obviously knows what she has been doing. First she moves the jewels around to avoid detection and then when they are found she is aware of the significance and, although she may not have demanded it, she was clearly relieved when a promise of secrecy was made." He turned to me again.

"At the time of finding the jewels, nurse, did you know that the police were investigating a charge of shoplifting brought by local costers?"

"Yes."

"And did it occur to you that the jewels might be relevant to police investigations?"

"I don't know."

"Nurse, I won't insult you by suggesting you are stupid!"

"Well, yes, I did think they were relevant."

"Were you aware that withholding evidence during a police investigation is a criminal offence?"

My mouth went dry and my head began to spin. It is one thing to engage in underhand behaviour but it is quite another matter to be told by a police sergeant that you have been guilty of a criminal offence. My voice was barely audible.

"I didn't know until yesterday that it was a criminal offence."

"And what happened yesterday?"

"I told the girls."

Sister Julienne exploded.

"You told the girls and you didn't tell me. This is outrageous!"

234

"Why did you tell the girls and not the Sister in Charge?"

"Because I knew that Sister Julienne would have to tell the police, but the girls wouldn't."

"And what did the girls say?"

"I can't quite remember. We had a couple of bottles of sherry and I'm not sure what we said. It all got a bit confused."

The constable taking notes gave a chortle, quickly smothered when the sergeant looked at him.

Sister Julienne's blood pressure was rising fast.

"This gets worse and worse. You girls had a couple of bottles of sherry when you were on duty! We will talk about this later."

I groaned in despair. Now I had got my friends into trouble.

The sergeant interrupted.

"Let's get back to the jewels. You decided to conceal the information from the police, but what did you intend to do?"

"I thought I could take the jewels from Sister Monica Joan's room and just leave them somewhere, in Hatton Garden, or outside a police station somewhere."

The sergeant and the constable exchanged glances.

"But I couldn't find them, so I couldn't do it."

"She had moved them from the bedside cabinet?"

"Yes."

"It's a very good thing for you, nurse, that you could not find the jewels. If you had done as you have suggested and been apprehended with the jewels on your person, you would have been in serious trouble with the police."

I went cold and numb with shock. Theft, prison. The end of my nursing career. The end of everything.

The sergeant was watching me carefully. Then he spoke.

"We are not going to take any further action, nurse. This is a caution, and will be recorded as such. You have been very foolish. I hesitate to call you a silly young girl, but that is what you are, and I hope this will be a lesson to you. You can go now."

I crept out of Sister's office in a state of shock. To be called a 'silly young girl' by a police sergeant when you think you are so mature and responsible is not a pleasant experience. The girls pressed me for information. We sat round the kitchen table eating cheese and pickle sandwiches and home made cake and I told them all about it. Narrowly missing prison was foremost in my mind.

"Not a chance, old scout. We'd have stood by you," said Chummy staunchly. Her loyalty reminded me of my own disloyalty — I had let the cat out of the bag about the sherry party. I was contrite in my apologies. Cynthia, as always, was soothing, pointing out that we were all in it together and no harm had come of it. She advised cocoa all round, an early night and try to forget the whole business.

The jewels were taken by the police for identification and the Hatton Garden jewellers, who had reported losses over several years, were asked to examine them.

One man, Samuelson by name, positively identified a rope of antique pearls and a diamond ring as having been stolen from his stock a few years previously. He produced record books verifying his statement.

The testimony of costers, who had seen Sister Monica Joan take small items from their stalls, was required. With their evidence, combined with that of Mr Samuelson, the police decided that on a variety of counts there was a case against Sister Monica Joan. However, her mental fitness was in doubt so a medical assessment was required.

The General Practitioner who had known Sister Monica Joan for many years and who had attended her through her recent bout of bronchitis, was consulted. He said that he was baffled and quite unable to decide whether she was senile or not, and advised obtaining the report of a psychiatrist.

The psychiatrist was a lady doctor, a senior consultant in psychiatry at the London Hospital, who examined Sister Monica Joan twice at Nonnatus House. Her report stated that in spite of her age, Sister's mind was remarkably clear. All her responses were swift and accurate; she was astute, observant and cryptic in her conversation; her understanding of past and present events was impressive; she had a clear understanding of the difference between right and wrong. No evidence of mental deterioration could be found and the psychiatrist considered that Sister Monica Joan could be held responsible for her actions.

Having considered the two medical reports, the police decided to prosecute and they referred the evidence to Old Street Magistrates Court for a preliminary hearing. Three magistrates presided. They agreed unanimously that there was a *prima facie* case of larceny, for which a younger person would undoubtedly stand trial at the London Quarter Sessions. However, the presiding magistrate was exceedingly doubtful about the age of the accused. He had a grandmother of ninety-three who did not know the time of day nor even recognise her own daughter. He was very sympathetic towards extreme old age.

Whilst the charges were being read by the police superintendent, Sister Monica Joan sat between her solicitor and Sister Julienne who was scarlet with embarrassment and distress and kept her eyes lowered. In contrast Sister Monica Joan sat upright and alert, looking around her with haughty grandeur, every now and then exclaiming something like "poof" or "tosh" or "fiddlesticks".

When the superintendent had finished, the presiding magistrate said, "You have heard the charges?"

"I most certainly have."

"And do you understand them?"

"Don't be impertinent, my man. Do you think I am stupid?"

"No Sister, I don't. But I must be quite sure that you understand the charges brought against you by the police."

Sister Monica Joan did not answer. She pursed her lips and half closed her hooded eyes. She looked towards the clock on the wall and raised her veined hand towards her chin like an actress posing for a photograph.

"I am not sure that she does, Sir," said Sister Julienne quietly to the solicitor who stood up to speak but, before he could do so, Sister Monica Joan turned on them with quiet rage.

"Do not presume to speak for me. Speak for yourselves. Bear witness to your own imperfections. We stand, each of us, alone and naked before the Judgement Throne, where none but the silent dead can testify."

The presiding magistrate was having second thoughts. This was very different from a grandmother whose conversation was confined to: "I'm ninety-three, you know, think of that, ninety-three." He addressed Sister Monica Joan very seriously.

"Have you understood the charges brought against you?"

"I have."

"Do you plead 'guilty' or 'not guilty'?"

"Guilty! Guilty? Do you imagine, my good fellow, that I accept a charge of guilt from the *hoi-polloi* I see before me?" She sniffed scornfully and drew out a laced handkerchief from beneath her scapular, which she applied to her nose with an affected gesture, as though an unpleasant smell had assailed her. "Guilty indeed — huh? 'Let he who is without sin throw the first stone.' Does your small mind understand the hidden meaning of 'guilt'? Before you use the word again, it behoves you find out, if perchance you are capable of such intellectual exercise, which I very much doubt."

Such rudeness to the presiding magistrate was Sister Monica Joan's undoing. Had she shown a little more humility, a little more uncertainty or even contrition, it is likely that, in their discretionary powers, the magistrates would have taken the matter no further. As it was, after a brief consultation, the decision was made to accept a plea of not guilty and to refer the case to the London Quarter Sessions for trial by judge and jury.

Sister Julienne was devastated by Sister Monica Joan's performance in the Magistrates Court. She had hoped that the matter would quietly end there, but now the full publicity of the Quarter Sessions would have to be faced. But Sister Julienne was not a woman easily beaten. She prayed about the matter. The inspiration granted to her from a heavenly source was that the defence of mental deterioration should be strengthened. She consulted the solicitor and it was decided to obtain a third medical opinion.

Sir Lorimer Elliott-Bartram had an enviable reputation as a psychologist. He was well known in London, having given medical evidence in several legal cases. Sir Lorimer was getting on in years but not so far on that he could not maintain a thriving practice in Harley Street. In fact the further on he got, the more patients came flocking to his doors and therefore the more money he made. It was all very satisfactory.

Sir Lorimer had qualified as a surgeon in 1912 having had a distinguished record as an army doctor in two world wars. Distinguished by the military commanders as a first-rate officer and doctor — and distinguished by the men in the ranks as a butcher.

Although Sir Lorimer had never qualified, nor attempted to qualify, as a psychiatrist, he had made a fortune in Harley Street by dabbling in psychotherapy, memory loss, personality change, mental block, hypomania, dypsomania, kleptomania and related subjects. He was a tall handsome man with a deep resonant voice that could easily adopt a silky quality. The majority of his patients were women.

There is an old saying in medical circles that if you want to make a study of invective, you should listen to two doctors talking about a third. In psychiatric circles Sir Lorimer, a mere psychologist, was regarded as a pompous old windbag and a lucky chancer, who fuelled the tank of his Rolls Royce with the blood of rich old ladies.

Oozing opulence, Sir Lorimer entered Nonnatus House and was taken to Sister Monica Joan's room. He kissed her hand and called her "Dear Reverend lady". She murmured, "What a relief to meet a mature gentleman of experience and understanding." He kissed her hand a second time, whispering: "I understand everything, dear lady, everything." She sighed and smiled, "I am sure you do, Sir Lorimer, quite sure."

Later that day, just before Compline, when I frequently spent time with Sister Monica Joan, I asked her how she liked Sir Lorimer. She was sitting comfortably by the window knitting. Her face assumed a bright, plastic smile as she cooed, "He is charming, my dear, perfectly charming ... ..." The smile

241

vanished, and a hard edge entered her voice — "and determined to be so."

Sir Lorimer's report was very long and technically complex. For the benefit of the lay reader who is unfamiliar with medical terminology, I have attempted to summarise and simplify it. The report stated:

Sister Monica Joan is a lady of the Leptosomatic type with a nervous affinity to the Cyclothymic make-up on the one hand and a tendency to Catatonic excitement on the other. Neologism and Disconnection, though slight, could not be discounted. Whereas elucidation of the former may throw light upon the latter, comprehension of the latter seldom throws light upon the former, from which it may be deduced that individual psychological symptomatology must be sought in personal biography. The Korsakaw Psychosis of Registration, Retention and Recall is important. A link between Retrograde Amnesia is consistent with the facility, richness and rapidity of association. Whilst Depersonalisation is not a factor, Derealisation is and Catatonic symptoms are not evidence of Catatonia, though significant to the trained mind. Kleptomania is consistent in Cyclothymic behaviour, but inconsistent with Leptosomatic tendencies.

Although he could not understand it, Counsel for the Defence was very impressed by this report.

★　★　★

The trial of Sister Monica Joan at the London Quarter Sessions attracted much attention. The public gallery was full. Many costers, and several jewellers from Hatton Garden, were present. Several older women, who remembered the accused as a young midwife and who owed their lives to her, had come out of sympathy. The press gallery was full.

Sister Monica Joan sat in the dock. She was sitting quietly and contentedly knitting and seemed completely unconcerned with what was going on around her. Sister Julienne sat just in front of her, and attended throughout.

The usher entered.

"Silence in Court," he shouted. "Be upstanding for his Lordship."

Everyone rose to their feet. Everyone, that is, except Sister Monica Joan who remained seated. "Stand for his Lordship," shouted the usher.

There was no movement from Sister Monica Joan. The usher moved towards her, banged the floor with his staff and shouted louder. Sister Monica Joan gave a surprised little squeak.

"Are you addressing me, young man?"

"I am."

"Then let it be known that I will not be addressed in this rude fashion."

"Be upstanding for his Lordship," shouted the usher.

"Did your mother never teach you to say 'please', young man?"

The usher swallowed hard and banged his staff down on the floor a second time. Sister Monica Joan sat immobile, her beautiful eyes half closed, her lips pursed in disdain.

"Please stand up, Madam." whispered the usher.

"That's better. That is very much better. Courtesy is a virtue and costs nothing. I am sure your mother would be proud of you." Sister Monica Joan leaned forward, patted him kindly on the shoulder and rose to her feet.

Cheers from the public gallery. "Be silent for his Lordship," screamed the usher, striving to restore his authority.

The Judge entered, murmured "Please be seated" and everyone sat down, including Sister Monica Joan.

Counsel for the Prosecution addressed the jury. He outlined the facts as they were known and said that he would call as witnesses three jewellers from Hatton Garden who had lost jewellery, and eight costers who had lost sundry items from their stalls. He would also call a psychiatrist who had examined the accused and considered her to be of sound mind and responsible for her actions.

The three jewellers were all reliable witnesses. The first, a Mr Samuelson, stated that he had inherited the business with its stock from his father. A rope of antique pearls and a diamond ring had disappeared from the stock four years previously. The police had been informed. The stolen jewels had never been recovered until the police had contacted him recently saying that a cache of jewellery had been found, and asking him to examine the jewels. With the help of his record books Mr Samuelson was able to identify the pearls and the diamond ring.

The second jeweller stated that Sister Monica Joan had entered his shop three years previously and asked to see a tray of small items of little value, such as charms and trinkets. He had been called away to attend to another customer and left her alone with the tray confident that, as the lady was a nun, it would be safe to do so. However, an assistant had seen the nun take a small item from the tray and slip it into her pocket. He had warned his employer, and together they had escorted Sister Monica Joan into a back room and challenged her. She had produced a small trinket, valued at about two shillings, from the folds of her dress. The jeweller said that he took the item back and told Sister that he would not call the police on this occasion but that she would not be admitted to his shop again.

The assistant was called to the witness box. He verified everything his employer had said and identified Sister Monica Joan as the nun referred to. He said that he had not seen her in the shop since but had seen her wandering around other shops in Hatton Garden. He concluded that she must have remembered that she was barred from entering his employer's premises and therefore he rejected any suggestion that she was suffering from memory loss or senile dementia.

Sister Monica Joan sat in the dock knitting. She displayed no interest in what was being said about her. Sister Julienne, on the other hand, looked on the verge of tears.

The costers were called to give evidence. They were a colourful group of seven men and one woman.

The first stepped confidently into the witness box to be sworn in giving his name as Cakey Crumb.

"Could you give your first name please?"

"Well I've allus bin known as Cakey. Wiv a name like Crumb, wha' would you expec'?"

"With what name were you christened?"

"Cuthbert." Shrieks of laughter from the costers, which were silenced by the judge. Counsel for the Prosecution continued: "Could you please describe your occupation?" Cakey stuck his thumbs into the armholes of his colourful waistcoat and drummed his fingers on his chest.

"I'm a business man. Managin' director of me own company. Bin a' i' since I was four'een, wiv a break for the war, when I was in the merchan' navy; 'orrible va' was, real 'orrible. Never did like wa'er, I never. We was torpedoed an' 'undreds of men was frown in ve wa'er. 'half of 'em drowned. 'orrible i' was to 'ear 'em cry for 'elp, poor sods. An' then another time we was . . ."

"Yes, Mr. Crumb. I am sure the court would like to hear your reminiscences but we must confine ourselves to the case against Sister Monica Joan. You are a business man you say?"

"Yerst. Costermonger. I 'as me own cock sparrer, an' sells in ve markets."

The Judge interrupted. "Did you say you sell cock sparrows in the markets?"

"No, no, m'lud. Cock sparrer is wha' we calls ve barrer."

"I see." The Judge makes a note. "Please go on."

"I sells ladies fings, and vis nun, she comes up to me stall and' afore you can blink an eye, she picks up a couple of bread an' cheeses, tucks 'em in 'er petticoats, an' is off round the Jack Horner, dahn ve frog an' toad, quick as shit of a stick. I couldn't Adam an' Eve it, bu' vats wot she done. When I tells me carvin' knife wot I seen, she calls me an 'oly friar an' says she'll land me one on me north and south if I calls Sister Monica Joan a tea-leaf. Very fond of Sister she is. So I never says nuffink to no-one, like."

The Judge had laid down his pen long before Cakey had finished his evidence.

"I think I am going to need an interpreter," he said.

The usher spoke.

"I think I can help you my Lord. My mother was a cockney and I was brought up with the rhyming slang. Mr. Crumb has testified that he saw Sister Monica Joan take a couple of handkerchiefs — bread and cheese is the usual expression for handkerchiefs — off his sparrow, or barrow, and set off round the Jack Horner — corner my Lord — down the frog and toad — meaning road — as quick as . . . . I need not go on, my Lord, a harmless vulgarity implying no disrespect to your Lordship — quick, stick — the rhyme is obvious my Lord."

"I am beginning to understand. Ingenious, very. But what was all that about Adam and Eve? We are not talking about the garden of Eden, you know."

"To Adam and Eve it is a very common expression my Lord. It means 'to believe it' or the negative. Mr.

Crumb could not Adam and Eve the evidence of his own eyes."

"You are very knowledgeable, usher, and I am indebted to you. But that was not all the evidence Mr. Crumb gave the court, and it has to be written down for the record."

The usher was standing up stiff and straight and feeling very important. All eyes were upon him.

"Mr Crumb said that he told his wife what had happened. There are several expressions for wife — carving knife, trouble and strife, Duchess of Fife spring readily to mind — and she called him a liar — holy friar, my Lord, and said she would hit him in the north and south — mouth is the anatomical term more commonly used — if he called Sister Monica Joan a thief — tea-leaf was the rhyming slang used by Mr Crumb."

"I understand now. Thank you usher." The Judge turned towards Cakey.

"Would you say that that interpretation is substantially correct, Mr. Crumb?"

"Oh yerst, yers. That's Isle of White."

"I suppose I am correct in understanding that it is — right?"

The Judge looked pleased with himself and smiled at Cakey. Counsel for the Prosecution continued.

"When did this all occur?"

"Abaht a year ago, I reckons."

"And you never told no-one — 'ahem, I mean — anyone?"

248

"Nah, nah. I'm no' daft. There'd 'ave bin a righ' 'ole bull and cow if I 'ad. I don't want me jackdaw broke, do I?"

The Judge sighed and looked towards the usher.

"Mr Crumb did not tell anyone, my Lord, because he was anxious to avert a row with his wife, whom he felt was capable of breaking his jaw."

"Is this correct, Mr Crumb?"

"Gor, not 'alf, an' all. Got an Oliver Twist like a piston she 'as. Knock yer 'ampstead 'eafs out soon as look at yer, she will."

"Mr Crumb, I was referring to the accuracy of the usher's translation, not to your wife's skill as a pugilist."

"Oh, I see. Well yers, 'e's got ve lingo taped an' all."

"Thank you Mr Crumb. Usher, I should be grateful if you would attend closely to what the witness says and interpret for me, should it be necessary."

"Certainly, my Lord."

Counsel for the Prosecution continued, "Having said nothing for a year, why have you come forward now?"

"Because I earwigged some of me mates 'ad seen ve same sort of fing; vis ole blackbird goin' round ve markets, lookin' all 'oly like, bu' pinchin' fings off stalls and then scarperin'. So we goes to ve grasshoppers, an vey took it to ve garden gate."

"I understand your evidence as far as the grasshoppers, Mr Crumb. Usher, perhaps you would enlighten me as to the meaning of the last sentence?" said the Judge.

"Grasshopper, my Lord, is rhyming slang for copper, which your Lordship may know is a colloquialism for police. And the police referred the case to the magistrate — the garden gate."

"I understand." The Judge turned to Mr Crumb.

"If the police are grasshoppers and magistrates are garden gates, what, may I enquire, is a Judge?" he asked politely.

"Barnaby Rudge, m'lud."

"Hmm. Not too bad. Could have been worse, I suppose. We might have gone down in local terminology as a pile of sludge, or something equally unsavoury. All things considered, I think we have been let off pretty lightly. Counsel, do you have any further questions?"

"No, my Lord."

Cakey Crumb stepped down from the witness box, and a costerwoman took his place. She stated that she had seen Sister Monica Joan take three skeins of embroidery silk from her stall and hide them under her scapular.

She continued: "I didn't do nuffink abaht it because ve Sisters are well respected arahnd vese parts, an' in fact saved my life when I was younger. The silks only cost a shillin' an' it just didn't seem worthwhile to make a fuss. I jus' thought to meself — poor ole girl she's goin' off 'er rocker, an left it, but when I heard from the other costers that she'd been pinchin' things left right and centre, I decided to go in with them an' go to the police. After all, we got a livin' to earn, an' thievin' is thievin' whoever is doin' it. We can't afford 'a be sentimental."

Five other costers told similar stories reporting the thefts of various sundry items, which they had seen Sister Monica Joan take. Lastly, the coster who had instigated the proceedings in the first place was called. He told the court that he had seen Sister Monica Joan take a child's bangle from his stall and hide it under her scapular. When he had challenged her, she had flung the bangle across the stall and stalked off. Five people were called to the witness box, each one declaring under oath that he or she had witnessed this scene.

Things looked black for Sister Monica Joan but she appeared completely unconcerned, as though the proceedings had nothing to do with her. She was knitting quietly, occasionally counting her stitches and noting them down on her knitting card. She would smile serenely at Sister Julienne who, in contrast, looked in a state of real anguish.

The day's proceedings ended and the Judge adjourned the court until 10 o'clock the following morning.

On the second day Counsel for the Prosecution called the psychiatrist to the witness box. She stated that she had examined Sister Monica Joan and could find nothing suggestive of senility or mental deterioration. On the contrary she found Sister to be exceedingly quick and accurate in her responses. Her memory was good and she had a clear perception of right and wrong. In conclusion, the psychiatrist stated that on the balance of medical evidence, Sister Monica Joan knew what she was doing and was responsible for her actions.

The general practitioner was less positive. He agreed with everything that his colleague had said but nevertheless had a feeling that something was amiss. He doubted if Sister Monica Joan could really be held responsible for her actions, although he was unable to say exactly why. In conclusion, he said that the Court should prefer the evidence of the specialists. He sat down next to the psychiatrist.

Sir Lorimer Elliott-Bartram was called to the witness box. Sister Monica Joan looked up from her knitting, caught his eye and gave him one of her ravishing smiles, then lowered her eyes again demurely.

The Counsel for the Defence asked the first question.

"From your examination of Sister Monica Joan, would you say she is of sound mind?"

Sir Lorimer paused for a long time before speaking. His pause was calculated for maximum effect. The jury was impressed and leaned forward attentively.

"That is an interesting question and one to which I have given much thought over many years. On mature reflection and after a lifetime of experience, with reference to Smellingworthy and Schmitzelburg on the subject and not forgetting the work of Crakenbaker, Corensky and Kokenbul as published in *The Lancet*, I have come to the conclusion that the sound mind is a figment of the imagination."

"What on earth is he on about?" whispered the general practitioner.

"He is making it up as he goes along," the psychiatrist murmured.

"Silence in Court!" warned the Judge. "For the benefit of the jury, Sir Lorimer, please elucidate. A figment of the imagination, you say."

"Indeed I do. Which of us can contemplate his friend and say 'he is of sound mind', gentlemen of the jury? Which of us can gaze upon the wife of his bosom and say 'her mind is sound'?"

The jury took notes and shook their heads.

Counsel for the Defence continued.

"Perhaps then you would say that the accused suffers from senile dementia?"

"Most certainly not," said Sir Lorimer indignantly. He was old himself, and senility or senile dementia were words that he never used.

"I have heard the evidence of the psychiatrist and would point out that normal sensory perception is far from being an objective picture of reality, but is conditioned and modified by many personal factors both sensory and extra-sensory. In my opinion, psychiatrists make the problems that are to be solved."

"Could you enlarge upon that, Sir Lorimer?"

"Certainly. Psychiatrists need to earn a living like everyone else. A similar syndrome can be observed in the fields of sociology and counselling. Left to themselves most people will sort out their problems for themselves. If it is suspected that someone else will sort them out, the problems multiply exponentially."

"The insufferable old hypocrite," whispered the psychiatrist.

Counsel for the defence continued.

253

"I have read your most erudite report, Sir Lorimer, and I am impressed by your reference to the Korsakaw Psychosis of Registration, Retention and Recall. Could you please enlighten the jury?"

"Certainly. A prominent feature of Korsakaw's Psychosis is that Registration may be interposed by Deregistration preventing the proper interpretation of happenings. Retention for shorter or longer periods may differ markedly, and Recall may be either voluntary or involuntary."

"That rubbish goes back to 1910," whispered the lady psychiatrist. "He ought to be struck off. I wonder if the General Medical Council knows about him?"

"Silence in Court," said the Judge. "Please continue, Sir Lorimer."

"Not infrequently psychological experiences are important as regards the origin of psychological symptoms. It is possible to ascribe to the psychological experiences that determine the genesis of the psychological symptoms aetiological importance in the production of the whole."

"This is an example of the three Bs," whispered the lady psychiatrist.

"The three whats?" replied her colleague.

"Three Bs — Bullshit Baffles Brains," she hissed.

Counsel for the Prosecution stood up.

"May I enquire what all this has to do with the theft of valuable jewellery from shops in Hatton Garden?"

"Here, here!" chorused the jewellers in the gallery.

"Silence in Court!" said the Judge. "Sir Lorimer, with respect to your eminent position in the field of mental health, I was wondering the same thing."

Sir Lorimer continued.

"Sister Monica Joan is a lady of great intelligence and fertile imagination. She was brought up in wealth and luxury. Association with her childhood is strong. If valuable jewellery was found in her possession, I have not the slightest doubt that by the Korsakaw Psychosis, the lady thought that the jewels belonged to her mother."

"Her mother!"

"That is what I said."

"I don't believe a word of it," whispered the lady psychiatrist. "She put him up to it. I told you she is as sharp as they come."

"If it is true it is a sign of senile dementia," whispered her colleague.

"Rubbish. The old girl's up to every trick. She pulls the wool over everyone's eyes."

Counsel for the Prosecution continued.

"A remarkable theory, Sir Lorimer. Fanciful would perhaps be a better description. But it does not get us any nearer to answering the question about how the jewels came to be in Sister Monica Joan's possession. Have you any theories, fanciful or otherwise, on that score?"

"No, I have not."

"No further questions, my Lord."

Sister Monica Joan had continued knitting placidly all afternoon, occasionally muttering to herself as she made notes on her knitting chart. She displayed not the slightest interest in the court proceedings. Sir Lorimer stepped down from the witness box and she smiled at him again. The time had reached 4.30p.m. and the Judge adjourned the court for the day to reassemble at 10 o'clock the following morning.

The Court was again crowded on the third morning when Sister Monica Joan was due to appear in the witness box. She was waiting in the dock quietly knitting, occasionally speaking to Sister Julienne who was sitting in front of her.

The usher entered and before anything else he went over to the two nuns and whispered, "When I call 'Be upstanding for his Lordship' would you be kind enough to stand up, Madam, please?" Sister Monica Joan smiled sweetly, "Of course I will," and she stood with everyone else.

Counsel for the Prosecution opened the morning's proceedings.

"I wish to call Sister Monica Joan of the Midwives of St. Raymund Nonnatus to the witness box."

A buzz of excitement ran through the courtroom and the jury leaned forward expectantly. Sister Monica Joan stood up. She wound up her ball of wool, stuck it on the end of the needles and placed it in her knitting bag, which she handed to Sister Julienne.

"Would you make a note, dear. The next row will be row 56. Slip one, knit two together, purl four, slip one, purl three, knit two together, pass slip stitch over, repeat to end."

"Yes dear, of course I will." Sister Julienne marked the knitting card.

"Did I say purl four, slip one, purl three, knit two together, pass the slip stitch over?"

"Yes you did, dear."

"That's wrong, it should be purl three after slipping the slip stitch over, not before."

"Oh yes of course, that makes sense."

The Judge leaned forward.

"Have you ladies sorted out your knitting?"

"Yes my Lord."

"Then perhaps we can start the morning's proceedings."

Sister Monica Joan made her way to the witness box. She looked completely composed; in fact she looked really beautiful in her full black habit with the halo of white linen around her face. A small smile lightened her features and her eyes sparkled mischievously. Naughty Sister Monica Joan always enjoyed the limelight.

Counsel for the Prosecution opened.

"The police report states that certain jewels were found in your knitting bag. Is this a true statement?"

Sister Monica Joan looked towards the jury, then to the visitors' gallery. She turned towards the judge and raised one eyebrow quizzically. Her composure held everyone captive as they waited for her reply. Her voice, always clear, had a ringing quality.

"Truth. The eternal mystery. 'What is truth?' asked Pilate. Mankind has been seeking the answer to that question for thousands of years. What would be your definition of truth, young man?"

"I am here to ask you the questions, Sister. Not the other way round."

"But it is a perfectly fair question. Before we can establish the truth, we must have a definition of it."

Counsel decided to humour her:

"Truth, I would say, is an accurate record of fact. Would you accept that, Sister?"

"You have studied Aristotle?"

"A little," replied Counsel modestly.

"Truth. Truth is a movement of inexhaustible power, containing within itself divine truth. In the depths of space matter is for ever being formed into the heavenly bodies and transformed into the speed of light and disappears from our ken. Would you say that this is an accurate record of fact when it has disappeared from our ken?"

"I am not a scientist, Sister, but a lawyer, and I am enquiring about jewels found in your possession."

"Ah, yes, the jewels. The stars are the jewels of heaven. But are they fact? Are they truth or are they a chimera? Do we see the stars? We think we see them, but we do not; we see what they were light years ago. Would you say that the stars are an accurate record of fact, young man?"

"You see, she is confused," whispered the general practitioner.

"She's clever. She is deliberately trying to confuse the issue. That's what she's doing," whispered the psychiatrist.

The judge interrupted.

"Silence in Court! Sister, this court is here to consider stolen jewellery. It is not here to discuss metaphysics. Please confine your answers to the matter in hand."

Sister Monica Joan turned her shapely head towards the judge.

"Matter, and what is matter? Einstein says that matter is energy. Are these jewels matter? Are they energy, moving at the speed of light into cosmic forces beyond the limits of our consciousness? Are these jewels living matter, living energy, circling the earth in the full moon of April, or are they mere clods of clay, dull and lifeless, as postulated by the police?"

Although Sister Monica Joan spoke to the Judge, her clear voice rang through the courtroom. An eloquent hand reached towards the jury, who sat spellbound although they did not understand a word she was talking about.

Counsel for the Prosecution continued.

"But how did the jewels come to be in your possession, Sister?"

She turned on him angrily.

"I do not know, young man. I am not a seer; I am but a humble seeker of eternal truths. These jewels, which seem to excite so much interest, have their own life, their own consciousness and their own energy force. When an atom gets excited it creates magnetic fields independent of human activity. Did they not teach you that at school, young man?"

Counsel, who was close on fifty, was beginning to look out of his depth.

"No, Madam, I was not taught that at school."

"Were you not taught that all matter is subject to the laws of gravity?"

Counsel refused to answer.

"Sister, I am enquiring into stolen jewellery. Are you trying to say that jewels were magnetised or gravitated from jewellers in Hatton Garden into your knitting bag by their own volition?"

"I do not know. I am not a seer. Only God knows the whole truth. Questions, foolish questions all the time. You wear me out with your questions, young man. Can I not expect a little repose in my old age?"

Sister Monica Joan raised her hand to her face and slightly tottered in the dock. A gasp of anxiety was heard in the courtroom. She murmured: "May I sit down, my Lord?" and the usher ran forward with a chair. She smiled weakly. "So kind, so very kind, my poor heart." She raised her eyes appealingly to the judge and murmured, "Thank you, my Lord. Are there any more questions?"

"No further questions," said the Counsel for the Prosecution.

Sister Monica Joan had created a good impression in the witness box. Even though most of the jury did not know what she was talking about, her sincerity and conviction was compelling. Her age and frailty were appealing and their sympathy was with her. A verdict of not guilty seemed likely.

The Judge adjourned the Court until 2p.m.

★ ★ ★

Counsel for the Defence opened the afternoon's proceedings. "Are you sitting comfortably, Sister?"

"Most comfortably, thank you."

"I will try not to fatigue you with my questions."

"You are most kind."

"The jury has heard you say that you do not know how the jewels came into your possession."

"I do not."

"But were they really in your possession?"

"I possess nothing."

"Nothing?"

"No, nothing. I renounced all worldly possessions with my profession. Poverty is one of the vows of the monastic life."

"So you do not and cannot possess anything?"

"No."

"And you have never possessed the jewels in question?"

"Never."

Counsel for the Prosecution stood up.

"Then what were they doing in your knitting bag?"

Counsel for the Defence was furious.

"My Lord, I really must protest at this interruption which is designed to intimidate the witness. I was coming to that point myself later, but without the bullying tactics adopted by my learned friend."

The Judge allowed the protest, but nonetheless he leaned forward and said more kindly.

"Sister, if as a professed nun you cannot own or possess anything, can you account for the fact that a quantity of jewels were found in your knitting bag?"

"No, I cannot."

"Did you put them there?"

"I don't know."

"Well, if you did not put them there, who did?"

Sister Monica Joan looked vague and tired. "I don't know, my Lord. I suppose I must have."

"And where did they come from?"

Sister Monica Joan was crumbling fast. The day had been too long. Her sparkle and confidence were fading away, leaving a tired old lady who did not really know what she was saying. She looked at the judge vaguely.

"I suppose they came from Hatton Garden, like everyone says they did." She leaned her forehead on her hand and sighed deeply. "I don't know why respectable elderly women do this sort of thing, but they do. Oh, they do, they do. Is it a sickness? Is it a madness? I do not know. I do not know myself."

A ripple of shocked sympathy spread through the courtroom. To incriminate oneself is sad, but for Sister Monica Joan to do so was tragic. If a pin had dropped it would have been heard in the silent courtroom. The Judge leaned back in his chair and sighed.

"I adjourn the Court for today. I will make my summing up tomorrow. The Court will reassemble at 10 o'clock.

★   ★   ★

The atmosphere in the courtroom was tense the following morning. A verdict of guilty was a foregone conclusion in the minds of the jury. Could it be prison for a lady of such advanced years? Perhaps the Judge would order confinement to a mental asylum. A recommendation for clemency was everyone's hope.

Sister Julienne was seated in court; her face was white with shock and sorrow, and showed signs of sleeplessness. On the other hand, Sister Monica Joan looked completely relaxed and unconcerned, knitting contentedly and smiling at people she recognised. She stood when the usher gave the order.

The Judge opened the morning's proceedings.

"Last evening, at seven o'clock, I was informed of new evidence which throws a different light on this case. The witness arrived in London this morning and is at present waiting outside. Call the Reverend Mother Jesu Emanuel, please usher."

A murmur of surprise spread through the Court. Sister Julienne gave a gasp of astonishment and stood up when her Superior entered. She was a good looking lady of about fifty with calm grey eyes. She walked firmly to the witness box to be sworn in.

Counsel for the Defence spoke:

"You are the Reverend Mother Jesu Emanuel, the Mother Superior of the Order of the Sisters of St. Raymund Nonnatus?"

"I am."

"And you have been in Africa recently."

"I have been to our mission in Africa for the past year. I returned yesterday."

"Would you please tell the Court what you have told me."

"On my return to our mother house in Chichester I learned that Sister Monica Joan had been accused of the theft of jewellery. I knew at once that this was a mistake. The jewels have not been stolen. The jewels belong to Sister Monica Joan."

Everyone started talking at once and uproar was imminent. The Judge ordered silence. "Please continue," he said.

The Reverend Mother continued.

"When a Sister takes her final vows all her property is given to the Order. In some Orders this is irrevocable, but not so in our Order. We hold the property in trust during the Sister's lifetime. If the Sister leaves the Order, or has need of the property for any reason whatever, the property reverts to her. Sister Monica Joan made her final vows in 1904. She had inherited great wealth from her mother, including a quantity of jewellery which has been kept in the security vaults of the convent's financiers ever since. Sister Monica Joan is now a very old lady. It is the policy of our Order to give special privileges to our retired Sisters, who have given a lifetime of service to our work. Knowing that Sister Monica Joan likes pretty things and that she would enjoy having her mother's jewels to play with, I gave them to her the last time I visited Nonnatus House."

"Have you any confirmation of this?"

"I have the certificate of withdrawal from the bank with me for your Lordship's inspection."

Counsel for the Defence spoke. "The jewels have been checked against the certificate, my Lord, and they can all be accounted for."

The Judge was handed the certificate, which he examined, then he said.

"Did you not tell anyone about this, Reverend Mother?"

"No my Lord, I did not, and in this respect I am entirely culpable. Sister Julienne was away on Retreat at the time of my visit to Nonnatus House, or I would probably have mentioned it to her. Immediately after that, preparations were made for my visit to Africa and it slipped my mind. I am devastated that my action should have caused so much trouble. But frankly, it was not something that I regarded as important. I looked upon the jewels not as objects of monetary value but as pretty things that would give innocent happiness to a very old lady, bringing back memories of her childhood and her mother."

The Judge adjourned the Court until two o'clock that afternoon to allow time for full consultation. The jeweller, Mr. Samuelson, who had earlier identified the pearls and the diamond, was called, and he acknowledged that he might have been mistaken. It was agreed by all parties that if Sister Monica Joan had forgotten how she came to be in possession of the jewels, she could not be held responsible for her actions, whatever the psychiatrist might have said, and the charges of petty theft from the costers were dropped.

265

After lunch the Judge informed the assembled Court that the Prosecution had withdrawn all charges. There was wild cheering and hat throwing in the public gallery.

The Judge motioned to the usher to call for silence. Then he addressed the Court.

"I think I speak for the popular voice of this courtroom when I say how pleasing is the outcome of this case. Much needless strain and anxiety has been caused to the Sisters of St. Raymund Nonnatus. However, I say to the Sisters, as I say to the Police, the Prosecution, the doctors and everyone involved in this case, including the press and the wider readership beyond these walls:

It is folly to jump to conclusions."

Part III

Mr Joseph Collett

Sister Julienne and I left Nonnatus House and cycled towards the tenements, known as the Canada Buildings. We made our way to Alberta House, to a patient I had not met before — a man with leg ulcers, requiring daily dressing. Sister had told me the ulcers were severe, and warned that dressing such wounds in the patient's home was very different from a surgically equipped and sterile hospital. The man was a Mr Joseph Collett, aged over eighty, and he lived alone in one of the ground floor flats.

We knocked at the door. There was no immediate response, but we heard movements inside. The door was opened by a very old and rather dirty man. He peered at us through thick lensed glasses, and it was obvious from the way he was looking and trying to adjust his focus that he could not see at all well. Nonetheless he must have recognised us, for he opened the door wide, drew himself up very straight, and slightly bowed, saying: "Mornin', Sister. I've been expecting you. Good of you to come. Who have you got with you today? Someone new?"

"This is Nurse Lee, and when I have shown her the routine, she will be looking after you."

He turned towards me, and put out a hand to touch my coat sleeve, as the partially sighted do. He couldn't quite see me, but he was obviously assessing my height and general contours, by which he would recognise me.

"It's nice to have you here, young lady, and I am sure we are going to get on famous. Allow me, Sister."

He said this with old world courtesy, and took her bag, and slowly walked with it to place it on the table.

"I've got the boilin' water ready for you, and the flavine, and lint. I think you'll find everything's there."

Sister Julienne started unpacking her bag, and I looked around the room. The smell was none too pleasant, but I had got used to that in the tenements. The walls were a dirty beige colour, with wallpaper peeling off. The paint was dark brown, blistering and cracking. A small gas stove was in one corner, by the stone sink. Next to the sink was a lavatory, which was an obvious addition to the room and not part of the original structure. The windows were so dirty that very little light could penetrate, and there were no curtains. An open doorway revealed the bedroom, with a brass bedstead. The whole area, living room, bedroom, kitchen area and lavatory could not have been more than about twelve feet square, and there was no bathroom. It was quite adequate for an old man living alone, but I knew that many such tenement flats housed whole families of ten or more people. How did they manage, and keep sane?

A fire was burning merrily, and a hod of coal stood beside it. I noticed a tin bath full of coal under the sink. A very beautiful grandfather clock stood proudly against the opposite wall, next to a large wooden crate full of sticks and old newspapers. A heavy wooden table — the sort antique dealers would fight over today — filled the centre of the room, and some grimy plates and mugs were spread out on a newspaper. The room was full of old military photographs, prints and maps, and what looked like medals and trophies, yellowed with age and dirt. I concluded that Mr Collett had been a soldier

Our patient sat down in a high wooden armchair next to the fire, took his slippers off and placed his right foot on a low stool. He pulled up his trouser leg revealing horrible blood and pus soaked bandages. Sister Julienne told me to do the dressing, whilst she watched me. I knew everything had to be disposed of in the patient's house, so I placed newspapers on the wooden floor. I kneeled down and started to undo the bandages with forceps. The stench was revolting, and I felt nausea rising as I struggled to peel off the layers of bandage, which were stuck to each other with slimy fluid. I let them fall onto the newspaper, to be burned on the fire. The ulcer was the worst I had ever seen, extending upwards from the ankle for about six to eight inches. It was deep and suppurating badly. I cleaned it with saline, packed the cavities with gauze soaked in flavine, and re-bandaged. Then the other leg had to be treated.

Mr Collett didn't murmur whilst I was attending to his legs, but sat back sucking an old pipe with no tobacco in it, talking now and then to Sister Julienne. The grandfather clock ticked loudly, and the fire crackled and blazed. The siren of a cargo boat echoed through the room as I completed the second dressing and bandaged up the leg, with the quiet satisfaction of knowing that I had made this dignified old soldier comfortable.

I cleaned up, saw that everything was burned, packed my bag, and Sister and I prepared to leave.

"Won't you stay for a cup of tea, Sister?" he asked. "It won't take me a minute."

"No, but thank you; we have other work to do."

I thought he looked crestfallen, but he said quickly, "Then I won't keep you, marm."

This old-fashioned use of the royal "marm" surprised me, but strangely it didn't sound out of place.

"Nurse Lee will come to you each morning from now on."

He laid his pipe on the mantelpiece and stood up. He was very tall, more than six feet, and very straight. He walked slowly over to the door and opened it for us. He bowed again very slightly as we left.

Out in the courtyard the air smelled sweet and fresh. A horse-drawn coal cart entered, and a huge man jumped out, lifting a tiny child of about two or three years onto the cobbles. The man strode through the courtyard calling in a distinctive and penetrating yodel: "Co-al, co-al," the second vowels rising a perfect fifth from the first. The long strides of the man took him swiftly through the court and the little boy, running as fast as he could to keep up, tumbled and fell. As he picked himself up, he lifted his fluffy blond head, and in a tiny, piping voice called out "Co-al, co-al". A perfect fifth!

Women came out of many doors, and hailed the coalman, who carried a bag, or half a bag, up the stone steps to the balcony where it was required. No-one had a real bunker or space to store coal, so small amounts, half a hundredweight, had to be bought frequently. Coal fires were to become obsolete, due to the subsequent Clean Air legislation, but in the middle fifties they were the only form of heating for most people.

Inevitably, if you see a person daily in his own home over several months, you will cease to regard him as a patient, and come to know him as a person. Treating Mr Collett's leg ulcers took about half an hour, during which time we talked and, as old people can always remember the long past more easily than they can remember yesterday, we talked about his early life.

Mr Collett was not a typical Cockney in appearance, speech, or manner. He was much taller than average, and had a slow, thoughtful way about him. His quiet dignity and formal way of speaking commanded respect and I never presumed to call him 'Joe'. He was a Londoner, of first generation, and spoke with a London accent, but it was not heavy Cockney, typified by an idiosyncratic use of grammar and idiom. He told me his parents were country people from Sussex, who had been tenant farmers. The family had been displaced by the Enclosure Acts of the nineteenth century and, unable to sustain even a subsistence level of economy, had drifted towards the city in search of work. They had settled in Croydon, where Mr Collett was born in the 1870s, the oldest of eight children. His father had been a painter and decorator, and an unskilled builder's labourer. He was often out of work, because painting was a trade at the mercy of the weather in the nineteenth century. Paints had no chemical quick-drying properties in them and would take about four days to dry, so in wet weather no painting was done externally, and the men were laid off. Building was in the same position, because cement would not dry in less than three days.

"But my father was a good man," said Mr Collett. "He would not see his wife and children go without. There was always stone breaking to be done for road building and railway construction, and he would go to the yards and break stones all day. He would come home at night wet through, aching all over, with a few pence in his pocket that he had earned, and my mother would rub his back and chest with liniment and apply flannel, soaked in hot mustard water to keep the cold out. He was a good man. He wouldn't go to the pub and drink away all his money, like many we came to see."

Mr Collett shook his head in disapproval, and cut off a chunk of tobacco which he proceeded to cut up finely in the palm of his gnarled old hand, and stuff into a leather pouch, in which he always kept a piece of apple peel "to keep the tobacco moist," he told me. I was fascinated by this tobacco, called shag or twist, which was sold in lengths. Tobacconists kept long coils of it, perhaps two or three feet long, like a curled, black sausage, and a few inches would be sawn off and sold to a customer. I thought the smell was lovely as he shredded it in his hand (or perhaps it was just an improvement on the usual fusty, dirty smell of the room), and I encouraged him to cut it up and smoke the stuff, which produced clouds of thick, grey smoke when a match was applied. Incidentally, shag was the same tobacco that men chewed. You would see a lot of old men chewing away on toothless gums, sucking the last drachm of juice from the tobacco, after which they would spit it out.

Mr Collett always asked me to join him in a cup of tea, and I always refused, for two reasons: I have never been able to drink strong tea, the unvarying brew of East Londoners; but, more importantly, the thought of drinking anything from the filthy mugs that I saw on the table made me feel sick. Neither of these reasons could I tell him, so I always said that I was too busy. He accepted this, but he always looked sad, and once he just nodded his head quietly and swallowed hard, as though there was a big lump in his throat. I could see him, of course, better than he could see me, and if he had known that I was studying his face, trying to read his thoughts, he would have stood up quickly and turned away. But I was packing up my bag and watching him at the same time. There was a patient weariness and sorrow written all over his strong features, which made me think he was lonely, and that

275

my visit was the bright spot of each day. I didn't like to leave him, even though it was always a relief to quit the all-pervading smell of the place.

Then I had a brilliant idea. Boiling water poured into those filthy mugs would melt the grease and accumulated dirt, which would then float to the top. If I asked for a cold drink, the dirt would remain stuck to the sides of the mug. It was foolproof. So I said that I didn't like hot drinks, but would enjoy something cold. I was thinking of orange juice.

His face burst into smiles, like the sun coming out on a grey day.

"That's what you shall have, my maiden."

He stood up, and went to a small cupboard near the sink. He fumbled about, feeling for the things that he could not see clearly, and came out with two handcut crystal glasses and a bottle of sherry.

"Oh no, no," I protested, "I can't drink alcohol, not when I'm on duty. I meant orange squash, or something."

His face fell. The sun went behind the clouds. I realised how much it meant to him, and how little it meant to me. The scales are unevenly balanced, I thought. I laughed and said: "All right, I'll just have half a glass. But don't you dare tell the Sisters, or I shall get the sack. No nurse is allowed, ever, to drink on duty."

I sat down on the wooden kitchen chair by the big mahogany table, and we drank a glass of sherry together, sharing the secret of my disobeying orders. The light was dim, because of the dirty windows, but the fire glowed red, transforming squalor into cosiness.

His eyes gleamed with pleasure, and I had the impression that he was so happy he could hardly speak. Two or three times he dabbed his eyes with a filthy old handkerchief, and muttered something about having a cold in the eye.

That moment was significant in my life, because I understood that he had wanted to give me something, but had not known how. A cup of tea was all he could think of. My refusal had been a rebuff. By joining him in a clandestine glass of sherry, we had shared more than just the drink; we had shared a conspiracy of silence. It obviously meant more to him than I could have imagined, and I felt all my youthful pride and arrogance crumbling to dust beside his humble, unaffected joy in my company.

That day was the beginning of a friendship which was to last until his death.

As I left and stepped out into the court, a woman with a shopping basket was just entering the flat next to Mr Collett's. She was old, but brisk and spritely. She looked up at me, challenge written all over her features.

"You seein' vat dirty old man agen — phew!"

She spat out the sound, with a hiss.

"Nasty old bugger, I says. I'm tellin' yer, you Sisters oughta have somefink better to do than run around after him all the time. Phew!"

She spat on the cobbles.

"Him, who is he, any road up? He's not nobody, he's not. He's not one of us, he ain't. Where's he come from that's what I wants 'a know. And look at 'ow he keeps 'is place. Filthy. It's disgustin', I says. He ain't not got

277

no right 'a be livin' there among God-fearing folks as likes to keep themselves respeckable." She leaned towards me and hissed, "Yer knows what? His son was shot, they says. I'm tellin' yer. Shot."

She nodded her head emphatically. The curlers under her scarf stuck out at angles, making her look particularly vicious. She smacked her gums together, and repeated "shot" as though she had delivered the ultimate condemnation of moral depravity, and disappeared into her doorway before I could say a word.

I was seething with fury. What right had this woman to speak to me, or anyone else, in that way about her neighbour? I felt deeply protective of Mr Collett, as obviously she would not hesitate to spread such venom about him to anyone who cared to listen. It was insufferable. He was dirty, admittedly, but no worse than many. And, anyway, he was partially sighted. The sherry had left me with a warm glow inside, and this gratuitous attack on a gentle old man, whom I respected, sent my blood racing. No wonder he was lonely, if he had her for a neighbour.

I mentioned the incident over lunch at Nonnatus House, with great indignation. Sister Julienne tried to calm me down.

"We meet a lot of this sort of thing among the older people of Poplar, who are deeply suspicious of someone from the next area of the Docklands, or even the next street sometimes. If we believed everything they tell us, we would believe everyone to be murderers and villains, and wife beaters, or granny bashers. Surely you've heard from all areas: 'ooh, them people darn Stepney (or Millwall, or Bow) they leave their babies on doorsteps, they do.'"

Everyone laughed. We had all heard it so often that if it was to be believed, every doorstep would be littered with abandoned babies from other boroughs.

I repeated the woman's words about a son being shot, and emphasised her nasty attitude. Sister said: "I cannot be quite sure, but I believe Mr Collett had two sons who died in the 1914-18 war. If this is the case, the deepest sympathy is due to him, and I hope you are wrong about the woman's attitude. Remember, we can all be mistaken sometimes."

She smiled at me quietly, and said no more.

The next day, a bottle of orange juice was standing on Mr Collett's table. Bless him, I thought, he must have made a special shopping journey on my account. I wanted to ask him about his sons, but decided it would be better left unasked. He could tell me if he wished to. I asked him to tell me more about his early life in Croydon, and about his family.

"It was a good life for children. Croydon was a small place in the countryside, then. There were fields and farmhouses around, and streams where the children played. We were poor, but not so poor as many, and my mother was always a good manager. She could make a meal out of a bone, she could, and my father kept an allotment so we always had fresh vegetables. But it all came to a tragic end."

279

He paused, cut off another chunk of tobacco, and filled his pipe. I bandaged up his first leg, and started the second.

"What happened?" I asked.

"My father died. The scaffolding on the building where he was working collapsed. Five men were killed. It was due to slip-shod workmanship on the part of the scaffold builders. There was no compensation for the wives and children of the dead men. My mother could not pay the rent, and we had to get out of the house. It was a nice house," he added, reflectively, and sucked his pipe. Clouds of smoke filled the room.

"I don't rightly remember where we moved to, but it was smaller and cheaper. We kept on moving to smaller and smaller places. I was thirteen, and the eldest of the children. I left school at once, and tried to get work but in 1890 there was no work." He told me how he tramped for miles trying for anything: on the land, on building sites, with horses, on the railways. But there was nothing. "The only job I could get was in the yard where my father used to break stones in the bad weather. But it was piece-work, and I wasn't really old enough or strong enough to break the granite boulders. I hardly got anything for a day's hard labour. I remember my mother cried when she saw me at the end of the day. She said, 'You are not going to do this, my son. I'm not going to have you die as well.' The men were rough, you know, really rough, and they were all swinging fifteen pound sledgehammers. Most of them were drunk. It would have been an unfortunate

280

accident if a lad of thirteen was hit by mistake for a stone."

I undid the second bandage. "So what did the family do?" I asked.

"We came up to London. I don't know why; perhaps my mother was told there was more chance of work for her, or for me. We came here, to Alberta Buildings. I can see the flat from where I am now — that one on the fifth floor, second from the end, by the stairway. It was just one room, like this one, but no water or lavatory, of course. I think there was gaslight, when we could afford to use it. The advantage was that it was cheap, but even at only three and sixpence a week my mother had to work day and night in order to keep a roof over our heads. From the day my father died, I never saw my mother when she wasn't working." With the childhood memories flooding back to him, he described how his mother did cleaning by day, portering, and took in washing and ironing. There were good washhouses at Alberta Buildings in those days, he said. On top of that she took in mending for the secondhand clothes dealers, did umbrella stitching in the winter and parasol making in summer.

He went on to tell me how she applied to the Poor Board for relief, but was told she was not of the Parish, and to go back where she came from. As a special concession, the chairman offered to take three of her children, saying that she would then be relieved of the burden of having to feed them, and would have only five children to feed. The three children would be put in the workhouse. When his mother refused, they called

281

her ungrateful and improvident, and told her that she need not trouble herself to come back, because the offer would not be repeated. They sent her away, saying she would have to manage as best she could.

"She did manage, but I don't know how. She kept a roof over our heads, and provided just enough food to keep us from starving. But we seldom had a fire, even in the coldest weather. We never had shoes, and our clothes were thin, of poor quality and mostly in rags. All the families around us were as poor, and it was made far worse by drunkenness. Most of the men drank, and this could cause awful violence in the home. Many women were in such despair that they drowned themselves. Every week the cry would go up 'A body in the Cuts', and it was always a woman. Every child's greatest terror was that mother would drown herself, if she was pushed beyond the end of her tether."

He sat thinking for a while, puffing his pipe, and chuckled.

"It's a funny thing, you know, but children accept everything when they feel loved and secure. In spite of being cold and hungry, my brothers and sisters were always laughing, always playing out in the court, always inventing new games. I never heard any of them complain. But I was different. I was thirteen when my father died, and I remembered the old life and hated our new one. I hated seeing my dear mother working eighteen or twenty hours a day for a pittance. She would sit late into the night, sewing shirts by candlelight, in a freezing room, with no food inside her, all for sixpence. I resented the injustice of it. Of course

I was out each day looking for work, but times were hard and the best I could find were odd jobs, like holding a horse, or running errands, or sweeping out a yard.

"I tried to get work in the docks. You would think there was plenty of work in London's docklands, wouldn't you? Well, there was, but there were thousands and thousands of men after this work. I reckon there were ten men for one job all the time. There was no chance for a young boy like me."

Such jobs as there were went mostly in those days to the boys whose fathers and grandfathers had been dockers all their lives, Mr Collett explained. There were frightening scenes at the dock gates: hundreds of half-starved labourers, clad in rags, crazed and desperate, fighting for the chance of a few hours' work. Perhaps fifty would be taken on for the day. Five hundred would be turned away to idle their time in the streets. No wonder men were violent.

"At low tide there was always scavenging to be done in the mud. Some lads found things of value, but I never did. The best I found was bits of coal, washed off the barges, and driftwood. At least that made a fire for the evening.

"The worst thing was the suspicion meted out by the gentry. I was looking for honest work, but I was called 'ragamuffin', 'varmin', 'lout', 'thieving dog'. Because I was thin and ill-clothed and looked hungry, they assumed I was a thief."

Mr Collett's mouth tightened. His proud face stiffened at the memory of insult. I had finished his second leg and sat on my heels looking up at him, thinking that the accumulated experience of old age is much more interesting than that of the young, who have experienced very little.

I had a glass of orange juice, whilst he drank a cup of tea. It had been a good compromise, because he gave me a glass which was dusty, but not filthy.

I was enjoying his company and conversation and didn't want to leave him, as he seemed so happy. On impulse I said:

"I must go now, but it's my evening off tonight. Can I come and have a glass of sherry with you, and you can continue your stories?"

The joy on his face answered my question.

"Can you come, my maiden? Can you come? I'll say you can come, and a thousand times welcome."

Young Joe

Cycling back to Nonnatus House I had misgivings about my quixotic suggestion of returning in the evening. All medical people are warned about the difficulties that can develop from forming friendships with patients. It is not something which is forbidden, but it is discouraged, for very good reasons. So after lunch I spoke to Sister Julienne in private. She didn't look disapproving, or even particularly concerned.

"Well, having said you will go this evening, you cannot possibly fail him. That would be needlessly cruel. I think he is a lonely old gentleman and your visit will give him pleasure. Enjoy yourself. He is a very interesting old man, I have found."

With Sister Julienne's blessing, all my misgivings vanished and I cycled round to Alberta Buildings at about 8p.m. with a light heart.

The smell nearly knocked me back when he opened the door. I took a good gulp of clean fresh air, and entered. He was so obviously overjoyed that I had come, that he seemed nervous. He had gone to some trouble, and put on a clean shirt and waistcoat. The dirty plates and mugs and newspapers had been removed from the table, and two fine crystal glasses and half a bottle of sherry put out in readiness. The fire burned brightly, casting flickering shadows over the dingy walls. He said, "I was so afraid you wouldn't come, but you are here."

He walked slowly and carefully over to his chair.

"You're here. It's good to have you. Sit down. It's so nice to see you."

I was overwhelmed and a bit embarrassed by all this, and sat down awkwardly, not knowing quite what to say. He said, almost nervously, "You've come. You are here. Ah, this is so lovely."

Obviously I had to say something. "Yes, I've come. Of course I have. I'm not going to run away, so let's have a glass of sherry, and we can talk about old times."

He laughed with delight and went towards the table, taking up the bottle. He felt around for the glasses and I moved to help him, but he said. "No, no, I can do it. I have to all the time, you know."

He poured out two glasses. His hands shook a little and he spilled a considerable quantity on the table, of which he was unaware. I realised that spilled food and liquid would probably account for much of the smell in the room. The rest was likely to be an uncleaned lavatory, unwashed clothes and the bugs that infested Alberta Buildings. I wondered if he had a home help.

But I wasn't going to think about that sort of thing. If he was unaware of, and quite content with his dirt, why should I criticise? Sister Julienne had told me to enjoy myself, and that I was going to do. I took a sip of the sherry, and said,

"Lovely. This is a cosy room, and you know how to make a nice fire. You were telling me about your childhood. I'd love to hear more."

He settled down comfortably in his wooden chair, and put his feet on the stool (ulcerated legs have to be kept raised as much as possible). He pulled out his shag and his penknife, and started cutting it up. I inhaled a sniff of the strong tobacco. He took a sip of his sherry.

"This is luxury. When I was young I could never have dreamed of such luxury. A fire every day! A warm bed at night! Enough food to eat! A welfare state that pays my rent because I am too old to work, and pays me a pension of ten shillings and sixpence a week, to buy all that I need, including a bottle of sherry when I want it! This is luxury my poor, dear mother never knew until the day she died."

He was cutting up his shag slowly and carefully, holding it in the palm of his left hand, and drawing the knife downwards. It looked alarming, as though he was going to cut his hand, because the tobacco was clearly tough, and needed a lot of pressure. But from long practice he knew just when to ease the pressure, and he never cut himself. He worked by feel, not by sight. He slowly unravelled strands of the villainous-looking stuff with which he filled the bowl of his pipe. He took a wooden spill, about eight inches long, from a pot at his side and stuck it into the fire. It burned up brightly, the flame leaping high into the air. He brought it towards him, sucking hard on the pipe, and the flame dipped downwards into the tobacco. He sucked and puffed contentedly, and smoke filled the air. Then he blew the flame out, and returned the half-burned spill to the pot.

"Sheer luxury," he said, smiling contentedly. "I was telling you about our first years in Poplar, after my father died; how my poor mother had to work day and night; and how I couldn't find work, except odd jobs, to help her. Well, there was one job I got, which was real good fun, for a lad who's looking for adventure.

"I was down Blackwall Steps, waiting for the tide to go out, so that I could go scavenging. A man came along and said to me:

'Here, boy, can you cook a stew?'

'Yes, sir,' I said (I would have said 'yes' to anything).

'Can you skin a rabbit?'

'Yes, sir.'

'Bone a fish?'

'Yessir.'

'Make tea and cocoa?'

'Yessir'.

'Clean a wick and fill a lamp?'

'Yessir.'

'You're the boy I want. My cabin boy's done a bunk. Can you sail today?'

'Anywhere, sir.'

'Be here at high tide. The British Lion's the barge you want. A florin a week all found.'

"It was all so quick I hadn't time to take breath. I raced back to Alberta Buildings, round to the wash-house where my mother was toiling away, and told her I had been hired as cabin boy on a Thames barge. My mother didn't look as thrilled as I had

288

expected. In fact, she was dead against it. We had words, and I shouted at her: 'Look, I'm off, whatever you say, and I'll come back a rich man. You'll see.'

"So I ran back to the Steps, no extra clothes, nothing like that. Sure enough, at high tide, the British Lion comes along, and I jumps aboard.

"It was the most wonderful time I ever had in my life, and I reckon every boy's dream. I was on the River for six months. The barge carried flints, coal, wood, bricks, sand, slates, anything. We would take a load of coal down to Kent, and pick up a cargo of bricks to bring back to Limehouse. In those days hundreds of trading vessels plied the River, huge ocean-going cargo boats down to little one-man skiffs. You could always tell a barge by the red sail, and often the sail and the cabin were all that could be seen. The barges were so low that, with a load, the whole deck would be under water. It's true."

He heard my incredulous gasp. He roared with laughter, and sucked his pipe.

"People would stare from the banks, because honestly, all they could see was a red sail, and men paddling about knee deep in water, with nothing apparently beneath them."

"I was as happy as a boy could be," he continued with another laugh. "I made the stews, trimmed the lamps, learned boat handling, and didn't mind I wasn't paid. The skipper always said he would pay after the next trip. After a bit, the mate whispered to me, 'That bloody monkey's not goin' 'a pay you. He never does. All the cabin boys do a bunk in the end.'

"That was a shock to me, that was. I had been counting up the florins in my mind, and had reckoned on £1 after working ten weeks, and £2 after twenty weeks. I thought I was rich — except that I hadn't got the money. So I asked the skipper and he said, 'After the next trip, lad. When I'm in funds.'

"Well, the next trip came and went, and no money. Three or four more trips — no money. I got cross and resentful and told him if he didn't pay me, I'd do a bunk. He just smiled pleasantly, and said, 'After the next trip, Joe, the next trip, trust me.'

"Well, of course, I knew he wouldn't, and the next time we reached Limehouse, I left the barge and didn't go back."

He paused, and sucked on his pipe, but it had gone out, so he scratched around in the bowl with a sharp implement that he pulled from his penknife, and lit another spill from the fire. The flame lept upwards again, narrowly missing his eyebrows. I thought with alarm that he might set himself, and the whole building, on fire. His eyesight was not good, and his hands shook. I wondered how many old men in a similar state of infirmity were playing with fire in Alberta Buildings that night. But he was speaking again.

"If I had known what I was doing, I don't think I would have left the barge, pay or no pay. You see, I was happy, and busy, which a boy needs. The skipper and his mate were nice men. We got on all right. I had enough food to eat, and a bunk to sleep on. What more can you ask in life? What does money matter? The trouble was, the skipper had hired me for a florin a week, so I was expecting it. When I didn't get it, I was resentful. If he'd asked me in the first place to join him to learn boatmanship, and navigation, with no pay while I was learning, I would have accepted. And my mother would have been pleased. But he lied to me, and that was his mistake, and my misfortune."

Joe left, fully expecting to find a similar job on another barge. But there were no jobs. The other barges supported just a skipper and a mate, but no cabin boy only because the skippers could not afford to pay a boy. The British Lion only had the luxury of a boy because he was never paid. Joe hung around the water's edge, and haunted the wharfs and jetties every day, begging to be taken on, but in vain.

After six months on the River, he was tanned and strong from long hours of work in the fresh air. He had trapped rabbits and caught fish, or pinched carrots and turnips from fields on the water's edge. He had grown taller and filled out, with good food inside him. The dense population of Poplar, the stuffy buildings and crowded streets suffocated him, and the lack of fresh air and sunlight nearly drove him to despair. Food was scarce, and he grew pale and thin with hunger.

On the barge, he had held himself upright, and his eyes sparkled with the pride of his position as cabin boy. Returning to the streets of Poplar, he slouched and dragged his feet, his eyes dull and downcast. Worst of all was his state of mind as it dawned upon him that he was one of the myriad flotsam drifting around the docklands, unwashed, under-fed, ill-clothed, barely educated, with no realistic hope of anything better. He was fifteen.

Of all the jobs that a boy could aspire to, casual dock labour was one of the least viable and most depressing. Joe could, and no doubt should, have looked further afield, but after a taste of river life and the thrill of handling cargo, he saw himself as a River Man. Most days, he would linger round the dock gates with a crowd of seedy, hungry, ignorant men, waiting for the chance of a job, if anything was left over after the regular dock hands had been employed. This seldom occurred and when it did, the older, tougher men got the work.

His poor mother worried about him, naturally. It had been a joy to see him fit, taller, stronger, after six months on the barge. When she learned that he had been cheated of his pay, she was justifiably furious. But there was nothing anyone could do, so she wisely said little, being thankful to have her son back, looking so well. But as the months passed, and she saw the degrading effects of poverty and unemployment biting deep, her worries increased. Furthermore, she had to feed him. She earned her money mainly from washing. The two eldest girls had left school and worked in a shirt-making factory. Joe knew that he was fed on sweated female labour, and his proud young heart rebelled at the knowledge. At thirteen he had seen himself taking his father's role and supporting the family. Now, two years later, he had to acknowledge that not only had he provided nothing, but that he was a burden on the female wage-earners.

"It was when I was at my lowest that I met the recruiting sergeant," he said. "But what time is it? I've been sitting here, talking nineteen to the dozen, and you, bless your heart, listening, as though an old boy rambling on can be interesting to you. You mustn't mind me. I don't often get the chance to talk. I hope I haven't bored you."

At that moment the grandfather clock sounded, solemn and stately, the quarter hour.

"What time is that? Quarter past ten?"

"No. Quarter past eleven."

"Eleven! It can't be. Oh, how time flies when you are enjoying yourself. I've talked far too much, and you must go, my maid. You've got a day's work to do tomorrow, and need your beauty sleep."

I had to assure him that he hadn't talked too much, that he couldn't possibly be a bore, that I was fascinated by his story and that I hadn't enjoyed myself so much for ages. Nonetheless, I had to go, but would certainly have another sherry with him, for the pleasure of his company, and in anticipation of hearing about the recruiting sergeant.

As I stood up, I glanced upwards above the fireplace. I was surprised to see a large area of the chimney breast black — about two feet in an irregular circular shape. In addition, it seemed to be moving slightly, or shimmering, like oil on a damp surface. I had not noticed this earlier, and curiosity compelled me to take a couple of steps nearer, to see what it was.

I saw, and I recoiled with horror, my hand over my mouth, to prevent a scream escaping. The moving mass

293

was thousands of bugs. I had heard that Alberta Buildings were infested with house bugs, but had not seen them before. They were behind the plaster of the walls and ceilings, where they crept along, infesting every level and every flat. They came out at night, attracted by the heat. It was impossible to get rid of them. Only with the demolition of the Canada Buildings, a few years later, were the bugs destroyed.

I stood there, rooted to the spot, my eyes darting around me to other areas of the room, feeling these vile creatures were everywhere, and would get on me. I imagined I was itching. My mind flitted to a horrible incident during my nurse training when an old gypsy woman was admitted to the ward on which I worked. She was gnarled and weather-beaten, and her long grey-black hair was matted and unwashed. On the third morning after her admission, the white pillow was entirely black, and we found it to be literally covered with fleas. Thousands of them had hatched from the eggs in her hair, due to the warmth of the hospital ward. I was one of the young nurses who had to clean her up. She was aggressively resistant, and fleas were hopping everywhere. It took days to get rid of them, and to rid ourselves of fleas. No wonder I began itching all over when I saw the bugs.

Mr. Collett could see neither the bugs on the wall nor the expression on my face, which was just as well. He rose, smiling, and held out his hand to say goodbye. With great difficulty I controlled myself and said goodbye, with renewed thanks for a lovely evening.

294

Outside, I shuddered and shivered, as much from shock as from the cold air after the warm room. I got on my bike and rode back to Nonnatus House. A hot bath was the only thing on my mind.

The Recruiting Sergeant

Bugs were creeping and crawling through my dreams during half the night and seriously disturbed my sleep. I was dreaming of a huge scaly creature getting bigger and bigger. It was poised to jump on me. It opened its horrible jaws and let out a ferocious 'Aaaarrrgh'. I awoke with a scream. It was the alarm clock. Shaken and trembling, I looked fearfully around the walls. No bugs. I pulled back the curtains and examined the whole room. None. "I can't go back there," I thought, "it's too horrible."

At breakfast, pale and heavy eyed, I picked at my cornflakes, my fingers twitching nervously.

"What the hell's the matter with you?" said Trixie, sharply. "I thought you had been to see an old man of nearly eighty last night. Or did we get it wrong? Was he nearly eighteen?"

"Oh shut up, you cynical cat," I muttered crossly, and told the girls about the bugs. They gasped with horror and Trixie, being the most affected, threatened to strangle me if I said another word. Cynthia gazed at me in silent sympathy, and Chummy said: "Great

Jehosaphat! how perfectly ghastly. What did you do, actually?"

A suppressed sound came from somewhere in the region of the boiler. It was a gurgling, spluttering sound, like a valve leaking. We had forgotten Fred, the boilerman and odd-job man for the convent, who was crouched on the floor among the ashes. The splutterings got louder and more frequent, ending in a long, drawn-out wheeze. I could see that Fred understood and sympathised with my experience. But did he? He took a deep breath, threw back his head, and bellowed with laughter. His eyes watered. He coughed, and the fag shot off his lower lip to a distance of three or four feet. His skinny body fell forward onto his knees, and he shook with laughter and coughing. He took a grimy handkerchief from his pocket, wiped his eyes, blew his nose, and spluttered.

"You girls will be the death of me, you will. Cor bli'! I'll shi' me breeks if you goes on like vis. You wai' till I tells ve ol' girl. She'll pee 'er drawers, she will. Likes a good laugh, she do, bu' can never' old 'er water, poor soul."

I was deeply offended. This was not a suitable reaction to my experience. Fred saw my expression, and went off into another paroxysm of wheezing and coughing.

"Wha' a lo' o' fuss abou' a few bugs!" he exclaimed when he could speak.

"There weren't a few, there were thousands," I said indignantly.

"Great Jehosaphat! how perfectly ghastly. Tell me, what did you do, actually?" he said wickedly, mimicking Chummy's genteel and plummy accent. She coloured deeply, and looked uncomfortable. Most of the Cockneys made fun of Chummy's accent, but Fred had not done so before. She was hurt, and I felt cross with Fred on her account.

"I didn't do anything," I said sharply. "It's none of your business anyway, and I assure you it was perfectly ghastly, so there."

He curled up again in another paroxysm of laughter.

"All righ', all righ', Miss Perfic'ly Ghastly, keep yer wig on, but don' ask me 'a git worked up. I've seen them bugs too offen 'a gi' excited."

The Sisters at that moment entered the kitchen, and wanted to know what was going on. I gave a graphic account, dwelling on the vast numbers of bugs, and my sleepless night, perhaps a little exaggerated.

If I had expected cries of sympathy and horror, I was to be disappointed. Sister Evangelina humphed.

"Well there are bugs in all the tenements and in many of the houses. I'm surprised you haven't seen them before. Don't make a fuss. They won't hurt you."

Sister Bernadette added, "I was delivering a baby one night, by gas light. I looked up and the gas mantle, which was fixed to the wall, had a circle of black around it, just as you have described. This was on the wall over the woman's bed!"

Sister Julienne, who had kept her hand firmly over her mouth, to prevent herself from laughing, I suspected, especially after Fred winked at her, said:

"It's a bit of a shock to us all, when we first see them. You have to understand that they live in buildings, and do not infest human beings. Their real danger is that they are suspected of carrying typhoid, but as there has not been an outbreak of typhoid since the nineteen thirties, I think you are quite safe. As for your never going back there, I'm afraid it is out of the question. You are going back this morning, to treat Mr Collett's legs."

With that she left the kitchen to start her morning's work.

I dug my nails into the palm of my hand and clenched my teeth. I had hoped to be relieved of treating Mr Collett. If he had been told that another nurse would be taking my place, he would have had to accept it, and not see me again. What could I do? Nothing. Sister Julienne was as firm as she was saintly. I had no choice but to go back. I realised I would have to take a firm grip on myself. Cynthia whispered to me, "Come on. Let's go to the clinical room, away from Fred." Her warm, soft voice was reassuring, but her first words unexpected.

"Now come off it. This isn't like you to get so worked up. If bugs are in all the tenements, we must work with them all the time, only we don't see them. Out of sight, out of mind. Now forget it. You will probably never see them again."

I knew she was right. Her slow, gentle grin put everything into perspective, and we laughed together as we got our bikes out and pumped up the tyres. District work tends to blow the cobwebs away.

299

Mr Collett was smiling and happy when he opened the door.

"Welcome, my lassie, and I hope you had a good night's sleep. Last evening was the happiest time I have had for ages."

I didn't tell him I was awake half the night, but wondered what his thoughts would have been if I had never come back. He would have suspected something, and supposed himself to blame. I didn't like to think of the hurt he would have suffered.

As I undid the bandage, I remarked: "These ulcers are improving — why did you not have regular treatment before?"

"Well, I didn't like to bother anyone. I've had them for years, and always bandaged them myself. I had to see the doctor about my eyes, and he saw I was limping a bit and asked to see my legs. Then he arranged for you Sisters to come. I didn't ask for treatment. I never thought they were bad enough."

They were the worst leg ulcers I had seen, and he didn't think they were bad enough to justify a nurse's treatment!

I asked him how they started.

"It was gun wounds during the war. They healed up all right, but there was always a weakness. As I got older, little patches started, and then spread. But I can't grumble. My legs have been good to me most of my life. You can expect these little things as you get old."

Little things, I thought, I don't call these ulcers 'little'!

The mention of gun wounds made me think of the recruiting sergeant, who had been driven from my mind by the bugs.

"Last night, before I left, you said you would tell me how you met the recruiting sergeant."

He settled back comfortably in his big wooden chair.

"Well, I was fifteen, going on sixteen, and I reckon if I hadn't met him, it would have been a life of crime for me. There was no work, and I met a lad who was into everything. He always seemed to have money. He was younger than me, but quicker and smarter. We palled up together. I'm not going to tell you what we did, because I'm not proud of it, but one day he suggested going up the West End, where the pickings would be better. I'd never been up West before. I remember feeling dazzled by the great buildings, the fine open streets, all the carriages, and ladies and gentlemen in their fine clothes. We went to Trafalgar Square and hung around. My eyes were popping out, especially at the sight of the soldiers in their crimson jackets and black trousers. One of them came over to where we were standing by a fountain. I was so flattered; I couldn't believe he wanted to talk to us."

He chuckled and blew a cloud of smoke across the room.

"I thought it was a special honour. No-one had told me they were at it every day, on the look out for lads like me.

" 'Nah then, nah then, my fine young man' (he was talking to me, not to my mate). 'Aint a fine young man like you got nothing to do on a day like this?'

301

"I must have shrugged and grinned sheepishly.

" 'Well then, did you ever see a soldier with nothing to do?'

"I hadn't, but then I had never seen soldiers before, and I was struck dumb with the honour of having this splendid figure of a man single me out for conversation.

"And then he asked me what I'd had for breakfast.

"Nothing, I said.

" 'Nothing!' he roared, 'nothing! I've never heard nothing like it. Did you say *nothing*?'

"I nodded.

" 'No wonder you're looking a bit skinny, begging your pardon for the liberty, squire, but one can't help noticing these things Look at me, now.'

"He patted a well-filled stomach with appreciation.

" 'Bacon and liver, and brawn and kidneys, with fresh farm eggs, and field mushrooms. As much bread and dripping as a man can eat, with beer if your tastes run to beer at breakfast, or tea and coffee, with fresh cream and sugar from Barbados. That's the sort of breakfast a man needs to line his stomach for the day. And did you tell me you had *nothing*? This is unbelievable. Unbelievable.'

"He shook his head as though he honestly had never heard anything like it and found it hard to believe.

" 'Well now, young man, you come along with me. A special friend of mine runs an ale house over there. As a great favour to me, I'm sure he can find you something to fill your stomach with. He's got a kind heart, he has, and when I tells him that my friend — if I can make so bold as to call you my friend — has had no breakfast, it will fair melt his tender old heart, it will . . . No, not you . . .' he said to my mate who had edged forward at the mention of breakfast. He put his hand on my shoulder and led me to the ale house.

"It was dark and smoky inside and, after the sunlight, I couldn't see anything, but the soldier led me to a table and sat me down.

" 'Bill' he roared, 'Bill. Does a man have to wait all day for a pint of porter? Look lively, man.'

"The fat, well-fed figure of the landlord emerged out of the gloom.

" 'A pint of your best for me, and for my friend — er — why, bless my soul, can you believe it, I don't even know your name. I've felt so comfortable with you, like I've known you all my life, but I don't even know your name.'

"I'm Joe Collett.

" 'Joe! What a coincidence. My young brother's called Joe. And a tall, handsome young man he is, just like you. Oh, what a lad he is, my brother Joe. Such larks! Remember the larks we've had in here with Joe, eh, Bill? Those were the days. My young brother Joe joined the Dragoons, and now he's a Commanding Officer, with a servant and a carriage at his pleasure, and as much money as he knows how to spend. But I was forgetting. Now, Bill, my old mate, my young friend Joe has had a bit of a night of it, and unfortunately has missed his breakfast.'

"The landlord sounded astonished.

" 'Missed his breakfuss? A man can't get through the day without a good breakfuss 'a warm him. That's terrible, that is.' He patted his large belly, and he looked at me with a very sympathetic face.

"The sergeant winked suggestively.

" 'There! I knew as how you'd see the gravity of the sitivation, Bill. I says to young Joe over by the fountain there, I'll take you over to my mate Bill, I said, and he'll see you right. Now what have you got out the back there that you've got a bit of spare of, that would satisfy young Joe? Not nothing too flash, like, because he ain't got much money on him at present.'

" I was alarmed. I hadn't got *any* money. But before I could speak, the landlord said, 'call it on the 'ouse, Sarj, on the 'ouse. It's an honour to entertain a Guardsman any time. And any friend of yours is a friend of mine. Now, young sir, would tripe, and faggots, and a good chunk of last night's pease pudding fried up crispy-like, suit you?'

"I couldn't believe my luck. It sounded like a meal fit for a king.

" 'Oh, an' do you like bread and drippin', young sir?'

"I loved bread and dripping!

"The meal arrived, and it was enough for two kings. I just ate and ate. The sergeant didn't say anything. He just smoked his pipe and drank his porter, and looked out of the window at the pigeons squabbling on the window sill.

"When I had finished, he said,

" 'You were hungry, lad.'

"I nodded. And I thanked him warmly.

" 'Don't thank me, lad. You heard what the landlord said — it's an honour to entertain a Guardsman. We gets that all the time, we do. We gets used to it. Treated like royalty, we are, wherever we go. No-one can do enough for us. Did you ever see a soldier hungry? Course not.'

"He puffed his pipe, and called for another pint of porter, saying, confidentially. 'Between ourselves, the ale in this house is rather special. Old Bill brews it himself. If you are a konosser of good ales, young squire, and I am sure you are, I don't think you will be disappointed. Unless, of course, you prefer coffee after breakfast.'

"What a suggestion to a fifteen-year-old, going on sixteen!

"Bill brought two pints of porter, and we became more confidential. I told the sergeant my father was dead.

"'Oh, your poor mother,' the Sergeant said, huskily, pulling out a handkerchief. 'My father died when I was a young lad — much younger than you, of course. I was sixteen when my father died, and my poor mother had a life of hard, hard work in order to keep us.' He blew his nose and dabbed his eyes. 'What would a man do without his mother? She sacrifices everything to bring up her family, and does without herself. A man can't do enough to repay his mother, he can't. My mother's settled comfortably in a nice little cottage in the country, which me and my brother John got her with our army pay.'

"'I thought your brother was Joe.'

"'I mean Joe. John's the other brother I haven't told you about. Here Bill, more ale, and look lively.'

" 'Did you say a cottage in the country?'

"He nodded.

" 'Yerse. It was the least we could do for our poor old mum. My brother Joe and me (he's a good lad, he is) we saves up our army pay, and now she lives like a princess, our old mother does. Wants for nothing.'

"I thought of my mother, sitting up half the night, mending for a rascally second-hand clothes dealer; going out at five in the morning to clean offices, and then toiling all day over the wash tub. I said, 'How do you get into the army?'

"He looked surprised, and raised his eyebrows.

" 'Oh, was you thinking of an army career, then?'

"I nodded. 'But how do you get in?'

"He drew his chair closer to mine, and lowered his voice.

" 'It's not easy. I can tell you that for a start. You needs hinfluence. It's not what you knows, but who you knows, as the saying goes. It's a lucky day for you, squire, that you met me, because I've taken a real fancy to you, seeing as you are like my young brother Joe. How old are you, Joe? Seventeen, eighteen, eh?'

" 'Seventeen,' I said. It was a lie, I was fifteen.

" 'I thought as much. A good judge of age, I am. It's lucky for you, you are seventeen, because you couldn't get into the army if you was only sixteen.'

"He leaned closer, and muttered out of the side of his mouth: 'Is your health good? No nasties, nothing like that, I take it?'

"I said my health was good.

" 'Are you a Christian? The army won't have none of them heathens and hatheists.'

"I said I was Church of England.

" 'Now, you're an intelligent lad, I can see that. Can you write your name?'

"I said I had been at school full time until I was thirteen.

" 'A scholar, my word. With your education, sir, you will rise to the rank of Brigadier General, you will.'

"He stretched out his hand, and took my porter from me, and drank it himself.

" 'If you are going to put pen to paper, young sir, you will need a steady hand. All the edification in the world is not going to help if your hand is shaking, on account of too much strong porter before lunch. Where was you planning lunch, by the way? Perhaps I can join you?'

"I said I hadn't any plans, but I was thinking about joining the Army, and how could I do it?

"He leaned closer, and tapped his nose. He looked all around, before whispering,

" 'It's your lucky day, lad. I reckons as how I can help. I knows where the recruiting office is sitivated, and if I recommends you to the company's Commanding Officer — I'm very well thought of in higher command, I am — I reckons you would be in with a chance. Without me you haven't a hope. They'd turn you away as soon as look at you, they would. Come on, let's go.'

"Out in the sunlight, I blinked, and lowered my head from the glare, but the sergeant turned on me.

"'Right now, Guardsman Joe — what did you say your name was? Collett? I must remember that — Collett. Guardsman Collett, stand up straight. Throw your head and shoulders back. Breathe deep, chest out. The Soldiers of the Queen don't slouch around the place. Now, pick your feet up. Left, right, left, right. Eyes straight ahead. Left, right.'

"We marched across the square at a cracking speed. People fell aside. Everyone looked at us. I felt so proud. We passed my mate, who just gawped. I didn't turn my head to look at him.

"We entered the recruiting office, and the sergeant snapped his heels together with a crack like a whip, and shot his right arm up in salute to the Officer who stepped forward.

"'Sar. Mr Joseph Collett, sar. Aged seventeen. Good health. Good education. Father dead, sar. Wants to be a soldier, sar. Highly recommended, sar.'

"There was a lot of saluting and 'sar-ing', and heel snapping, and the Sergeant said,

"'Right, young Joe. I'll leave you with the Commanding Officer. I'll be off now. Good luck, lad.'

"And I never saw him again."

With bewildering speed Joe was hustled into the medical room, and asked to stick his tongue out, and to drop his trousers. A doctor gave him a quick look over, and passed him as fit. He was taken to a desk and told to write his name and address at the top of a printed form, then to sign his name at the end of the page. Confused but confident, Joe did so.

"Guardsman Collett, you are now a soldier in Her Majesty's Scots Guards. You will receive full uniform, full rations, full billetting, and a shilling a day. Here is a travel warrant to take you from Waterloo to Aldershot, which will be your first camp. You may go home now to tell your mother and collect your personal belongings. The last train from Waterloo goes at 10p.m. If you are not on it, remember, you are now a fully enlisted guardsman, and failure to report at barracks will be counted as desertion, which is punishable by a flogging and six months in prison on bread and water. Here is your first day's pay of one shilling. Now follow the uniform sergeant downstairs where you will be fitted with boots and uniform. Stand to attention, Guardsman Collett, and salute when you are leaving a superior officer."

In the wardrobe room Joe was fitted up with full uniform and boots. He looked exceedingly handsome in the scarlet jacket and black trousers, and he gazed at his reflection with barely suppressed joy. He put the shilling and his travel warrant in his pocket, and was given a brown paper parcel containing his old clothes. He was given directions as to how to get to Waterloo Station and, with dire warnings about prison and flogging if he failed to turn up, was sent on his way.

Joe marched all the way back to Poplar, his newly acquired military swagger getting stronger with every step. His buttons gleamed, his boots shone, his red tunic dazzled the eye. People stood aside. Older men touched their caps. Small boys marched beside him, imitating his step. Best of all, young girls giggled and whispered and tried to attract his attention. But 'eyes straight ahead', as ordered by the recruiting sergeant, was Joe's rule, and never once did he glance back, however enticing the female attentions. Girls had never looked at him before. 'A soldier's life is the life for me' — and his young heart sang in tune to his step.

He marched into the court of Alberta Buildings, round to the wash-house, and flung open the door. The chatter stopped and a gasp of admiration went up from the women at the wash tubs. But his mother had her back to him. Turning round, she gazed uncomprehendingly at the figure in the doorway, staring for a few seconds, as though not recognizing him. Then a low moan escaped her lips, rising to a high, terrible scream, and she fainted.

Joe rushed forward in alarm. Women crowded round. Water was splashed over her face and neck, and she opened her eyes which, seeing Joe in his scarlet tunic, flooded with tears. She sobbed uncontrollably, unable to speak. A woman said, "You best get her back to your place an' all, Joe. Poor soul. She's that took she can't hardly stand, poor lamb. Oh Joe, you didn't never oughta done it, you never."

Alarmed and bewildered, Joe helped his mother across the cobbled court and up the stone stairway to their flat. Doors opened, and women came out onto the balconies to witness the drama. A neighbour brought in a cup of tea, and gave it to her with the words,

"I've laced it with a drop of something soothing, Mrs Collett, to keep yer strength up. Lor' knows, yer goin' 'a need it," and she gave Joe a nasty, reproachful glance.

His mother drank the tea, and the sobs grew less. When she could speak, Joe asked her why she cried. She clung to him, and rubbed her swollen face on his sleeve.

"A soldier, Joe! My eldest son, my comfort, my hope, a soldier. They draw them in, young men, thousands of them, every year. Cannon fodder, they calls them. 'The scum of the earth'. They draws them in to die."

Tears again flooded her eyes, and she wiped them away with her shawl.

"Go an' ask Mrs Willoughby three doors down if I could have another cup of tha' tea of hers, will you, dear? She's a kind soul, an' won't mind, I knows that. She feels for me. She's lost sons in the Army, she has."

Joe was not merely deflated. He was shattered. He had expected a hero's welcome. He took his jacket off, not wanting to step onto the balcony in scarlet, and fetched another cup of tea, laced with a drop of rum, which many good Poplar housewives kept for moments of crisis.

While gratefully sipping the tea, his mother said: "I had four older brothers, and they all died in the Crimean War. I was only a little girl, and hardly remember them, but I remember my mother crying, and how she never recovered. The dreadful grief seemed to cling to her for the rest of her life. My older sister was engaged to be married to a young man who died at Sebastapol. The suffering was terrible by all accounts. Terrible."

"But the Crimean War was ages ago," Joe protested, "it's all over and done with. The Empire's strong. There are no wars now. No-one would dare to attack the British Empire. And I'm a soldier of the Queen Empress, and proud of it."

She forced a smile.

"You're a good lad, my son, and your mother's a silly old fuss-pot. She's not going to spoil your last afternoon with tears. When do you have to report to barracks?"

He remembered the travel warrant and the shilling in his tunic pocket. He pulled it out and laid it proudly on the table beside her.

"I'm paid a shilling a day and it's all for you. I get my billet and my food and my uniform, so I don't need money. I'll bring it all to you, and you won't want no more."

Poor woman! She cried all over again. What mother wouldn't?

"You must keep some for yourself, my son."

"Nope. Not a penny. I done it for you, and you shall get the pay."

"My boy! Oh, my lad!" She kissed his hands and wiped her tears on his sleeve. "My dear boy. But I fears for you. My heart is heavy. I fears for you."

She finished the tea, and pulled herself together. The rum helped. The children would soon be in from school, and later the girls from the factory. She couldn't present a sniffy face to them.

"You start getting your things together in a bundle, while I go down to the yard to wash my face. Then we'll use your shilling to buy some whelks and a loaf, and some real butter and a saucer of jam for the little ones. We'll have a real feast your last evening at home."

And that is exactly what they did. The younger brothers were over the moon about their big brother's uniform. Each of them tried on the jacket, and the six-year-old pranced around the room with the jacket trailing on the floor and the sleeves flapping wildly. The sisters were agog with admiration. Suddenly Joe had become a man in their eyes. Only the mother was silent, but she kept a brave smile on her face.

Time passed all too quickly. The laughter, the cheers, the songs, had to come to an end. Joe had a train to catch from Waterloo at ten o'clock that night. He dared not miss it.

Army Life

Guardsman Joe Collett arrived at Waterloo Station at 9.30p.m., along with about sixty other young men recruited on that day. Each of them thought that he had been singled out for special consideration by the kindness and favour of a recruiting sergeant. They were all surprised to see each other. None of them knew that the Army was obliged to recruit twelve thousand men each year to make up the numbers, mostly lost through death.

Also at Waterloo Station were around a hundred girls, dressed to kill. Oh, the skirts, the ribbons, the laces, the tucks, the frills and flounces! Oh, the boots with dainty buttons, and the wide brimmed hats, heavy with fruit and flowers and feathers! And what was that Joe saw? Could it be paint? Joe had never seen rouged lips and cheeks before, and he was enchanted.

The girls clung to the soldiers, two or three to each. Some of them carried a phial of gin or rum in their garters, and these were brought out with much skirtrustling and mock modesty. There was only half an hour before the train was due to leave, but the girls knew how to use the time to advantage. Much can happen in half an hour, and each girl knew that the recruits had been paid a shilling that day.

Most of the new recruits had gone alone to the station, but some were accompanied by mothers, aunts or sisters. These young men were put to great embarrassment by the girls, who openly sneered at them, and cast bold, contemptuous eyes on their womenfolk. These good women were scandalised by the wanton behaviour of the girls, and tried to protect and warn their sons, which made matters worse.

Joe, being alone, taller than average and undoubtedly good-looking, was mobbed. He was offered a phial of rum which, laughing, he swallowed in one gulp. It went straight to his head. He clung to a brunette, who cuddled him, and led him round the station, singing. Joe felt he had never been so happy in his life. Two more girls joined them and led him out of the station into the little lanes. It was a quarter to ten. In the lanes the girls cuddled and kissed him, and fondled him all over. In his intoxicated state Joe felt that more than his blood was rising. It was then that the girls discovered that Joe did not have his shilling on him. They screamed with rage. They kicked him and pushed him; he fell against a wall, hitting his head. They tore his jacket off him, frantically going through the pockets, threw it on the ground — Joe's beautiful red tunic — and trampled it in the mud. He cried out, but could not stop them. They pulled his hair and scratched his face until the blood ran. They spat on him. Then they rushed off, with a flick of skirts, around the corner.

Dazed, bewildered, dirty and bleeding, Joe leaned against the wall. He tried to gather his senses, but couldn't think what had happened. His head hurt from the blow against the wall. He was sliding comfortably down the wall, when a sharp noise penetrated his fuddled hearing. What was it? It was repeated. Dear Heaven, it was the train whistle. Aldershot . . . the last train . . . must catch it . . . desertion . . . flogging . . . prison. He snatched up his jacket, nearly falling flat on his face as he did so, staggered towards the station, hurtled towards the moving train, was pushed onto it by a porter and fell into a seat.

"Blimey, mate, you look as if you've had a good time," said his companion, with a sardonic grin, and a slow wink.

The train gathered speed, and Joe fell asleep. He was awakened by a rough hand shaking him.

"Wakey, wakey, Sleeping Beauty. You're a soldier now, and we're at Aldershot. You can dream of her another time."

Aldershot? What was that? Joe woke to see half a dozen grinning faces above scarlet tunics staring at him, and it all came back. He was a soldier now . . . .the Recruiting Sergeant . . . that was it . . . .head up, shoulders back, chest out, breathe deeply, no slouching now. He jerked himself upright, and pain split his head from ear to ear. He groaned. The men roared with laughter.

"He's only a kid, leave 'im be. He'll learn. Here, mate, give us yer arm."

Joe staggered off the train on the arm of his unknown companion, and a Staff Sergeant stepped forward.

"Right men. In line. Roll call. Look sharpish."

The motley group of raw recruits shuffled backwards and forwards, sideways and hitherways, trying to make a line. The Staff Sergeant bellowed and swore and brandished his regimental swagger cane, trying to get them into military line. He was not successful, but had to make do with second best.

"Right, you horrible men. You wait till I get you on the parade ground. You'll damned soon learn how to form a line. Roll call."

An old Duty Sergeant stepped forward with two sheets of paper in his hand, containing lists of names which he proceeded to read out. His reading was not very good. No doubt it would have been better if a Duty Sergeant who could read properly had been sent, but the ability to read was not an accomplishment rated very highly in the army.

He got through several simple names without mishap — Brown, Smith, Cole, Bragg — but then got stuck.

"Warrarramb . . ." he shouted. No-one answered.

"Warrarrnad . . ." Louder. No response.

"What you say?" yelled the Staff Sergeant.

The Duty Sergeant tried to look confident, and shouted "Warrarrandy . . ." No response.

The Staff Sergeant strode over to him, his cane swishing, his boots clicking, and snatched the paper. In the flickering gas light of the station he squinted at the page.

"Warrenden," he shouted. A man stepped forward.

317

Roll call proceeded in this manner. The Duty
Sergeant did his best, but got stuck on Ashcroft,
shouting "Askafoot". Bengerfield, Willowby, Waterton
set him mumbling and stuttering, until everyone
thought roll call would never be finished.

One man was missing. The name was shouted
backwards and forwards several times, but no one
stepped forward. The Staff Sergeant struck the calf of
his leg with his swagger cane and the Duty Sergeant,
with great deliberation, pulled out a stub of pencil and
underlined the name.

"Right men, form a column, four abreast, quick
march."

Forming a column for untrained men is as difficult
as forming a line. The Staff Sergeant swore and cursed
and used his cane liberally, eventually getting some sort
of ragged column together. With "left, right, left, right"
they marched off.

It was four miles to the camp, which did Joe good.
By the time he got there, his head had cleared from the
effects of the rum, and ached only a bit from the crack
on the wall. The night air refreshed him, and the men
surrounding him gave him a feeling of security.

The sentry guards at Aldershot barracks leapt swiftly
to attention when they heard the column approaching.
An incomprehensible word was barked out by the Staff
Sergeant, sounding something like 'awt'. No-one in the
column thought it meant anything and continued
marching. The four at the front were confronted by a
menacing row of Guards, each with bayonet raised at
45 degrees, and pointing directly at their stomachs.

Another step, and they would have been on the bayonets. They halted. The men behind carried on marching, straight into the backs of the men in front. About half the column fell upon each other in this way. The men, being fresh from a sane world where this sort of thing is considered funny, fell about laughing, but the Staff Sergeant failed to see the joke, and swore and raged at their imbecility.

The column re-assembled inside the gates and marched another quarter mile to the billet, a grey rectangular building, four storeys high. A little way from this building the Staff Sergeant shouted.

"In a minute, I am going to say 'halt', and that means 'stop', and when I say 'halt' I want you to stop. Got it?" They continued marching.

"Awt". Half the men stopped, the other half didn't. The result was exactly the same as at the gate. The Staff Sergeant nearly went berserk.

Somehow he managed to re-assemble them. He marched them another fifty yards and shouted 'halt'.

Everyone stopped.

"Right. In line."

This was no easier than it had been on the station. In fact it was harder, because it was pitch dark. Men stumbled and fell over each other, muttering and laughing.

"Silence!" roared the Staff Sergeant.

"Silence yerself, yer bloody windbag," shouted a voice.

"Who said that?" roared the Sergeant.

"Father Christmas," said the voice.

"Corporal, open the door," roared the Sergeant.

The Corporal on duty opened the door of the billet.

"Forward. Quick march," roared the Sergeant, leading the way up four flights of stone steps. At the top, the Corporal in charge of the billet opened the door, and the disorderly line of men entered.

"New recruits, Corporal, and a bigger bunch of stupid bastards I've never met." The Staff Sergeant turned to go. He turned to the men. "You wait. You just bloody wait. You'll wish you'd never been bloody born, you will."

And with those pleasant words, he departed.

I roared with laughter at this story. We both laughed, Mr Collett and I. Nothing unifies and binds people more strongly than the same sense of humour, and the ability to laugh together. I was thoroughly enjoying my evenings of sherry and an old soldier's reminiscences round at Alberta Buildings. The British Army of the 1890s was not something I would have expected to be interesting, but in the firelight, with a good storyteller as my companion, the years became alive, and a young soldier's life of absorbing interest.

I was also aware that Mr Collett had become deeply fond of me, which was touching. One of the pictures on his walls was of a pretty young girl in 1920s dress. I understood that this was his only daughter, who had been killed in the bombing in the Second World War. Perhaps I was becoming a substitute granddaughter to him. I didn't mind. I liked him. He was a dear old man, and reminded me of my grandfather, whom I had loved and admired very deeply, and who had been more of a father to me than my own father. He had died some five years previously at the age of 84, and I still felt the loss. If Mr Collett and I were both substituting another person in our growing affection, it was all right by me.

He refilled my glass.

"Do you like chocolates, my dear? I bought a box of Milk Tray this morning, with you in mind."

He reached to the mantel-shelf, and felt for them. I was still a bit chary about eating anything, because of all the filth around the place, and once, when he had produced a grubby plate of biscuits, which I had seen him drop on the dirty floor and pick up, I had said that I didn't like biscuits. But an unopened box of chocolates was a different matter. Anyway, I loved them. After that, it was always sherry and chocolates. Incidentally, I never saw the bugs again, and after a bit I ceased to look for them.

"So you got to your billet, and your head wasn't too bad. What happened then?"

"We were told to make up our cots. A soldier sleeps in a cot, not a bed. They are constructed in two halves, the bottom half of which pushes into the upper half. This allows for more space during the day in the centre of the billet. The Corporal showed us how to do it. The biscuit, which is a soldier's straw-filled mattress, and two rough blankets, were folded on the top part of the shortened bed. We had no pillows, no sheets. Nothing fancy like that. The Corporal told us the sip-but was on the landing."

"What on earth is a sip-but?" I interrupted.

"Oh, that's back slang for a piss-tub. There's a lot of rhyming slang and back slang in the army. At least there was in my day. It may have been dropped by now.

"I remember my first night very well. It was so new, so exciting, that I couldn't sleep. Apart from which I had a headache from the girls pushing me against the wall. My thoughts were racing . . . those girls, my mother, the Recruiting Sergeant, the Staff Sergeant, the station, the march through the night. I must have dozed off towards dawn and vaguely in my dreams heard a bugle call. Seconds later the Corporal burst into the billet, shouting: 'Show a leg now, get out of it. Open those blasted windows and let some fresh air in. It smells like a bloody farmyard in here. Get out of it now, do you hear me?'

"Perhaps I didn't move, but the next thing I knew was that my cot collapsed, and I landed on the floor. The Corporal had pulled the bottom half away from the top half, which was a very effective way of rousing anyone who did not leap out of bed on the instant the reveille was blown. This was 5 a.m. summer or winter.

"The Corporal ordered us to dress and put away our cots and fold the biscuit and blankets. I was in a daze, but the roar of the Corporal kept me on my toes. He kept bellowing out about the blankets not being folded straight, and how he'd never seen such a useless, slovenly bunch of recruits, and how we would be licked into shape and no mistake. He ordered two men next to the door to carry the sip-but, to empty it down the drains and clean it at the pump where it would be left until the following evening.

" 'Right now. Stand by your cots. This is only the Reception Centre, where you are treated gentle-like. Later you will learn what army life is, when you have been sorted into the Regiments what you have enlisted for. Get me. You will have an hour's drill before breakfast. Then your breakfast, then an hour's parade, then present to the Colour Sergeants for sorting. Got it? Right. In line. Down to the parade ground.'

"We got into some sort of line and filed down the stone stairs. In the darkness outside we could hear from all sides voices rather like the Staff Sergeant's barking out orders. We were put to physical exercises — press-ups, star-jumps, squatting with straight back, step-ups. Imagine all that with a headache and no sleep! But I kept thinking this is better than hanging around the dock gates looking for work, and it was. The last quarter of an hour consisted of the most violent exercise so far — running with knees lifted high at each step. After this, as you can imagine, we were starving for our breakfast. This consisted of dry bread and sweet tea. It tasted delicious. After that we were led to the parade ground for an hour of drill. At 9a.m. a bugle sounded and the Colour Sergeants marched onto the square, each followed by a Duty Sergeant carrying a list of names which they read out in turn. The recruits were sectioned into their Colours, and marched off. This happened every day, because the Recruiting Sergeants were busy enlisting unsuspecting young lads like me every day of the week.

"There were only four Scots Guards recruits that day. It's a crack Regiment." (He said this with great

323

pride, lifting his chin high). "We were taken — in marching order, of course — to the Quartermaster's stores where we were issued with top-coat, cape, leggings, one suit of scarlet, one of blue for drills, boots, shirts, socks, and numerous pieces of regimental dress. We were issued with a rifle, bayonet, and two white buff straps, with pouches that could hold fifty rounds apiece. We were also issued with a busby, the tall fur head dress reserved for Guards. Everyone in the regiment was very proud of these.

"We, the four of us, that is, were shown to a white-washed barrack room overlooking the square. A corporal was in charge of each billet, and a couple of older duty-men also kept billet there. They showed us how to fix straps for drill purposes, how to roll the top-coat and fix it to the kit-bag, how to fix leggings, what cleaning materials we should need, how to place our cape and scarlet top-coat, when not in use, on the racks above our cots, and even how the straps of the kit-bag should hang from pegs above the head of the cot."

The pettiness of it all, the meticulous attention to detail, reminded me of my nurse's training in the 1950s. I told Mr Collett about it. We were issued with three fitted dresses, twelve aprons, five caps and a cape. We were instructed minutely on how they must be worn at all times. Dresses had to be fifteen inches from the floor, no more, no less. Caps, which were flat pieces of starched linen, had to be folded and pinned to an exact shape and size. Aprons had to be pinned at an exact point above the bosom, and adjusted to the precise length of the dress. Shoes had to be black lace-ups, of a specific style, with rubber soles for quietness. Stockings were black, with seams. Belts and epaulettes were of differing colours, distinguishing the different years of training a student nurse had undergone. Full uniform had to be worn at all times when on duty. I recall, in my first year of training, being ordered out of the dining room by a third year nurse, because I had forgotten to put on my cap. Later, when I became a Ward Sister, I forgot my cuffs on one occasion when I went to the Matron's office, and was sent back to the ward to get them before I could address the Matron!

We discussed whether this sort of discipline was necessary. Mr Collett said. "Well, it certainly is for men. Because large numbers of men living together can easily and quickly become like wild animals. Men are brutes at heart, and without the civilising influence of women quickly revert to savagery. The discipline of the armed forces is the only thing that keeps them under control. I wouldn't have thought it was necessary for women, though, would you? But I maintain that nurses always look very lovely, and so therefore I approve of the uniform."

I chuckled at this. There is no doubt in my mind that the nurse's uniform of the early and middle 1900s was just about the sexiest thing ever invented. Nothing has ever surpassed it for allure. I was not the only young nurse to be acutely conscious of a heightened sex appeal when in uniform. Ironically, the draconian old

Sisters and Matrons who rigidly enforced the uniform seemed unaware of the effect it had on the male sex!

Those were the repressive days when student nurses had to live in barrack-like nurses' homes, and be in by 10p.m. No men were allowed, and a nurse who smuggled one in would be dismissed if she was caught. Student nurses could not marry. All this was to repress our sexuality. Yet we were dressed up like sex kittens!

With exquisite irony, in today's permissive society, when anything goes, and nurses can do anything they like sexually, uniform has changed out of all recognition, and the average nurse now looks like a sack of potatoes tied in the middle, often wearing trousers rather than sexy black stockings.

I asked Mr Collett how he coped with all the regulation of army life. Was he as bad as I had been in my early nurse's training? I must have driven Ward Sisters mad. He laughed, and said he didn't believe it.

"But I had a hard time at first. We all did. The Scots Guards prided themselves on being a crack regiment, so we had more hours of drill, rifle and bayonet training, longer marches, and heavier pack-weights than other regiments. Also we had less time off. We were so exhausted in the evening that we seldom went to the wet canteen. Often I just made up my cot at 8.00p.m. and went fast asleep until reveille.

"I had more money than I had ever had. On a shilling a day I was able to send home to my mother four shillings a week. I knew that would pay the rent, and I swore to myself that I would always pay the rent, so that she need never again fear the workhouse. And I kept it up for years and years, even when I married."

I asked him about his marriage.

"Well, after three months at Aldershot, I was given forty-eight hours' leave to go to see my family, before being posted to Plymouth. Across the court of Alberta Buildings lived a girl I had known for years, but she seemed so much more grown up than I had remembered her to be, and I reckon she must have thought the same about me. She was the prettiest little thing I had ever seen in my life."

He chuckled fondly, and slowly refilled his pipe. He rubbed it in his hands, and stroked his cheek with the warm bowl.

"We were only sixteen apiece, and forty-eight hours isn't long, but I knew she was the only girl in the world for me. We reached an understanding that she would wait for me until I was in a position to marry her. Long engagements were common in those days, and couples thought nothing of waiting ten or fifteen years before they could get married. As it happened we had to wait only three years."

He lit a spill from the fire, applied it to the tobacco, and sucked hard. He looked thoughtful.

"It's a damned good thing I did meet my Sally during that forty-eight hours, because the promises we had made kept me clean while I was at Plymouth. It was a lively town, and ten or twelve regiments were garrisoned there, as well as sailors and marines. Pubs and bawdy houses were in every street, and prostitutes at every bar. I learned fast. You do in the Army, and it

327

didn't take long to figure out that if I went with one of them girls I was likely to pick up VD. That would have been the end of my army career, the end of my hopes for winning Sally and the end of the rent for my mother. So I kept myself clean. All the other chaps said I was mad, and I should enjoy myself while I could. But I saw enough of them go into the venereal wards of the sick bay, to know who it was who was mad."

He looked severe, and spat into the fire.

"But hadn't you better go, young lady? Are you going to be locked out at 10 o'clock? I don't want to be the cause of getting you into trouble."

"I will go, but I want to hear about your marriage first," I said eagerly. "It sounds so romantic. Anyway, there are no restrictions with the nuns. They are much too sensible for that. Now tell me about how you got married."

He patted my hand fondly.

"After Plymouth, I was posted to Windsor Castle, as one of Her Majesty's Foot Guards. It was the best posting I had, and I loved it. There wasn't really a lot to do. It was all marching and square drill. There were several hours of sentry duty, day and night, but we relieved each other every two hours, and then we had two hours off, until the next relief. At Windsor Castle I started reading. I knew I was not educated properly, and wanted to do something about it. There was a library in the barracks, and I just took anything I could get hold of. It became a passion with me. The more I read, the more I realised how ignorant I was. I devoured history like other chaps devoured booze. I spent all my spare time reading, and it was a habit that never left me, until my eyes began to go, and it became impossible."

He looked sad, but perked up.

"But I can listen to the wireless. There's nothing wrong with my hearing.

"Anyway, what with one thing and another, I loved it at Windsor Castle. Now, it's a funny thing but in the army, I've noticed, the less work you have to do the more you get paid. We were paid nine pence extra per day for Royal Duties. I was now earning good money, and was able to apply to my Colonel for permission to marry. He said I was too young, but when I told him that I had known the girl since I was thirteen, he relented. Married quarters were sometimes available to soldiers and their wives, and that was what I was after. I wasn't going to get married and have my Sal living in a room in the town, and me in barracks. The Colonel said we would have to wait until a cottage became available, which we did, and within two years Sally and I were married at All Saints Church, Poplar, just over the way there, and I took her down to Windsor soon after. Our twins were born at Windsor Castle, and I was the proudest young father in the Regiment. But our happiness was too good to last. News from South Africa was bad. Infantrymen were being sent out every week. I had a feeling, though I didn't say it to Sal, that my turn would come, and it did. On 1st November 1899 I sailed for South Africa."

South Africa 1899–1902

Mr Collett's legs were greatly improving with daily treatment. The ulcers were reduced from about eight inches in diameter to two inches. They were more superficial and were also drying out. Consequently, the smell in the room was improving. The room was still dirty, with a faint whiff of urine hanging in the air, but the sickly-sweet, choking stench had definitely gone. I realised that the smell must have been due to the suppuration of the wounds. If only he had sought treatment earlier, and not tried 'do-it-yourself' remedies, the ulcers would never have got into such a state in the first place. I reduced the visits to alternate days, and then every third day, and improvement was maintained.

Our sherry evenings continued as a regular feature, and I knew how much he loved me coming. He made no pretence about his joy at seeing me. I began to think that I was the only person who visited him and wondered about his family and friends. It was unusual, if not unknown, to see a Poplar man without either. Family life was close, and old people were valued. Neighbours lived on top of each other and were always in and out of each others' doors, especially in the tenements. Yet I never saw or heard of anyone popping in on Mr Collett to see if he was all right, to ask if he needed anything, or just to pass the time of day, and I wondered why.

He said to me once, regarding his neighbours: "I'm not one of them, you know. I was not born and bred in Alberta Buildings, so they will never accept me. Besides, neighbours can be nosy, and it's best that they shouldn't ask."

Once, at about 10.30p.m. as I was leaving his flat, the curtains next door were pulled aside. The sharp, suspicious features of the old woman who had accosted me on one of my early visits, stared hard at me. I remembered the vicious things she had said about him. Sister Julienne's words about two sons being killed in France came back to me.

I asked him about his family. He said, simply and sadly, "I have outlived them all. It is God's will that I should be left. And one day we will be reunited."

He wouldn't say any more, but I hoped that as time went on he might. In the meantime, if he looked upon me as a granddaughter, I was happy for him to do so.

One evening, I asked him to tell me more about the Boer War.

"I was drafted in the Autumn of 1899. My poor Sally was heartbroken. We were so happy at Windsor. We had a nice little army cottage. She did washing and mending for the officers and earned some money that way. She was happy, and as pretty as a picture. What's that jingle now, let me think:

'The Colonel's wife looks like a horse
The Captain's wife is not much worse
The Sergeant's wife looks a bit slicker
But the Private knows how to pick 'er.'

"Or something like that. Anyway, my Sal was the prettiest little girl in the Regiment. Our twins were born, and they were on their feet and running around, when the postings came. We knew it would be a long time. Sally and the boys couldn't stay at Windsor, so they went back home to live with her mother. The flat is just above where we are sitting now. That's why I like living here. I can sit of an evening, and think of Sally and the twins, when she was so young, living right above me more than fifty years ago."

"We sailed from Plymouth. There were crowds on the quayside, cheering, waving, singing. Some of the lads were happy and excited at going, but my heart was heavy, and a lot of others felt the same. I reckon that single men make the best soldiers, because they have few regrets about what they leave behind."

He went on to describe the troop ship, crowded with men and horses, carts and waggons, guns and munitions, food and supplies. The journey took five weeks. Discipline had to be very strict, because of living in a close, crowded space. The men did hours of drill on deck. But they were in good spirits, because it all seemed like an adventure. "We were going to knock hell out of those Boer farmers who dared to defy the British Empire," he said.

They landed at Durban and were ordered to form ranks and march. They weren't told where they were going, just told to march. They marched for eight days in full winter uniform in boiling heat, carrying 150 lb packs. The sun baked down relentlessly, and flies and mosquitoes followed all the way. There were no roads, so they marched through open scrubland, and along rough tracks. The countryside was beautiful, and wild, nothing like home, but they were too tired and too hot to take it in.

"I was in a Highland Regiment, as you know — the Scots Guards — and I'll tell you something: there is nothing in the world like the sound of the bagpipes to raise a man's morale, to lift his spirits, and give him strength. I can tell you, however tired and thirsty we were, the bagpipes at the front of the column only had to strike up and within seconds, you felt your feet lifted off the ground, your step lighten, your spirits lift, and every man-Jack was marching strong, in rhythm to the bagpipes."

Mr Collett chuckled, straightened his shoulders, threw back his head, and swung his arms as though he were marching.

"There's a photograph of my regiment hanging on the wall over there, if you like to have a look."

I peered at the grey and yellow photo of a column of soldiers, which didn't really mean a lot to me, and said it looked very impressive.

"Yes, it was impressive, you're right. But, at the same time, it was insanity."

I was surprised to hear him say that.

"Well, you imagine. Going to war, and marching through open country, soldiers in scarlet, playing bagpipes! Talk about secrecy or surprise tactics! The enemy could see and hear us for God knows how many miles around. And we never saw them. All over South Africa columns like ours were marching, and being attacked by an unseen enemy. Yet still the British generals didn't seem to learn. We carried on in our old swagger ways, and we lost countless thousands of young men because of it."

He told me how they were ordered to climb a hill one night. He didn't know where, because none of them were told. It was steep and treacherous, more like mountain terrain than a hill. They had no special climbing equipment. They wore their military uniform with full pack, as well as rifle and bayonet, and were wearing boots made for marching, not for climbing. Nor were the men trained for climbing.

By dawn they had got to what they thought was the top, only to find that there were higher ridges all around that were not seen from below. When the whole brigade had gained the first ridge, fire opened up from all around them, from cannons, rifles and long range muskets. They were completely unprepared. Hundreds of men were mown down before they could retaliate. "I shall never forget the scene," said Mr Collett. "The cries and screams were terrible to hear. We formed ranks and fired back, but our position was hopeless. We were in full view of an enemy we could not see. It was a day of gunfire, under a baking sun. No shelter, no water. Just relentless gunfire."

334

By nightfall the barrage from the guns died away, and in the darkness all that could be heard were the cries and groans of the wounded. "We tried to help them, but we were stumbling over rocks and dead bodies. In any case, we had no water, no supplies. There were no doctors or medical orderlies, no bandages, no morphine, no stretchers; nothing." The men were ordered to retreat, and to leave the dead. The injured would die the following day in the sun. "That was the moment when I knew the truth of my mother's words 'cannon fodder'. Young private soldiers were ordered, time and time again, to march out directly into gunfire, and High Command didn't give a damn how many died, nor the cost in human suffering."

Mr Collett was trembling and his voice was shaky. He bit his lip to control himself.

"And would you believe it, it was all unnecessary. Of course, we didn't know at the time, the ordinary soldier didn't, but there had been no reconnaissance. There were no maps of the terrain, and no scouts had been sent ahead to assess the area and the heights of the various hills. Had a ground map been available and studied, the incident would never have occurred. The British lost two thousand men that day, the Boers two hundred. All because of lack of reconnaissance.

"I have read a lot of history in my life, and bad leadership seems to crop up time after time in the British Army. Of course, we had some good colonels, and generals as well, but it was always a lottery."

Mr Collett spoke with some bitterness about the effect in those days of the class system when, as he put it, only the aristocracy and upper classes could hold a commission, and they bought their rank. Working class men could not afford to buy a commission. On the other hand this meant that a young man with money, however stupid he might be, however lazy, or indifferent to army life, could buy a rank and be in charge of men. The tradition of an easy life for the officers, with nothing but parties and races, was well entrenched. Any friendship between officers and men was forbidden. "They did not know us as human beings," said Mr Collett. "We meant nothing to them. We were merely 'the scum of the earth', utterly disposable.

"I don't know how it was that I wasn't killed. In my regiment, more than three quarters of the men who went out to South Africa died either in battle or in the military hospitals. Yet somehow I was spared."

Another killer was disease. Mr Collett suffered slight leg wounds in one skirmish, and had a short stay in hospital. While there he saw a constant stream of men brought in with what was called dysentery. It was, in fact, typhoid fever, due to infected water and it spread like wildfire. At one stage it seemed to be out of control. He commented: "I don't know if anyone recovered who caught the disease, but I know that I never saw a man walk out. I only saw the bodies carried out — ten or twenty a day from one ward, and they were quickly replaced by as many new patients with the same disease. The small hospital that I was in had been built for three hundred patients, and it was carrying two thousand. There were nowhere near enough doctors or nurses or orderlies to treat all those men, so most of them died. It was published later that three times as many men died in the hospitals as died on the battlefields. I don't know how it was that I didn't catch typhoid. I was to be spared for worse."

I wondered what could be worse, and imagined the heartache and frustration of trying to nurse sick and dying men under impossible conditions. But he was continuing.

"Somehow I survived and had to take part in what was called 'the bitter end'. After two and a half years of fighting we were no closer to victory than we had been at the beginning. We couldn't engage the enemy. They were always hiding, and attacking our lines, our communications, our stores, always surprising us. So our generals decided to attack their food supplies. This meant attacking their farms. A 'scorched earth' policy was approved and we private soldiers had to carry it out. We hated it. Most of us felt degraded and unmanned, attacking women and children. We turned them out of their homes and burned their farms and barns. We killed their animals and burned their fields. Nothing was left after we had finished. They were turned out to wander on the Veldt with no water, no food, a prey to wild animals. I remember one young Boer woman with two little children and a baby. She was sobbing and begging us to spare her. I wanted to, but refusal to obey military orders is unthinkable. It would have meant execution by the firing squad if I had done so. Perhaps I would have risked it if I had been single. But my money was going to Sally and the boys, and to my mother for the rent. What could I do? Apart

337

from this, even if I had disobeyed orders, it would have done no good. Other men would have carried out the job."

He looked very grim and bitter and chewed the stem of his pipe angrily.

"It was humiliating to us, and to our Commanding Officers. We were sent out to fight men, not defenceless women and children. We should never have done it. Never."

Mr Collett spat into the fire, and clenched his hands tightly.

"It was a black time for the British Empire. Thirty thousand women and children died, mostly small children, and we were disgraced in the eyes of the world. We outnumbered the Boer fighting men by twenty-five to one, yet even then we couldn't win without attacking their homes, their womenfolk and their children.

"In the Spring of 1903 I sailed for home, and I was discharged from the Army in 1906."

"Did you regret your army years, or do you look back with pleasure?" I asked.

"Mixed feelings. It certainly educated me and broadened my mind. I mixed with men from other backgrounds and experienced other ideas and points of view. Without the Army, I would have been a casual dock labourer, mostly unemployed, so I am grateful for that. With my army record, I was able to get a good job as a postman. And a postman I remained for the rest of my life, until I retired with a pension to keep me comfortably in my old age."

His ingenuous simplicity had always charmed me. He looked upon his squalid, bug-ridden flat as comfort and even luxury; he was grateful for a modest pension enabling him to buy food and coal, sufficient for his needs. He saw himself as a wealthy man, who could afford to buy a bottle of sherry and a box of chocolates with which to entertain a young nurse whom he had grown fond of. He was completely content, and I leaned forward and squeezed his hand with affection.

"I think it's getting late and I must go, but next time you must tell me about re-adjusting to civvy life. I guess your twins didn't know you?"

He didn't reply, but looked dreamily and sadly into the fire.

"You go, my maiden, you go," he said, softly. I left an old man to his memories, the consolation of loneliness.

My next visit to Mr Collett was a morning about three days later. His legs had improved beyond all recognition with regular treatment, and the ulcers were now completely dry. It was very gratifying.

On the mantelpiece, amid all the dingy and faded old photographs, was a gleaming white card, with a gold border and an embossed crown on it, requesting the pleasure of the company of Mr Joseph Collett and lady at the Old Guards' reunion at Caterham Barracks on a Saturday in June. I remarked on the card. He told me that for several years he had enjoyed going to the Old Guards' Day, but had not been able to go in recent years, due to deteriorating eyesight, and also bad legs.

Impulsively I said, "Look, your legs are so much better now. It won't be any trouble to you to get around. Let's go together. It looks like a bit of good fun. It's not everyone has an opportunity like this, and I don't want to miss it."

He positively lit up. He took my hands and kissed them.

"You darling girl! What a wonderful idea. It hadn't even crossed my mind. We'll go, and we'll make a day of it. I can tell you, the Guards do us old soldiers proud. What a day we'll have! What a day!"

I requested the day off duty well in advance, telling Sister Julienne about the invitation, and the plans. The girls were most intrigued; what on earth would it be like? Trixie suggested that a Young Guards' Reunion might be more exciting, but wished me pleasure with my old ones.

The June day dawned bright and fair. I was round at Alberta Buildings shortly after 8 o'clock. Mr Collett was excited and chatty. He was dressed for the occasion in a faded old suit. His shoes had been polished, and he carried a new trilby hat. Most important of all, and by far the most impressive, he was wearing a row of medals on his chest. It had not occurred to me that he had medals, and I looked at them closely. He was proud and happy, telling me what they were for.

We took the bus from Blackwall to Victoria Coach Station, and then a coach to Caterham, and arrived at about 10 o'clock. I was excited, having never been inside a barracks before. For a young, inexperienced girl it was a stupendous occasion, and my excitement and enthusiasm communicated itself to Mr Collett. We kept very close together, because of the crowds, and I held his arm all the time as he couldn't see very clearly. I had expected a rather solemn occasion with a lot of old men talking about old times. But it was nothing like that. It was an Open Day, with full military honours and pageantry. The Reunion was an evening event.

The day was exhilarating. The British Army really knows how to put on a show. The colour, the flags, the pipes and drums, the drills. The scarlet uniforms, black busbies, the marching, with the Pipe Major throwing the staff into the air. I was thrilled. Mr Collett had seen it all before, and couldn't see it very clearly this time, but he heard my cheers and gasps of amazement and he was delighted to be showing it to me.

Towards evening, when the marching and the drilling had ceased, and the tired crowds were starting to leave, I thought we would be leaving also. But Mr Collett pulled me back.

"Now is the time for the Regimental dinner, and the Reunion. Come on, my beauty. This way. They'll see 'the privates know how to pick 'em'."

We went to the great dining room by special invitation. We were a little late, because Mr Collett's walking was slow. We passed young soldiers who clicked their heels and saluted. We entered, the doorman took our card, and called: 'Mr Joseph Collett and Miss Jenny Lee.' There were about two hundred men and women seated at the tables, talking. Heads looked up, and then a voice called out: 'Gentlemen — now here is a really old soldier.' And everyone in the room stood up and raised their glasses. "To a really old soldier."

Tears of emotion sprang to Mr Collett's eyes. We were led to the Colonel's table, and placed at his side. The dinner was sumptuous, and the Colonel and his lady so gracious to the old man. They talked about the Boer War, and Africa, and army life sixty years earlier. He was treated with the respect and recognition that he so well deserved.

France 1914–1918

The joyous day at Caterham Barracks cemented our friendship and I knew then that, come what may, I was bound to Mr Collett for life. We chatted and laughed all the way home, and parted at the bus stop near Blackwall Tunnel. He insisted that he didn't need me to go back with him, as he was perfectly capable of finding his way in the dark. As I returned to the warm, happy atmosphere of Nonnatus House, I thought of the suspicious eyes watching him, and the vicious tongues talking about him in Alberta Buildings. It was beyond me why they didn't like him. It gladdened my heart remembering the respect, even deference, with which he had been treated at the Barracks by the Colonel. He would not forget that day in a hurry.

One day, whilst treating his legs, I asked him about his life after leaving the Army. I knew Sally and the twins were then in Alberta Buildings. Did they continue to live there when he came back?

"No. I got a job in the Post Office you see, and so we had to move near to the sorting office in Mile End," and he went on to tell me about his new life. Postmen had to sort their mail in those days, and had to be in the sorting house by 4 o'clock each morning to receive the night mail. Sorting took a couple of hours, then they would be out on the road delivering until about 1p.m. After a couple of hours off, they went back to sort and deliver the evening mail, which finished about 7p.m. Mr Collett thought it was a good life.

"The twins were getting bigger. Pete and Jack were about six or seven, and the spitting image of each other. No-one except their mother could tell them apart and even she got it wrong sometimes. They were lovely boys."

He bit his lip and swallowed hard, choking down emotion, but continued in a firmer tone.

"You've heard, I suppose, that identical twins often seem to live for each other. Well, I can tell you how true this is. They were two people, but I often thought that neither of them could be quite sure where he ended and the other began. They were always together, you couldn't separate them. They didn't seem to need anyone else. They even spoke their own language. Yes, it's true! We would listen to them playing, Sally and me, and they spoke different words to each other to what they spoke to everyone else. It was a mixture of ordinary English and their own language. They could understand it, but we couldn't. You can never be quite sure what's going on in a child's mind, and identical twins are more of a mystery than other children. Pete and Jack lived in a world created out of their combined imaginations, filled with giants and dwarves, kings and queens, castles and caverns, and wondrous people and talking animals. They didn't really have any friends. They didn't need them. They had each other."

"Didn't their mother feel left out?"

"You're right there. She did. The boys weren't lacking in affection, or anything like that. They were just totally sufficient in each other. In fact, Sally said once, 'I reckon you and me could die, Joe, and they wouldn't notice. But if one of the boys died, I reckon the other would just fade away'."

Tears glistened in the corners of his eyes, and he murmured, "Perhaps it was best, all for the best. The Lord giveth, and the Lord taketh away."

He was completely silent, lost in thought. I had heard of two sons being killed in France, and looked at the picture of two handsome little boys on the wall.

I asked, "Did you have any more children?"

"Yes, we had a little girl, and Sally nearly died in childbirth. I don't know what went wrong, and the midwife didn't know either, but my Sal was near to death for weeks after. Her sister took the baby and wet-nursed her for the first three months, and the boys went to my mother. It frightened the life out of me, so I never let her go through it again. That's one thing you learn in the Army, if nothing else — contraception. I never could understand these men who let their wives have ten or fifteen children, when they could prevent it.

"But Sally recovered, thank God, and the children came home. We called the little girl Shirley — don't you think that's a pretty name? She was the loveliest little thing in all the world and a blessing to us both."

As I left that morning the woman next door approached me again.

"You 'anging arahn va' dirty ol' man still? I'd 'ave thought you would find somefink be'er 'a do wiv yer toim."

I was so furious, I was tempted to hit her — but professional nurses can't do that sort of thing.

During one of our sherry evenings he told me the story of Pete and Jack. I don't think he could have told me without a few sherries inside him and he broke down many times, the words faltering between sobs. I didn't force him to tell me, but I think in a way that it did him good. In fact he said: "You are the only person in the world I've told this story to. We kept it hidden so long, and tried to run away from it. But it's still there, and no escape. I'm glad I've told you."

Pete and Jack were sixteen when the Great War started. They both had good jobs as telegraph boys in the Post Office, but with youthful enthusiasm they were desperate to enlist in the Army. Their father was against it. He knew the realities of war. In 1915 social pressure was mounting, and able-bodied young men were called 'cowards' for not responding to the posters of Kitchener saying darkly: 'Your country needs YOU'.

That powerful message was surely one of the most successful advertising campaigns of all time, still remembered to this day. Young men, in their hundreds of thousands, queued up to march to their deaths as a result of that poster.

Mr Collett, as a post office worker was in a special occupation, because all information between France and England was handled by the Post Office. He did not have to enlist, and told me he had regretted it all his life. "I should have enlisted in the same regiment as the twins. Then I might have been able to stop the tragedy," he said.

When the twins enlisted they were marched off to three months' rifle and bayonet training. That was all they received before being shipped to France. News from the front was consistently good — 'it will all be over in a few weeks' — but as 1916 dawned the number of dead and wounded rose steadily.

The boys came home on a five-day leave a few times. They kept very close to each other and didn't communicate very much with their parents, preferring the company of little Shirley, who was about ten or eleven. They played with her, and took her out, and would not talk about France and the war.

Their parents, meanwhile, read the newspapers every day and picked up every scrap of information they could. Letters came from the boys, which reassured the Colletts they were alive. Several neighbours suffered news of the death of their loved ones, but the twins seemed to be spared, even though they had been in front line battles at Bois Grenier, Loos, the Somme, and Ypres. Then came Passchendaele.

Mr Collett gripped the arms of his wooden chair until his knuckles showed white. I got up from my chair and took his hands, and kissed his wrinkled face.

"Don't tell me if you can't. I understand. The boys were killed at Passchendaele, weren't they?"

He touched the place on his cheek where I had kissed him, and nodded.

"Worse than that, much worse. I've never told anyone, although many have guessed the truth, but I'll tell you, dear. If I put it into words, perhaps it will help to lay the ghosts before I die.

"It was a week before Christmas 1917. A telegram came from the War Office informing us that Pete had been killed by enemy action, and that Jack was missing.

"Oh, the grief, and also the hope, for Jack. It was little Shirley, with the insight of a child, who said: 'But how can Jack be missing? If Pete is dead, Jack must be dead, too'.

"Sally and I looked at each other and knew in our hearts that she must be right. The twins could not live without each other."

In the middle of January, on a bitterly cold day, the Colletts received a letter from the Commanding Officer informing them that Jack was confined to the military prison awaiting Court Martial for cowardice in the face of the enemy.

"I was beside myself. Cowardice! My boys were no cowards. They had fought at the front line for three years. I rushed to the War Office in Whitehall and demanded to see Lord Kitchener himself. Of course I didn't see him, but I saw some high ranking big-wig, who coldly informed me that there was nothing he could do, and that justice would be done."

"Justice!" He spat the word out. "Justice! After three years of trench warfare. Court Martialled! And for what? I didn't know, and I couldn't find out. They didn't know at the War Office, and they wouldn't have told me if they did. I had to be led, forcibly, out of the building and I was told I would be kept informed by letter but that I would not be admitted to the War Office again. If I tried to force entry, I would be arrested.

"We waited. We waited for three weeks, and were informed that Jack would be tried by Military Court Martial on the 28th February, in France.

"I wrote letters to the King, the War Office, the Colonel of the Regiment, the Divisional Commanding Officer — everyone I could think of. The reply was always the same — giving the data of 28th February. I wrote to Jack, but the letters were returned to me by the Company Commander, saying he regretted that correspondence with a prisoner was not permitted. I tried to go over to France, but was not allowed, because the war was still on and I was a civilian. I could do nothing. I was helpless. Then came the thought that has never left me — I should have enlisted as a reservist, and I would have been there, and perhaps, been able to speak for Jack.

"Early in March we were informed that Jack had been tried by Military Court Marshall, found guilty, and executed by firing squad at dawn on the morning of 3rd March 1918."

That is all he said, just the bare facts, no more. There is a grief that is too deep for tears. He sat motionless, his face drained of colour, his eyes blank. Only his hand, which I was holding, trembled slightly. The clock ticked several minutes away, and sparks shot up the chimney as a coal shifted and fell. And still we sat in silence. He lifted my hands to his face and kissed them repeatedly, and then I felt the hot tears flowing over my wrists, as he murmured: "My boy, my dear boy. Why couldn't it have been me?"

He fumbled for a handkerchief and blew his nose vigorously.

"I thought I would go mad. I was raving and delirious. Sally had to go to the Post Office and tell the Postmaster that I was ill. I had never had a day off work in my life. Sally told me later that she feared for me and feared to leave me, in case I did something desperate. Women are stronger than men in some ways. She was suffering just as much from the news, but I was the one that had a breakdown.

"It was Shirley who pulled me together, and gave her mother and me the strength to go on. She was a child of thirteen when it happened, and she became a woman within a few weeks. She had been close to her brothers, as close as anyone can be to identical twins, and she was torn apart, but she kept strong and steady and helped her mother and me through that terrible time. I think we would have just given up without little Shirley.

"The three of us spoke only in whispers about . . ." — he hesitated — 'it'. We never told a soul outside, not even our closest family. My mother went to her grave thinking that the twins had both been killed fighting the enemy."

"Why did you not tell anyone?" I asked, innocently.

"The shame, my dear. The bitter shame. You cannot know what the public attitude was to 'cowardice'. If people had known they would have cursed his name. Our Jack had suffered enough, and we were determined to protect his name in death. We knew he wasn't a coward. We knew there had been some terrible mistake. But we also knew no-one would believe it, and once chattering neighbours started there would be no end to the gossip flying around, and the stain they would cast upon Jack's memory."

His words brought into my mind the image of the woman next door, and her spiteful look, as she hissed. "They say his son was shot. Shot!" and then she had spat on the ground and stamped on her spittle.

His tears started again, so I stood up beside his chair and took his head in my arms. There were no curtains and anyone could have looked straight in at us. The woman next door would have had a fit of rage, if she had been looking in. He whispered. "You are the only one I have ever told, my maiden, the only one and I feel it is good that I do so. Jack is at rest now. They are all at rest, and I hope to die in peace soon, to join them."

He wiped his tears away on my dress, and then pulled his head away abruptly, and sat up straight.

"You'll think me a silly, sentimental old man, going on like this. Don't mind me. I've lived with it all these years and I gets emotional thinking about it. Have another sherry, and some chocolates, they're Black Magic — I thought you would like them. You don't come here to be made miserable."

351

I poured two more sherries, and took a chocolate, but it would have been impossible to start chatting idly about other things. As I put the glass into his hand, I said, "I'm terribly sorry, and honoured that you feel you can tell me. Did you ever find out the circumstances leading up to . . ." I hesitated to say 'the execution' and whispered ". . . leading up to — 'it'?"

"Yes, I did," he said firmly. "I couldn't rest without knowing."

He handed back the glass of sherry to me, and said, abruptly, "Look in the bottom of that cupboard, will you? You'll find half a bottle of brandy. I don't want this stuff, you drink it, and pour me out a stiff brandy, will you lass, then I'll be able to tell you."

He cut up his tobacco whilst I fetched the brandy. He was slicing it with savage fury and filled the bowl of his pipe with strong, angry pokes of his middle finger. He lit a spill from the fire, and it went out. He cursed, and jabbed it again into the flames. This time it flared up, and the flame dipped into the strong tobacco as he sucked his pipe fiercely, and puffed clouds of grey smoke across the room. He took the brandy from me, and swallowed it in a gulp. I replenished the glass.

"I couldn't rest. I would have gone mad if I hadn't done something. I couldn't undo the past, but at least I could find out the truth.

"While the war lasted, I was helpless, because all information was top secret. But in November of the same year the armistice was declared, and I knew what I was going to do.

352

"I obtained the names of every man in the Division, every officer, infantryman, doctors, chaplains, stretcher bearers, storemen, signallers — no-one was left out. Some had moved to other Divisions, most had been killed. It was pathetic — out of a Division of 35,000 men, only 650 were alive. But that was enough. I resolved to see them all, and get at the truth.

"It took hours of my time, sorting through thousands of names. Sally tried to restrain me, saying it would do no good, it wouldn't bring the twins back. But Shirley was behind me. She said we owed it to Jack's memory."

Mr Collett wrote hundreds of letters asking the men if they remembered the twins, and whether they would talk to him about them. He had quite a lot of replies, and travelled all over the British Isles to meet these veterans. He built up not only a picture of his sons, but a picture of the war as it was for the ordinary soldier, which was a very different story from that issued by the War Office.

I asked him to tell me about it, and refilled his brandy glass as encouragement.

The civilians at home, he said, were not told that the soldiers were for months living underground, in trenches half full of water, with their dead comrades lying in the water under their feet. Conditions were so cramped that the men were tightly packed side by side and their only way of sleeping was to lay their heads on the parapet. The War Office issued no reports on 'trench foot', frostbite, gangrene, filthy clothes unchanged for weeks, no hot food for weeks, no sanitation, drinking-water contaminated by sewage, or rats, or dead bodies. None of this was reported to civilians at home. The term 'trench warfare' was talked about — but few people knew that the trenches stretched from the North Sea to Switzerland and that millions of men, on both sides, lived, slept and died in those hell-holes for four long years. If a wall fell, men would be buried alive. If a man slipped and fell, he would be likely to drown. The War Office failed to report on the plague of rats that thrived on an unlimited supply of human flesh, or on the lice that covered every man from head to foot.

"Perhaps they didn't know, here in London," he said. "Perhaps they hadn't been informed. I met hundreds of men over a period of four or five years, and every one of them told me that he never once saw a general in the front lines. The generals, and the chiefs of staff, were always miles behind the lines and only reported what *they* saw. They never saw the grim reality."

He snarled savagely, and spat into the fire.

"I had seen it in South Africa. Military incompetence. Gentlemen in the rear and cannon fodder in the front. Cannon fodder. That's what my boys were.

"The gunfire never stopped. Both armies were entrenched in their dug-outs, you see, often only fifty yards apart, and both sides were ordered to blow the other to smithereens. So shelling and gunfire never stopped day and night for four years. Men were blown to pieces all around; arms, heads and legs were blown off, men were disembowelled, faces torn open, eyes shot out. And mostly there was no chance of burying the dead — they just had to lie where they had fallen, beside the living, to be consumed by the rats. And all the time there was the never ending gunfire. Many men went stark raving mad, and I met some of them.

"This was the war that my boys had lived and fought through for three years. And one of them was accused of cowardice and shot in cold blood."

His voice rose.

"Cowardice! Every man at the front line was a hero, and my Jack was a hero."

Mr. Collett was trembling all over, his face was red, veins stood out on his forehead and I became alarmed, thinking of his great age, the amount of brandy consumed, and the effect of the rage and emotion upon his heart and blood pressure.

"Perhaps you had better not tell me any more. It is too much for you."

"I'll finish now that I have started."

He cut another chunk of tobacco with fierce strokes, and began to shred it as he told me of his search for the facts about his sons' lives in the war.

He met several men who had fought alongside the twins. All of them said they were reserved, didn't mix much, or talk much, except to each other. Several former comrades mentioned another language the twins spoke. One man said they had saved his life in the winter of 1917. He had slipped and fallen into the mud, which was two feet deep. He couldn't pull himself out because of the weight of his pack, and the added weight of the water and mud, which were sucking him down. The twins pulled him out. He would have drowned if they hadn't, he told Mr Collett.

After seeing about two hundred old soldiers in different parts of the country, he met one who was with them the night Pete was killed. He recalled for Mr Collett the night when they were marching in a column to relieve the southern flank which had sustained heavy losses. They were expected to be there before midnight, and to go into battle the following day. It was a clear, bright winter evening, stars shining. There had been a quiet few days, and the men had had some cooked food which had put them into good spirits. One of the men started singing as they tramped along and the Captain ordered him to stop, in case of snipers. The twins were marching on the nearside when, without warning, a single shot rang out. One of the twins cried out, threw up his arms, and fell. Ranks were formed, and a volley of gun fire directed at the point from which the shot had come, but they heard nothing more, and there was no movement. The Captain looked at the fallen twin, declared him dead, and ordered the men to re-form and march on, which they did. But the other twin wouldn't leave his brother. Several of his comrades tried to get him to join the column, saying there was nothing he could do, because Pete was obviously dead, but he was cradling his brother in his arms, and sobbing, and trying to breathe life into his mouth.

Mr Collett's informant, the soldier who witnessed the tragedy, stayed behind a little while, saying to Jack, the surviving twin: "You've got to come. We have parade tomorrow morning before battle. If you're not on parade then, you know the penalty — death." But Jack didn't seem to hear. He was talking in another language to the body in his arms. "I tried shaking him to get him to see sense. I shouted, 'If you don't report for battle, it will be the firing squad for you, son,' but he didn't take no notice. I had to leave him and catch up with the column, or it would have been chips for me an' all."

The rest of the story is brief and inevitable. Jack was not present on parade before battle, and was declared a deserter. He was found five days later, two miles from where Pete had fallen. He had carried his brother two miles away from the battle lines, towards a deserted farmyard. On the quiet outskirts of a wood, with bayonet and hands, he had dug a shallow grave, and placed his brother's body in it. The grave was covered with evergreen leaves, mingled with red berries, and white winter aconytes. He had fashioned a rough wooden cross and set it at the head of the grave. Carved into the wood, with a bayonet point, were the words: 'Peter Joseph Collett. I die with you.'

London 1939–1945

The story of Pete and Jack was so profoundly affecting that I could not sleep that night. The horrors of a judicial execution filled my mind. In my imagination I re-lived Jack's last hours in captivity, knowing that dawn was approaching; his walk from the cell to the firing rank; the command to halt; turning round; being blindfolded. We all know that we must die, and only the unpredictability makes it acceptable. To know the hour and minute of death is where hell opens up for us, in all its ghastly detail. I tossed and turned all night, telling myself that Jack had been glad to die and had sought death, but it was hollow comfort.

Falling asleep fitfully around dawn did little to ease my mind and the lighthearted chatter over breakfast irritated me, so I went quickly to the clinical room to prepare for the morning visits. Sister Julienne brought in the daywork lists and we were alone for a few moments.

Briefly, I told her the story. She looked sad, and said: "Poor man, poor dear old man. 'God loves greatly those whom he requires to suffer greatly.' Suffering is one of the great mysteries of life, which we will never be able to understand. It can sometimes be a source of grace. There has been much suffering in these docklands over the centuries, but there is also much grace and spirituality, have you noticed? I am glad you are friends with Mr Collett, Jenny, because he values it."

She gave a little grin, and wrinkled her nose.

"What a good thing you managed to overcome your aversion to bugs."

She put down the day-lists and trotted out of the clinical room, leaving me to ponder her strange words about suffering.

I saw more of Mr Collett after that, but we never again mentioned the twins. He told me that Shirley, the pride of his heart, had had a good education, and passed the School Certificate, an achievement attained by very few East End girls in those days. This enabled her to go into the Post Office to be trained in accountancy and book-keeping, to work as one of the counter staff. She also studied telegraphy and Morse Code.

"It was a two-year study," Mr Collett said. "The system was based on long and short sounds, or flashes of light. We spent many hours, the three of us, tapping and flashing messages to each other. Sally and I picked up some of the Code, enough to learn the alphabet, but Shirley became a real expert. She had to be a touch typist as well and could sit blindfolded, listening to a message tapped out, typing the words with never a mistake. Then we darkened the room, and I sat flashing the Code to her with a torch while she typed the message. Still no mistakes. She became an expert, and

359

this was greatly valued when the Second World War came. In 1939 she was put straight away onto the reserve Special Occupation List."

I asked him for his memories about the War and his admiration for Winston Churchill shone through.

"From 1935 onwards you had to be blind not to see that something was going to happen. Hitler was re-arming and mobilising, casting fear and unrest all over Europe. Unfortunately, most of our leaders seemed to be both blind and deaf. Only Churchill could see clearly and he poured out warnings, but his words fell on deaf ears, and the Government refused to re-arm. Consequently, when war came in 1939, we were completely unprepared. We had the minimum trained army and navy, and virtually no equipment.

"Now, Churchill is a man who has interested me all my life. He is a contemporary of mine, and was also in the South African War. The first I heard of him was his famous escape from Pretoria Prison, which electrified the troops, and the whole of England, when the news got back to London. The funniest thing about it was the letter which he left behind for the Boer Minister of Defence. Something like: 'Sir, I have the honour to inform you that I do not consider your Government has any right to detain me as a prisoner. I have therefore decided to escape from your custody', and ending up 'I remain, Sir, your humble and obedient servant, Winston Churchill'."

"In 1916 Churchill became a Lieutenant Colonel of the Royal Scots Fusiliers (I was a Scots Guardsman, you remember). He served in the front line alongside his men, which was more than most of the officers did. After the War he dabbled in politics, but was never very successful. He made a lot of mistakes — but whatever he did, he did it on a grand scale, and he was always fascinating, with a magnetic personality.

"I tell you, I have never been more relieved in all my life than when he became Prime Minister and Minister of Defence in 1940. He had moral strength and a command of words which put fire in your belly, and united the people to stand up to Hitler and Fascism, even though we only had broken bottles and carving knives to fight with. I honestly believe that without Churchill we would have lost the War, and Britain would be a Nazi state today."

It was a sobering thought. I had always taken freedom for granted. I had been a child during the war, and had seen things with a child's understanding. It was not until after the war, when I was about ten years old, that I saw on the cinema newsreel the ghastly pictures of Belsen, Auschwitz, Dachau, and the many other death camps dotted across Europe. This was when I began to understand the evil we had been fighting.

Also, being a country-born child, I had seen very little of war. We lived only thirty miles from London, but life was peaceful and untroubled. My mother took in evacuees, which was good fun as far as I was concerned. Food was scarce and I didn't see a banana or an orange until I was ten, but apart from that there might not have been a war going on at all.

Where, I wondered, had Mr Collett spent the war?

361

His response was firm. London was home to him and it was where he lived throughout the war years. Also, Sally didn't want to leave London where she had been born and bred. They both felt there really was no other option. This attitude was fairly typical of Cockneys. In 1939 large-scale evacuations of women and children occurred, but within six months most of them had returned. They couldn't cope with the countryside. They returned in droves, preferring the risks of London bombing to the quiet of the countryside.

I had heard a similar story from the Sisters. About seventy Poplar women, all of them pregnant, had been evacuated with two of the midwifery Sisters to Cornwall. One by one these young women returned, always giving the same story: the silence got on their nerves; they were frightened of the trees and the fields; they couldn't stand the wind moaning. At the end of six months there were only about a dozen left, so the Sisters themselves returned to where their work was most needed — in the heart of Poplar.

In 1940 Mr Collett retired from the Post-Office. Straight away he joined the ARP (Air Raid Patrol) and Sally joined with him. In the early months of 1940 the duties were to see that Government directives were carried out. This mainly involved checking that people carried gas-masks, that black-out regulations were being observed, that sandbags were filled and that air-raid shelters were suitably equipped. At first, ARP wardens were often called snoopers and laughed at, but in September 1940 the Blitz started and their work really began.

For three long months London was bombed every night, and there were sometimes daylight raids as well. Bombing was concentrated mainly on the dockland, but this was also the area of the highest civilian population and hundreds of thousands of Londoners died or lost their homes.

If one looks at a map of London, the Thames and the horseshoe loop going round the Isle of Dogs is pretty obvious. From the air it is a landmark, and the German bomber pilots could not fail to see it. Bombs only had to be dropped at that target, and they were sure to hit either the docks or the housing around. Thousands of tons of high explosive fell in less than three months. Poplar was a sitting target, housing around 50,000 people to the square mile.

There were never enough air-raid shelters for such huge numbers of people. In other parts of London people went into the underground stations, but Poplar has none. The nearest underground was Aldgate. The Government provided corrugated iron for people to build Anderson shelters in their gardens, but most Poplar people did not have a garden, so that was no help to them. Fortunately, many houses had cellars where people slept. The crypts of churches provided shelter for hundreds of people, and whole communities lived day and night in the churches. More than one baby was born in All Saints crypt, as I learnt from the Sisters. The overcrowding was terrible. Each person had just enough room to lie down, and no more.

There was always the fear that plague or disease would sweep through the shelters. Water and sewage pipes were frequently hit, but somehow they were always repaired, at least enough to prevent any spread of disease. Gas and electricity supplies were often hit, but they were always patched up too.

Mr Collett said to me: "Looking back it seems impossible, but everyone worked day and night, with amazing good spirit.

"When you are living in such conditions, close to death, every day is a gift. You are happy every morning to see the dawn break, and to know that you are still alive. Also, death was no stranger to us. The Poplar people were used to suffering. Poverty, hunger, cold, disease, and death have stalked amongst us for generations, and we have just accepted it as normal, so a few bombs couldn't break our spirit.

"We were used to overcrowding, so the shelters didn't seem too bad. The loss of house or rooms was no worse than eviction, and most people didn't have much furniture to lose, anyway. A family would just move in with neighbours who still had a roof over their heads.

"It was an extraordinary time. Suffering and anguish were all around us, but also, in a strange way, exhilaration. We were determined not to be beaten. Two fingers up to Hitler was the attitude. I remember one old woman we pulled out of the rubble. She wasn't hurt. She gripped my arm, and said. 'That bugger Hitler. 'E's killed me old man, good riddance, e's killed me kids, more's the pity. 'E's bombed me 'ouse, so I got nowhere 'a live, bu' 'e ain't got me. And I've got sixpence in me pocket an' vat pub on' corner, Master's Arms, ain't been bombed, so let's go an' 'ave a drink an' a good laugh an' a sing-song.' "

There was even more devastation when the fire bombs came, and it was these that were responsible for Sally's death. Both Mr Collett and his wife had a premonition, sensing that one of them would be killed, but they didn't know which, or when. The fire bombs were small, and just burst into flames when they hit the ground. They were easy to put out — it could be done with a sandbag, or even a couple of blankets — but if the fire spread it would set whole buildings alight. So the Government appealed for volunteer fire-watchers who would go to the top of tall buildings to keep a watch on the area all around. They gave the alert when a fire bomb fell, and at once the men with sandbags rushed to the spot to put the fire out. These fire-watchers had to know the area, and were mostly old people who hadn't got the physical strength to deal with all the digging and heavy lifting required in the streets. Sally volunteered. She and others went up the highest buildings with nothing but a tin hat to protect them from the explosives and fire bombs falling all around. One night the building Sally was in got a direct hit. Mr Collett never saw her again. Her body was not even found.

After telling me this sad story he paused, and just stared into the fire, unspeaking, for a few minutes, then said softly: "She knew the risk. We both did. I'm glad that she was taken first, and not left on her own. Death

365

is kinder than life. There is no more suffering beyond the grave. We will meet again soon, I hope."

He said the words "soon, I hope," a second time, and I didn't know what to say, so I asked him about his daughter.

Shirley's skills in Morse Code and telegraphy were classed as a 'special occupation.' She joined the WAAF in 1940 and entered the Intelligence and Communications Corps at RAF Benson. Her father saw a little of her when she could come home on leave, but mostly he didn't even know where she was stationed, because all her work was confidential, and secrecy was tight. She had never married, and had always been very close to her parents. After her mother's death she just threw herself into her work.

Mr Collett, too, found that hard work was the only remedy for unhappiness. After Sally's death he just worked day and night, not bothering much about food or sleep. As an ARP Warden he did anything and everything that needed doing: helping ambulance men, digging away rubble, carrying water, filling sandbags, and mending burst pipes. He went out at night when bombs were dropping all around, not caring if he got killed. He helped people out of burning buildings, got them to shelters, carried babies, pushed prams. "It was a hard time, but satisfying," he told me "and all the while I fancied Sal was looking down on me, and sharing the experience."

Many of his experiences from those days he could still vividly recall. He told me about one little boy he said he would never forget. He was about six or seven years old. The wardens dug him out of the rubble where he had been buried for several hours. He was underneath the body of his mother. She must have thrown herself over her son in order to protect him when the bomb fell. She was quite stiff and cold, and he was quite safe underneath her. But one does not know the psychological damage that such an experience can inflict. He said his name was Paul. Mr Collett mused: "He would be in his twenties now, and I often wondered how he grew up, and if there was any lasting mental damage." He continued his tragic story.

"During the next five years I saw Shirley occasionally. She was flourishing. War has that effect sometimes. The unusual circumstances bring out the best in some people. All her intelligence and qualities of leadership placed her in positions of command, and she thrived on it. I was so proud of her.

"In 1944 it seemed that the war was ending and we dared to plan for her demob and picking up life again together. But it never does to plan ahead in wartime. The V1 and V2 rocket attacks started. At Christmas 1944 I was told by the RAF that a rocket had fallen on the staff headquarters where Shirley was stationed, and that she had been killed. I have been alone ever since."

The Shadow of the Workhouse

'Jenny kissed me when we met
Jumping from the chair she sat in . . .
Say I'm weary, say I'm sad,
Say that health and wealth have missed me,
Say I'm growing old, but add,
Jenny kissed me.'

Leigh Hunt

Poplar was destined for change. Town planners had a new broom with which to sweep clean, and they were so successful that they swept virtually everything away. Poplar had survived the war, the blitz, the doodlebugs and the V2 rockets. The people had picked themselves up, brushed off the debris, and formed themselves into a community again, almost indistinguishable from the communities of their parents and grandparents. But Poplar was finally destroyed by the good intentions of bureaucracy and social planning.

The tenements were to be demolished. In 1958 and 1959 notice was served to thousands of tenants and alternative accommodation was offered. This could be as far away as Harlow, Bracknell, Basildon, Crawley, or Hemel Hempstead — as far away as the North Pole, for most of the older people. Social workers and housing officers buzzed in and out of the tenements all day with sheaves of forms and good advice and forced good cheer. The residents were not taken in. Most were wary or apprehensive. Some were distraught.

This was the time, and the only time, when I felt sympathy with Mr. Collett's neighbour. She came up to me piteously one day as I entered the court of Alberta Buildings.

"Vey sez we go' 'a go. Go where? Somewhere we don't know, somewhere a long way off. Somewhere no-one'll know me, an' I won' know no-one. It ain't right, it aint. I've always paid me ren', you can look a' me book. Never a day la'e. I keeps me flat clean, like me mum used 'a. You can see for yourself. Can' chew do somefink? Ve Sisters 'ave a lo' of say in fings round here."

All the Sisters experienced scenes like this. The idea amongst the older generation that the Sisters would somehow intervene and help them to save their little homes was touchingly persistent, but quite erroneous, of course. We tried to comfort the people as best we could, but I doubt if it did much good. The community was doomed. The people, who had seen off Hitler by sticking two fingers up and carrying on, were themselves seen off the premises. Then the demolition men took over. The land became valuable. Then big business stepped in. The ordinary people didn't stand a chance. Tower blocks were built, which were supposed to be so much better than tenements. In fact they were the same thing, only far worse, because interaction between neighbours had been stripped away. The courtyards had gone, the inner facing balconies had gone, walkways and stairways had gone, and upstairs and downstairs neighbours were strangers, with no obvious points of contact. The communal life of the tenements, with all its fraternity and friendship, all its enmity and fighting, was replaced by locked doors and heads turned away. It was a disaster in social planning. A community that had knitted itself together over centuries to form the vital, vibrant people known as "the Cockneys" was destroyed within a generation.

But this was all in the future. We did not know, in 1959, that the effects would be so catastrophic to the Poplar people. We only knew what was happening at the time — namely that the Canada Buildings were to go. We discussed it endlessly over the luncheon table, and one of the nuns said, "Well, if the tenements go, it won't be long before we have to go, because we won't be needed here."

We all looked at each other in sadness and silence, but Sister Julienne said, without a trace of sadness or regret: "For more than eighty years we have served God in Poplar. If we are no longer needed, He will give us other work to do. In the meantime, I suggest we stop speculating on the future and get on with the job in hand."

When I next visited Mr Collett a social worker was leaving. She looked harassed, poor soul, and was besieged by women as she stepped across the courtyard. I felt sorry for her. 'What a job! You are on a hiding to nothing' I thought as I looked after her.

Mr. Collett's legs were virtually better now, and as he was quite capable of dressing the superficial wounds himself, I called only once a fortnight to check that there was no deterioration. His walking was much better and he was able to get about easily, which was entirely due to simple, regular treatment. Nursing is one of the most satisfying jobs in the world.

He was silent and thoughtful as I undid the bandages. I think we were both wondering what the other was thinking. He was the first to break the silence.

"You've heard, I suppose, that the Buildings are being demolished? Yes, of course you know all about it. I don't understand why. These buildings are sound. They are still here after the blitz, when thousands of terraces went down like packs of cards. The Canada Buildings will last for a couple more centuries. Yet they are pulling them down. All my ghosts will be cleared away in the rubble. Will they be laid to rest, I wonder? Will I?"

His words sounded like a premonition.

"What are they offering you?" I asked.

He started, as though I had interrupted a dream.

"Offering me? Oh, I don't know. Several things; a flat in Harlow; another in somewhere called Hemel Hempstead. I've got to think about it. I must say, it's very good of them to offer me anything at all. When I was a boy, if a landlord gave notice to quit, he was not obliged to offer anything else. So I'm grateful for that, and I told the lady social worker so."

I smiled at his generous disposition. There can't have been many social workers at that troubled time who heard an expression of gratitude.

"How long have you got to decide?" I asked.

"A few weeks. Perhaps a month. No longer. It's come very sudden."

It was indeed sudden. The sounds of children playing were the first to go. Flats were vacated, and removal men were in and out of the courtyards; windows were boarded up; the stairways were left dirty and increasingly derelict; dustbins rolled across the cobbles. The constant hum of human activity was replaced by empty echoes, as the courts picked up the sound of a single voice and threw it backwards and forwards, till it fell silent in the still air.

I wondered how much more I would see of Mr Collett. If he was going miles away into the countryside of Hertfordshire or Essex how often would I be able to visit him? Our cosy evenings of sherry and chocolates and chats seemed to be coming to an end.

I popped in on him about a week later to ask if he had come to a decision. He had.

"I'm going to St Mark's in Mile End," he said. "When I was young, it used to be the workhouse. But that was long ago. Now it is a residential home for old codgers like myself. I think it will be for the best. The lady social worker tells me I will be well looked after. I am going next week."

I was shocked and alarmed by the news. The shadow of the workhouse had darkened the lives of countless people for more than a century. Although officially closed in 1930 by Acts of Parliament, workhouses had merely lingered on under another name. I feared for Mr Collett but I did not like to express doubts, or even to sound negative, so I simply said: "I'll come and see you, I promise."

Back at Nonnatus House, I poured out my misgivings to Sister Julienne. She was thoughtful, and looked grave, but said: "You must understand that this is his decision. He is intelligent, and I think he probably realises that he will not be able to manage to look after himself, alone, in a new place."

I was young and passionate, and argued the case.

"But he's so much better now. He can get around without any trouble. Although his eyesight is dim, he's not blind, and he can find everything he needs."

Sister Julienne smiled her sweet, beautiful smile.

"Yes, my dear, I know, but that is only because he knows where everything is, and habit makes it possible for him to continue living alone. In other surroundings he would be lost and helpless. It is the same for most old people."

My unease persisted, but I knew there was nothing I could do.

A few days later, when I was in the area, I thought I would pop in to arrange a final evening with my old friend. To my astonishment the flat was empty. I peered through the curtainless window. Everything was the same — but different. Inanimate objects have a life of their own, especially when they are the daily companions of a living soul. Without that life, they take on a bleak, desolate appearance, like furniture piled up in a warehouse. I knew he was gone, and didn't need anyone to confirm it, although the woman next door stepped out, or rather shuffled out. Gone was her self-righteous aggression; gone, her busy-body ways and manners. Instead, she exuded a dull, helpless apathy and despair. Her voice was subdued and husky.

"E's gorn. Vey took him vis mornin' wiv 'is case. Vey'll take me an' all, vey will."

She shuffled back into her flat, and bolted the door. Poplar people never bolted their doors in daytime, unless they were afraid of someone.

At Nonnatus House, I felt a heavy sense of loss as I climbed the stairs. It had all been so sudden. My first thought was to go and see him at once, but then I dithered around, thinking that he needed time to settle in and to get to know other people. Perhaps it was all for the best. If a thing has to be, it's best to do it quickly. He was a wise old man; he would not have agreed to go so soon if he had thought there was anything to be gained by delay.

It was about a fortnight later, after lunch, when I cycled up to Mile End, to find St Mark's. I entered by the huge iron gate, and looked at the bleak grey buildings. I was accustomed to the old workhouse buildings, because most of them had been converted into hospitals or isolation units. I knew that they all had a particularly grim appearance, but I had never seen anything as grim and forbidding as St Mark's. My heart sank as I looked around.

I enquired for Mr Collett. Perhaps I had imagined that some helpful, pretty young nurse in a natty little uniform would take me straight to him. Not so. The only person I saw was a rather dirty-looking porter pushing a trolley of bins. He spoke no English, but pointed to a door. Inside was a sort of office area with no-one around. It was cold and high-ceilinged, with plaster cracking and crumbling off the walls. I called, and my voice echoed up the stairwell. Still no-one came.

I wandered out, and into another door. A wide, empty corridor stretched ahead, with doors going off. I opened one, and entered a large, square room, with a lot of old men sitting around formica-topped tables. For a room so full of humanity it was eerily quiet. Faces looked up at me, blank and expressionless, and I looked all round, but could not see Mr Collett. Nor could I see anyone to ask. Some plates rattled, which indicated a kitchen, and I went towards it. Two young men were inside, and neither of them spoke English. They repeated the name 'Collett' several times, but shook their heads. One of them indicated another building to go to. I followed the advice, and was fortunate to meet a porter, who said, "You need Reception, dear, over there," pointing to the first door I had entered.

Back in the hall with the echoing stairwell I hung around, and "hello-ed" for about twenty minutes. Eventually a middle-aged man entered, carrying a sheaf of papers. I gave my request. He looked at me in astonishment.

"You want to see a Mr Collett? Is that what you are saying?"

"Yes."

"Why? Are you a social worker?"

"No. I just want to see him. Have I come at the wrong time, then? Am I out of visiting hours?"

375

"No. We don't have any visiting hours. We don't generally get any visitors. I'll have to open the office and find out where this Mr Collett is."

In the office, he thumbed through piles of papers.

"I think I've found him. Mr Joseph Collett. Is that the name you want? Block E, Fifth Floor. Go up that staircase you see opposite."

He pointed to an iron staircase going up the outside of the building. I climbed five flights and pushed open the heavy door, entering at once into a room similar to that which I had seen on the ground floor. It was large, and about twenty formica-topped tables filled the room with four hard-backed chairs at each table. On most of the chairs old men were sitting, with their arms on the table, staring at the man opposite. Some had their heads down, resting on their arms. No-one spoke. The room smelt acrid with urine and body odour. The high windows let in the light, but they were too high for anyone to see out.

I looked around until I saw Mr Collett at the far end of the room. He was looking down at the table at which he was sitting, and did not know I was approaching. I went straight up to him, and kissed him. He gasped, looked up, and tears filled his eyes. His hands trembled, and the tears fell. He whispered, "My maiden, my Jenny, you've come, then."

He was too overwhelmed to say anything more. The chair opposite was empty, so I sat down and we held hands across the table.

"I would have come sooner, only I thought you should have a chance to settle in, and get to know your companions. I'm so sorry if you thought I wasn't coming."

He muttered, "Yes — no — I mean, that's all right, my pet, that's all right. You're here, and I love you for it, and I'm so grateful." He squeezed my hand.

I bit my lip, close to tears myself, and looked round at the cheerless room, filled with lethargic old men saying nothing. I didn't know what to say myself. We had never had any difficulty with conversation before; in fact, time had always seemed too short for all that we had to say. But now I was tongue-tied. I asked empty questions like: "Are you all right, then?" "What's the food like?" "Are you comfortable here?" to all of which he replied, bleakly, "Yes, I do very nicely, thank you. You don't want to worry your head about me."

Minutes ticked by, and there were long silences. I knew I would have to go, because I had my evening visits to start at 4.00p.m. It had taken me at least forty-five minutes to find him, and time was short. It had been only the briefest of visits, and I hated leaving him, as I tried, haltingly, to explain. He said, simply,

"You go, my maid, and don't mind me."

I kissed him again, and fled from the room. At the door, I turned. He was stroking the cheek where my lips had touched him, and his tears were falling fast onto the table.

I don't know how it was I didn't have an accident as I cycled back to Nonnatus House. I was trembling with sorrow and emotion. After supper, I spoke to Sister Julienne. She listened in silence to what I had to say, and didn't speak for a long time. Thinking she hadn't taken it in, I said. "You do understand what I am saying, don't you? It is simply dreadful. He shouldn't be there."

"Oh yes, my dear, I understand all right. I was thinking of our Lord's words to Peter, as recorded in St. John's Gospel: 'When you are young, you go where you wish, but when you are old, others will take you where you do not wish to go.' This was taken to indicate the manner in which St. Peter would die, but I have always thought that it is a general reflection about us all. For we all grow old, and very few of us retain health and strength to the last. Most of us become helpless and completely dependent on others, whether we like it or not. Old age is a time when we learn the virtue of humility."

I didn't know what to say. I had often found myself this way with Sister Julienne. She had a purity of thought and a simplicity of expression that were quite unanswerable. She continued:

"Mr Collett's tragedy is that all his family have been killed in the wars of this century. The tragedy is loneliness, not the surroundings, which I doubt he notices. What you see as intolerable living conditions may be all par for the course to him. If he were living in luxury in a palace, he would be just as lonely. You are his only friend, Jenny, and he loves you. You must stay with him."

I said that I had pledged myself to do that, and then I started to rail against the folly and inhumanity of turning him out of the flat where he was comfortable and independent.

378

She stopped me in mid-sentence.

"Yes, I know all about that. But you must understand that the Canada Buildings have long been due for demolition. People are not going to put up with a bug-infested environment and insanitary conditions today. The Buildings must go, so the people must go. I am well aware of the fact that most of the old people who are being moved will not be able to adjust to new surroundings, and that many of them will die in consequence. Which brings me back to the words of Jesus: 'When you are old, men will take you where you do not want to go'."

She smiled at me, because I must have looked so sad, and said: "Now I must go and take Compline. Why not join us this evening?"

The beauty and timelessness of the monastic office of Compline eased my troubled soul.

"The Lord grant us a quiet night and a perfect end."

I thought of Mr Collett and all the other old men, isolated even from each other by loneliness.

"In thee, oh Lord, have I put my trust. Let me never be put to confusion."

The candles lighting the altar were reflected on the windows, shutting the dark without, and enclosing the nuns within.

"Be thou my strong rock and house of defence."

Jews and Christians have drawn strength and wisdom from these psalms for two to three thousand years.

"Thou shalt not be afraid of any terror by night."

All those sad old men — were they afraid? Afraid of living, yet more afraid of dying?

"*For He shall give his angels charge over thee.*"

Did they know any joy, in their joyless surroundings?

"*Lighten our darkness, we beseech thee, oh Lord.*"

Just hold them in your prayers, as Sister Julienne will in hers.

"*Protect us through the silent hours of the night, so that we who are wearied by the changes and chances of this fleeting world may repose upon Thy eternal changelessness.*"

The Sisters left the Chapel quietly. The Greater Silence had begun.

I saw Mr Collett as much as I could after that. I never stayed very long, half an hour perhaps, not more, and this was mainly because we both found it difficult to know what to say. The circumstances were just not right for cosy chats, and I was no good at small talk. Also the inertia, I think, was dulling his mind, once so alert. Knowing how much he used to enjoy the radio documentary programmes and plays, I asked him if he listened to his wireless. He looked at me blankly, so I repeated the question.

"No, I haven't got my wireless. I don't know what they did with it. I don't think I could have it here, anyway, so it doesn't matter."

I asked what had happened to his things.

"I don't know. The lady social worker said she would look after all that. I suppose they were sold, and the money put into my account. I've got a bank account, you know. I gave her the number."

"Have you seen her since?"

"Oh yes, she came here. She is very pleasant. She gave me this."

He fumbled in the inside pocket of his waistcoat, and produced a bit of paper. It was a receipt for £96.14s.6d for the sale of furniture. I thought of the grandfather clock, the fine old table, and his high wooden armchair. Now all that was left was a bit of paper.

The big room with its high windows was oppressive, and the all-pervading smell of urine nauseating, but I doubt if the old men noticed this (after all, the sense of smell fades along with the other senses as age advances.) The worst thing for them, I could see, was the boredom of having absolutely nothing to do, hour after hour, day after day. One or two got up and shuffled off to the lavatory, or to another room which I was later to discover was the sleeping dormitory. But apart from that, they did nothing. A few played cards or dominoes, but the games never seemed to excite much interest. The *Daily Mirror* and the *Express* were passed around, and some of the men glanced at them but, from what I observed, most of them just sat at the tables, looking at each other. I never saw any other visitor, and I wondered how it was possible that so many old men could have no-one at all who wanted to see them. I saw only Block E, Fifth Floor, and I did not know how many other blocks and floors there were filled with old men, seemingly abandoned, each day killing the time, until time killed them.

One day I asked Mr Collett where his pipe was and if he smoked it. He said, "We are only allowed to smoke on the balcony."

"Well, do you do so, then?"

"No, I don't know where the balcony is."

I felt really cross at such thoughtlessness on the part of the staff. They were not unkind, as far as I could see, but they were mostly Phillipino or Indonesian young men, who spoke little or no English, and it obviously had not occurred to any of them to take a nearly blind man to the balcony and make sure that he knew how to find his way there and back.

"Well, let's go onto the balcony then, and you can have a smoke, and we can get some fresh air at the same time. Have you got your pipe, your twist, and some matches?"

"Not on me. They are in my locker. I'll go and get them. You can come with me. I don't suppose anyone would mind."

He stood up, and felt his way along the tables to a short corridor at the end of which was a wide double door leading into the dormitory. My experienced eye saw at once that it was the size of the average hospital ward, designed for twenty-eight or thirty beds. It held, at a rough guess, sixty or seventy. They lined each wall, and the far end wall also. They were small two foot six inch iron bedsteads, with thin mattresses over sagging springs. Each had a tiny locker about twelve inches wide beside it, and the beds touched the lockers on each side, so that the space between each bed was no wider than twelve inches. I looked down the far end of the dormitory. There were no lockers, and the beds were so close to each other that, presumably, the only way the occupant could get in and out was by climbing over the end. Some were occupied by old men lying in them, sleeping or just staring at the ceiling. My critical nurse's eye looked at the bed linen and blankets. All were filthy, and the stench of urine and faeces was evidence that fresh linen was a rarity. As a ward sister I would have had a team of cleaners in there. But I saw no staff at all that day.

Mr Collett felt his way along fifteen beds, and then went to the locker beside the fifteenth. I watched him, and noticed that he was walking with difficulty again. I thought, with alarm, about his leg ulcers — so much better, but only because of regular treatment. Was he still getting it? I looked around at the general neglect, and had misgivings. Perhaps he was treating the ulcers himself, quite satisfactorily. I resolved to ask him before leaving that day.

He found his pipe and chuckled as he cradled his old friend in the palm of his hand. We made our way, first to the table where he had been sitting, and then to the balcony, counting the number of tables, and the direction he would have to take. I wanted to be sure he knew how to get there by himself. The door was big and heavy, with a metal safety bar, but he could manage to open it, and would be able to do so by himself.

The fresh air was lovely, though cold, and the balcony was pleasant, but there was nowhere to sit down. I had to hold Mr. Collett's pipe and matches whilst he cut up the tobacco. He filled the pipe and lit it, and, with a satisfied sigh, exhaled clouds of thick smoke. "Luxury," he murmured, "sheer luxury."

I noticed the way he was standing. It was not good. He was shuffling from one leg to the other, and taking a few steps backwards and forwards. I didn't like the omens. People with leg ulcers can usually walk, but standing still in one place is nearly impossible for them. I asked how his legs were, and who was treating them.

"Well, I can do it myself."

"Yes, but do you?"

"Now and again, lass, now and again."

"How often? Every day?"

"Well, not quite every day; but enough, quite enough."

"Do the staff here renew the dressings?"

"They looked at them when I first came here, but I don't recall since."

I was silent. Two months, and no trained person dressing the ulcers, or supervising his treatment. It was not good enough. I said, "I would like to have a look at them."

"Another time. Another time. I'm enjoying the fresh air, and the pipe, and above all, your company. I know you'll have to go soon and I don't want to spoil it. You can look at my legs another day."

He was right. Time was drawing near to 4.00p.m., and my evening visits. I could not linger, so I kissed him tenderly, and left him with his pipe, and a rare smile on his face.

The Last Post

Something told me that Mr. Collett did not have long to live. I was anxious about his legs, but apart from that I could see that he would never adapt to the communal life of St Marks. Sister Julienne had been quite right, I discovered. The unpleasant, even squalid surroundings meant nothing to him at all. The tiny bed in a dormitory with about seventy other men was quite acceptable. In fact, he described himself as "Very comfortable. Doing nicely. They are very good to us here". So if he had no complaints about the conditions, I realised that I should not. His trouble was chronic loneliness, and the inability to adjust to change.

On two occasions when I visited I asked to see his legs, but he prevaricated, making different excuses, and I didn't think I could force the issue. The next occasion when I called he was not at his usual table. The man who generally sat opposite him pointed to the dormitory and said, "He ain't got up today".

I went to the dormitory, and in the fifteenth bed on the right Mr. Collett lay motionless. I looked at him for a long time from the doorway, hating myself for hating the smell, and not wanting to approach the bed. A sort of dread had entered my heart, and I wanted to turn and run. He moved and coughed slightly, and this set me in action. I went up to his bed, kissed him, and whispered, "It's me. Are you all right? It's not like you to stop in bed."

He took my hands and kissed them, and murmured that he would be all right by and by.

I sat beside him, not talking, squeezing his hand from time to time, thinking, if he stays here not moving for several days he will get pneumonia, and that will be it. Pneumonia is the old man's friend, they say. A quiet and peaceful end. I hope he goes that way in his sleep. What greater blessing can we ask at the end of life?

Then it occurred to me that, whilst he was lying in bed, it would be easy to look at his legs, so I asked him if I could. He neither agreed, nor disagreed, but seemed indifferent.

I pulled the blankets away from the foot of the bed, and the stench of decaying flesh rose to greet me. A rough, fluid-sodden bandage covered each leg, and I unwound them with difficulty. I had no surgical forceps, or scissors, and had to do it with my fingers. The bandages looked as though they had not been changed for a fortnight, and were stuck to the flesh underneath. As I tried to ease them away I thought I would be hurting him, but he did not move, nor show any sign of pain or distress.

At last the wounds were fully exposed. I had to grip the iron bedstead, and call upon all my nurse's training of discipline and self-control to avoid crying out. From the knee to the ankle there was no skin at all, just livid, suppurating flesh, oozing pus and blood. Daylight was fast fading, and the dim electric light bulb hanging from the ceiling was not a great help, but I thought I saw traces of black around the edge of the wound. I looked down at his feet. The toes looked greyish and swollen, one or two of them a darker colour than the others.

"Oh, my God, it can't be. Oh, please, no. Don't let it be. Not him. It's not fair."

There was only one way to tell. I unfastened the brooch I was wearing and dug the pin deep into the centre of the wound on each leg. He didn't move. Then I dug it really hard into his toes. He didn't feel a thing. There could not be the slightest doubt of it — gangrene.

He said, "They are feeling better today. They've been giving me jip the last few weeks, but they don't hurt now, and I guess they're getting better."

I had to control myself. Fortunately he could not see my face, but he was sensitive to my voice.

"As long as you are comfortable, you just stay there. I'll go and get someone to put another dressing on, because I've taken the bandages off. I won't be long."

I raised the alarm, and later the superintendent and a doctor came to the dormitory, but in the meantime, I had to leave for my evening work. After I had finished my visits, I cycled back to St Mark's and, for the last time, climbed the iron staircase to the fifth floor of Block E. Mr Collett had been transferred to Mile End Hospital.

I was relieved to hear it, and I cycled the half mile down the road to the hospital in order to find out which ward he had been admitted to. It was too late to see him, but I was told that he was comfortable and sleeping.

Immediately after lunch the next day, I cycled up to the hospital and went straight to the ward. The ward sister told me that Mr Collett had been operated on that morning, and had not yet come round from the anaesthetic. The operation had been mid-thigh amputation of both legs.

I was taken to the side-room where he lay. The calm cleanliness and efficiency of the hospital was reassuring after the shambolic dirt of St. Mark's. Mr Collett lay in spotless white sheets, his face calm and relaxed. A nasal tube was in situ, and a nurse was sucking the mucus from his throat with an aspirator. She then counted his pulse and checked the flow-rate of the blood-drip that was running into his arm. She smiled at me as she turned to go. Hospital protocol and discipline had the upper hand, and Mr Collett was now a part of it.

I sat with him for a little while, but he was deeply asleep, and looked quite peaceful, and so I left, resolving to come back after my evening visits, by which time he might have come round from the anaesthetic and would recognise me.

It was about 7.30p.m. when I approached the ward, and the screams assailed me long before I pushed open the door. A harassed-looking staff nurse was on duty, and as I ran towards the side-ward a frightened nurse whispered: "I think he's gone mad."

Mr Collett was sitting bolt upright in bed, his blind eyes staring, wide with terror. He was waving his arms and screaming: "Watch out, to your left, a grenade exploding." He screamed and ducked to escape an invisible missile flying over his head.

I ran to him, and took him in my arms.

"It's me, Jenny. Me, I'm here."

He grabbed me with superhuman strength and pushed me down to the floor.

"Get down, keep your head down. They'll blow you to bits. A bloke over there had his head blown off a minute ago. That one over there has lost both his legs. It's a terrible place to be. Gunfire all around. Down. GET DOWN!"

He screamed with all his strength and hurled himself forward. The stumps of his legs twitched violently and he fell out of bed. He seemed impervious to the fall, and grabbed me, pulling me under the bed with him.

"Stay here. You'll be safe here, in the shelter. I'll keep a look-out for any other poor soul to get under cover. Look out!" He screamed and looked up. "That plane, see, it's just dropped its load of bombs, they're coming for us. It'll be a direct hit." He screamed louder than ever, "KEEP DOWN!"

A doctor and two male orderlies rushed into the ward. The staff nurse had a syringe filled and ready. The orderlies crawled under the bed and held Mr Collett, who was fighting and screaming about capture and court martial and the firing squad. The doctor injected a powerful anaesthetic and a few minutes later, Mr Collett rolled over onto his side, deeply asleep, but the stumps of his legs twitched violently with involuntary nervous spasms.

We were all shaken and trembling. The two orderlies picked the old man up and put him back into bed. He looked peaceful again. The hospital staff left, but I sat by his bedside for a long time, crying quietly.

At 9.30 the night sister asked me to leave, saying he would be kept sedated all night, and telling me to ring in the morning.

Before breakfast, I rang the hospital, and was told that Mr. Collett had died peacefully at 3.30 a.m.

There was no Last Post for the old soldier; no solemn drum roll; no final salute, no lowering of the Colours. There was just a contract funeral, arranged by the hospital, leaving from a hidden back area next to the morgue. A priest and one mourner followed the coffin, and we travelled in the hearse, next to the driver. I had not thought of flowers until nearly at the hospital gate, so I had bought a bunch of Michaelmas daisies from a street flower-seller. We were driven to a cemetery somewhere in North London. I don't remember where it was. I only remember a cold, bleak November day, as we stood on either side of the open grave, the priest and I, reciting the office for the burial of the dead, "Dust to dust, ashes to ashes." The men shovelled the soil over the coffin, and I laid the purple daisies on the rich brown earth.

Coda

It was many years later — perhaps fifteen or twenty years — when Mr Collett visited me. I was happily married, my daughters growing up, my life in full flow. I had not thought of Mr Collett for years.

I woke in the middle of the night, and he was standing at the side of my bed. He was as real as my husband sleeping beside me. He was tall, and upright, but looked a little younger than when I had known him, like a handsome man of about sixty or sixty-five. He was smiling, and then he said,

"You know the secret of my life, my dear, because you know how to love."

And then he disappeared.

Also available in ISIS Large Print:

My Life as a Spy

Leslie Woodhead

A wry and poignant memoir of coming of age in the Cold War

Woodhead's memories exude a wonderful sense of nostalgia for a world of lost innocence that, to anyone over 60, is instantly recognisable **The Times**

An only child, living above a shop in post-war Halifax, Woodhead grew up with austerity and secrets. But nothing prepared him for the comically bleak RAF training camps he now found himself in, nor the isolated Joint Services School for Linguistics on the East coast of Scotland. Here he was trained by a colourful staff of émigrés, who taught a course of total immersion in Russian for purposes not always clear to their pupils. A posting to an ex-Luftwaffe base in a war-scarred Berlin provided only partial explanations. In the ruins of a city gripped by espionage and paranoia, he discovers adulthood and his vocation as an observer and documenter of people.

ISBN 0-7531-9366-3 (hb)
ISBN 0-7531-9367-1 (pb)

Myths & Legends of the Second World War

James Hayward

The Second World War gave rise to a rich crop of legends, many of which persist in the public consciousness of today. Some are well known, such as the escape of an undead Hitler to South America, Allied aircraft buzzed by "Foo Fighters" and UFOs, German parachutists dressed as nuns and a failed German invasion in Suffolk in 1940.

Then there are tales of betrayal at Dieppe and Arnhem, Coventry and Scapa Flow, Hitler's obsession with the occult, the real identity of The Man Who Never Was, the Glenn Miller mystery, Nazi U-boat bases in Ireland, and a wealth of other true lies and propaganda falsehoods.

This is a new and refreshing persective on the history and legacy of the Second World War, through its myths, legends and folk memories.

ISBN 0-7531-5663-6 (hb)
ISBN 0-7531-5664-4 (pb)

D-Day to Berlin

Andrew Williams

The defining moment of the Second World War through the voices of the British, American and German soldiers who were there

Williams has drawn on the memories of an eloquent band of interviewees. A valuable and sobering re-evaluation of the liberation of northwest Europe
Sunday Times

This is the remarkable story of the Allied struggle for survival — the battle from the beaches of Normandy to the heart of Hitler's Reich and ultimate victory just eleven months later. The campaign to free Europe from Nazi oppression through the collective operations from D-Day to Berlin marks one of the greatest ever military offensives. The Allies overcame initial setbacks to inflict a devastating defeat on Hitler's crack divisions in France — a victory that was threatened just months later in the bitter winter fighting of the Battle of the Bulge. The final crossing of the Rhine and the advance into Germany changed the course of European history forever.

ISBN 0-7531-5653-9 (hb)
ISBN 0-7531-5654-7 (pb)

Mosaic

Michael Holroyd

By the author of **Basil Street Blues**

Praise for Basil Street Blues:"A touching and cunningly constructed self-portrait . . . a minor masterpiece"
Jeremy Lewis, Sunday Times

When Michael Holroyd published *Basil Street Blues*, in which one of our finest biographers turned his attentions to his own family, it was the beginning of a story rather than the end. For as the letters from readers started to arrive, the author discovered an extraordinary narrative that his own memoir had only touched upon.

Mosaic is Michael's piecing together of these remarkable revelations: some of which are pleasant surprises, others more startling. There is a discovery that his Swedish grandmother was the mistress of the French anarchist writer Jacques Prevert; and a letter from Margaret Forster that leads to his remarkable account of a decade-long affair. A love story, a detective story, a book of secrets, this is a beautifully written journey into a forest of family trees and a fascinating insight into the workings of genealogy.

ISBN 0-7531-9976-9 (hb)
ISBN 0-7531-9977-7 (pb)

Call the Midwife

Jennifer Worth

Jennifer Worth can rival James Herriot with her descriptions of childbirth in Poplar tenements
Fiona McDonald Smith, Sunday Express

Jennifer Worth was just 22 when she volunteered to spend her early years of midwifery training in the heart of London's East End in the 1950s.

Coming from a sheltered background, there were tough lessons to be learned. The conditions in which many women gave birth just half a century ago were horrifying, not only because of their grimly impoverished surroundings but because of what they were expected to endure.

Working with an order of nuns who were nurses and midwives, Jennifer saw brutality and tragedy first hand. She dealt with it with amazing kindness and understanding — and a great deal of Cockney humour. She also earned the confidences of some whose lives were more strange, poignant and terrifying than any fiction.

ISBN 0-7531-9878-9 (hb)
ISBN 0-7531-9879-7 (pb)

ISIS publish a wide range of books in large print, from fiction to biography. Any suggestions for books you would like to see in large print or audio are always welcome. Please send to the Editorial Department at:

ISIS Publishing Limited
7 Centremead
Osney Mead
Oxford OX2 0ES

A full list of titles is available free of charge from:

Ulverscroft Large Print Books Limited

(UK)
The Green
Bradgate Road, Anstey
Leicester LE7 7FU
Tel: (0116) 236 4325

(Australia)
P.O. Box 314
St Leonards
NSW 1590
Tel: (02) 9436 2622

(USA)
P.O. Box 1230
West Seneca
N.Y. 14224-1230
Tel: (716) 674 4270

(Canada)
P.O. Box 80038
Burlington
Ontario L7L 6B1
Tel: (905) 637 8734

(New Zealand)
P.O. Box 456
Feilding
Tel: (06) 323 6828

Details of **ISIS** complete and unabridged audio books are also available from these offices. Alternatively, contact your local library for details of their collection of **ISIS** large print and unabridged audio books.